Leave Me Alone and I'll Make You Rich

Leave Me Alone and
I'LL MAKE YOU RICH

HOW THE BOURGEOIS DEAL
ENRICHED THE WORLD

Deirdre Nansen McCloskey
and Art Carden

The University of Chicago Press   *Chicago and London*

The University of Chicago Press, Chicago 60637
The University of Chicago Press, Ltd., London
© 2020 by The University of Chicago
Published 2020
Paperback edition 2022
Printed in the United States of America

31 30 29 28 27 26 25 24 23 22   1 2 3 4 5

ISBN-13: 978-0-226-73966-3 (cloth)
ISBN-13: 978-0-226-82398-0 (paper)
ISBN-13: 978-0-226-73983-0 (e-book)
DOI: https://doi.org/10.7208/chicago/9780226739830.001.0001

Library of Congress Cataloging-in-Publication Data

Names: McCloskey, Deirdre N., author. | Carden, Art, author.
Title: Leave me alone and I'll make you rich : how the bourgeois deal
enriched the world / Deirdre Nansen McCloskey and Art Carden.
Other titles: How the bourgeois deal enriched the world
Description: Chicago ; London : The University of Chicago Press,
2020. | Includes bibliographical references and index.
Identifiers: LCCN 2020022827 | ISBN 9780226739663 (cloth) |
ISBN 9780226739830 (ebook)
Subjects: LCSH: Economic history—1750–1918. | Economic
history—1918– | Economic history—Moral and ethical aspects. |
Free enterprise—Social aspects. | Liberty—Economic aspects. |
Liberalism—Economic aspects. | Libertarianism—Economic
aspects. | Capitalism. | Progress. | Economics—Philosophy.
Classification: LCC HC51 .M396 2020 | DDC 330.12/209—dc23
LC record available at https://lccn.loc.gov/2020022827

♾ This paper meets the requirements of ANSI/NISO Z39.48-1992
(Permanence of Paper).

What is crucial is our ability to engage in continuous conversation, testing one another, discovering our hidden presuppositions, changing our minds because we have listened to the voices of our fellows. Lunatics also change their minds, but their minds change with the tides of the moon and not because they have listened, really listened, to their friends' questions and objections.

AMÉLIE OKSENBERG RORTY[1]

To the socialists of all parties

F. A. HAYEK

I give you the toast . . . of economics and economists, who are the trustees not of civilization, but of the possibility of civilization.

JOHN MAYNARD KEYNES

Contents

Preface

The theme of our book is simple and true. But controversial.

It is that human liberty—and not the machinery of coercion or investment, or even science by itself—is what made for a Great Enrichment, from 1800 to the present. The Enrichment was really, really "great": three *thousand* percent per person. Liberated people devising new technologies and institutions did an amazing job from 1800 to the present and will keep doing it. Liberty will make the Enrichment worldwide. And the Enrichment will not corrupt the human soul. The news, in short, is very, very good.

The Enrichment wasn't achieved by governmental coercion, which is usually counterproductive—except maybe in plagues and invasions. Nor was it achieved by science unassisted, or the exploitation of slaves, or the routine accumulation of capital, or a profound dialectic of history, or a deep specialness of Europeans. It was achieved by liberty alone, a necessary and pretty much sufficient cause, which came tentatively to northwestern Europe in the eighteenth century. Give people liberty, and by uncoerced cooperation through commerce they become adults, enriched in body and soul.

You are doubtful and pessimistic. You worry quite understandably about populism or the environment or the decay of standards. We offer, though, an optimistic prediction and give ample evidence for it. The world will prosper mightily, if people play their cards right to favor liberty and its theory, liberalism—"liberalism" in the classic sense, born two centuries ago.

We make a little joke in the title of the book and throughout, in referring to "the Bourgeois Deal." The word *bourgeois* (*boor-ZWAH*) means "of the urban middle class, businesslike." Imagine our master proposition, articulated by either a bourgeois man in a London coffeehouse in 1820 or a bourgeois woman (Deirdre Nansen McCloskey) addressing a chapter of the National Association of Women Business Owners in 2020:

> Leave me, a bourgeois businessperson, pretty much alone, subject to sober ethics learned at my mother's knee, and a few good and restrained laws, with an effective social safety net. In a word, give me and my fellow citizens liberty. Do not envy the rewards I get for selling innovations. They are tested by your willingness to buy them. If you don't like them, and I fail, I won't ask the government to coerce you into buying. The happy result will be that the innovations will make everyone enormously better off, by 3,000 percent, especially the formerly poor—your ancestors and mine.

You've heard a lot of dismal chatter since the Great Recession of 2008. As it, the most recent of the successively trademarked "Final Crises of Capitalism," recedes into memory, we do well to remind ourselves that median weekly real earning of wage and salary workers is setting all-time highs every time the data are reported and is, the COVID-19 dip aside, about 10 percent above where it was at the depths of the Great Recession—and is well above its recent nadir in the second quarter of 2014.[1]

You might recoil at the notion that we live in a blessed age. After all, hundreds of millions of people around the world remain in dire poverty. The United States government is separating immigrant children from their parents, holding them in cages, on the economically silly and morally obnoxious notion that by doing so they are somehow making America great again. We aren't saying there aren't serious problems. We are saying that things have gotten better, are getting better, and will continue to get better for the vast majority of humanity, and in a few generations for everyone on the planet—as long as we keep our ethical wits about us and opt for true liberalism.

Think it possible that the nonstop torrent of bad news filling your newspapers and e-readers and social media time lines is not giving you the complete story. Be wary, for example, of headlines about the exploits of "Florida Man," a popular meme spawned by a loose public records law in the Sunshine State. It makes it exceptionally easy to write stories with headlines like "Florida Man Arrested for Burglarizing Cars in Jail Parking Lot Moments after Being Released" and "Florida Man Charged with Impersonating Officer for McDonald's Discount."[2] There are roughly 10.5 million actual Florida men. If only 0.01 percent of them are idiotic criminals, it's still enough for about three outrageous "Florida Man" stories every day for a year. We admit that even in an innovation-embracing, bourgeois-dealing society, an occasional evil nitwit will show up and an occasional paragon of virtue will slip through the cracks into a life of destitution or just plain bad luck. We are claiming, on the basis of overwhelming evidence, that the bourgeois deal has made the cracks a lot smaller. Long may it reign.

So we beseech you, dear reader: don't let the much larger positive story get lost amid the vivid and rare counterexamples, or even the miseries of mishandled plagues. On a long view, even since 2008, and since 1960 or 1900 or 1800, the economic world has leapt far, far beyond the zero-sum game of olden days. You need to stop thinking zero-sum. A liberal world is stunningly positive sum. The hands-off ideology of liberalism has allowed an invisible hand to push forward any society that permits it to work—not toward *capitalism* (a silly word, as we'll show) but toward what we call "innovism." The evidence is overwhelming that liberty, not coercion by a private master or a public state, inspires people to continuous betterment. For the poorest.

The political side of innovism, we note, is *liberalism*. We use the word, you see, *not* in its strange US sense, of "bigger and bigger government." Such a "liberalism" usually gets the economy wrong and often enough slips into tyranny. Look at the misuse of the FBI and the IRS and ICE, the Palmer raids and the fugitive slave laws. Nor do we use the word in its even stranger Latin American sense of "suppressing the people with military tyranny," which likewise usually gets the economy wrong, and is tyranny already. There's something in the water of the Western Hemisphere. We use the honored *L*-word in its original and international sense of "no involuntary masters"—no masters over slaves, no husbands over wives, no kings or priests or politicians over citizens. On the contrary, you are permitted to say "take this job and shove it." Or "take this marriage and shove it." Or "take this politician and shove him." It turns out that, like the free working of language or newspapers or fashion or rock music or cookery or most other human enterprises, permitting people in the economy to have a go, free of involuntary masters to whom they can't say no, usually gets the economy right. Not perfect, but pretty darned good. Three thousand percent good.

Not anarchy: we accept that some government is necessary. Well, McCloskey thinks so, at any rate. Carden is more sanguine about the viability of a sort of anarchy, understood not as nihilism but as no rulers.[3] In opposition to liberalism, people will often say, taking an indignant tone, "There must be *some* role for government!" To which we reply, "Yes, though 'some role,' such as safety nets and plague response, doesn't justify grotesquely large and illiberal governments pushing you around." That there is at least a plausible argument for carbon taxes does not give the government license to regulate in withering detail the domestic and international trade in sauerkraut. James Madison said in *Federalist* 51, "If men were angels, no government would be necessary." Humans are not angels. The trick is to frame a government for nonangels, whether the rulers or the ruled. It had better be small, because any government tends to corrupt. Power is the ability to physically coerce people to do things they can't be persuaded to do voluntarily, such as paying taxes or getting inoculations or serving on the eastern front. Big governments exercise more power over more people—people harmlessly chatting or strumming or knitting or dealing in the economy. We believe, and so should you, that the more involuntary masters the citizens have, the worse they do, materially and spiritually. With too many masters with too much power, they are reduced to children. Absolute power corrupts absolutely.

Madison himself, like Jefferson and Washington, was not a consistent liberal. Though talking a good deal about liberty, all three had large numbers of slaves. Our own special heroes of the Revolutionary era are rather Adam Smith and Thomas Paine and Mary Wollstonecraft, who thoroughly rejected the ancient impulse to employ a visible hand of masterful coercion to push people around. A new and liberal ideology of hands-off, leave-alone, no-push, combined with a wise generosity toward the poor and the disabled, gave the masses permission to flourish. They did, spectacularly.

The result contradicts an ever-fashionable itch to make up more and more "polices" directed from above. "Let's expropriate the rich people," says the left. "Let's do more policing of the poor people," says the right. We say: Give permission to all the people, and give effective, non-demeaning help to the poor and disabled among them, and all will continue to flourish in body and mind. Sang the African American poet Langston Hughes in 1936, "O, let America be America again—/ The land that never has been yet—/ And yet must be—the land where *every* man is free." Hallelujah.

§

That is, the McCloskey-Carden team is properly, honorably "liberal," in the old and international sense, and does not sit anywhere along the conventional left-right spectrum. The disagreements along the spectrum are merely about *whom* to push around with government-sanctioned coercion. Pick your favorite pushees, and take your place along the spectrum. Immigrants. Workers. Customers. Entrepreneurs. Members of the United Auto Workers in Dearborn on May 26, 1937. Democratic protestors in Hong Kong late in 2019. Our friends sitting self-satisfied on the left or right or middle of the spectrum of coercion mistakenly think that *they* can claim the honorable title of champions of liberty/freedom. They can't.

Real liberals like us say that personal liberty and political liberty and economic liberty are all of a piece. Latin *liber*, says the *Cambridge Latin Dictionary*, was long understood by the slave-holding ancients as "possessing the social and legal status of a free man (as opp. to slave)," and then *libertas* as "the civil status of a free man, freedom." The new liberal plan born in the eighteenth century came to mean the startling notion of a society consisting *entirely*, if ideally, of free people. No slaves at all. Equality of status and permission. No pushing around. Minimally coercive. Sweet-talking. Persuasive. Rhetorical. Voluntary. Humane. Tolerant. No racism. No Jim Crow. No voter suppression. No abusing of immigrants. No imperialism. No reign of terror over gay people. No unnecessary taxes. No imprudent collective projects. No domination of women by men. No casting couch. No beating of children. No messing with other people's stuff or persons.

That is, liberty is liberty. It's meaningless by parts. To put it in terms of the Abrahamic religions, God wants humans to have free will. Only then is their choice of bad or good, sin or redemption, meaningful. To put it in secular terms, you are still a slave if only on odd days of the month. As a free person you seek the permission, equal to anyone else's, to braid hair for a living, to open a factory, to love whom you wish, to call out a tyrant in the newspaper. But the left or right or middle on the spectrum want to deny you one or another permission. Shame on them.

§

This book is a popular riff from Carden's pen on McCloskey's Bourgeois Era trilogy (2006, 2010, 2016)—three long, academic, heavily footnoted, and (McCloskey claims) decisively argued volumes, 1,700 pages in total.[4] It says that bourgeois life is not evil and that approval of it led to a Great Enrichment. It says too that the usual materialist explanations for the Enrichment are wrong. It says, on the contrary, that changes in the ethics, rhetoric, and ideology of northwestern Europeans, and now the world, led to liberalism, innovism, and enrichment.

The trilogy relies on a large body of scientific and humanistic literature, ranging from national income accounts to Shakespeare. Here Carden substitutes, with McCloskey's more or less heavy editing, brief examples and quickie arguments—adding a bit of corny clowning around, in which both authors idiotically delight. In ancient Greece a dramatist would put on a trilogy of serious plays but then add a fourth, short, comical "satyr play." So here.

The motto at the outset, by Amélie Oksenberg Rorty, is not clowning around or satirical. It urges us to "engage in continuous conversation, testing one another, discovering our hidden presuppositions, changing our minds because we have listened to the voices of our fellows." That's good advice in thinking about auto repair or marital issues. So too we believe it's good advice in thinking about history and economics.

If in the end you're not persuaded that the world has been very lucky indeed to have embraced, even if only partially, the liberalism and the innovism of the Bourgeois Deal, go in peace. Yet we hope, dear reader, that at least you leave with some doubts rattling in your brain.

Part One
POVERTY IS ON THE RUN

1
Liberalism Liberated

In 2005 a coalition of groups organized a campaign to "Make Poverty History." The very idea—making poverty *history*—startles, considering the grind that was once the life of virtually everyone on the planet, a few nobles and priests excepted. To be quantitative about it, the beginning of scientific wisdom about economic history is to realize that in the year 1800 worldwide, the miserable average of production and consumption per person was about $3 day. Even in the newly prosperous United States, Holland, and Britain, it was a mere $6. Gak. Those are the figures in terms of roughly present-day prices, understand: no tricks with money involved. Try living in your neighborhood on $3 or $6 a day. And realize by contrast that in the United States it's now about $130 a day, and $33 as a world average, doubling in every long generation. The poorest have been the biggest beneficiaries. Contrary to what you hear, further, since the mid-twentieth century, inequality in the world has fallen dramatically.[1] The wretched of the earth are coming to a dignified level of income, and more. Wow.

Our task is to convey the gak and to explain the wow—and to show that the change from gak to wow came from liberty.

The view in 1651 of the English philosopher Thomas Hobbes was that without an all-powerful king there must have been once upon a time a "war of all against all." We doubt he was correct about the king or about the once upon a time, in light of modern scholarship in history and anthropology. But his famous vision of the poverty of a society without *some* sort of discipline, whether a coercive visible hand or a voluntary *in*visible hand, can serve to characterize the world that the campaign to Make Poverty History wants to escape:

> In such condition [as he imagined, "the state of nature," with no discipline] there is no place for industry, because the fruit thereof is uncertain [think: no incentive if the fruit will anyway be stolen]: and consequently no culture of the earth, no navigation [think: no caravels of Prince Henry the Navigator exploring the coast of Africa], nor use of commodities that may be imported by sea [think: no pepper from the East]; no commodious building [think: no Amsterdam city hall on the Dam]; no instruments of moving, and removing such things as require much force [think: no coaches on the king's highway]; no knowledge of the face of the earth [think: "Don't know much about geography"]; no account of time [no clocks, no history: "Don't know much about the Middle Ages"]; no arts; no letters, no society; and which is worst of all, continual fear and danger of violent death; and the life of man solitary, poor, nasty, brutish, and short.

Double gak. Not nice. People on their own, Hobbes supposed, are cruel and selfish and above all unable to organize themselves voluntarily. To tame them, they need a "leviathan," as he called it in the title of his 1651 work—that is, a great beast of a government. Only a top-down king, like his beloved if recently beheaded master, Charles I of England, or Charles's son hiding out in France, the future Charles II, would protect peace and civilization. (His is rather similar, we note, to the argument on the left nowadays that a leviathan government, much more powerful than anything Charles I could have imagined, is necessary to protect peace and civilization and the poor.) The choice, he said, was between *utter* misery without a masterful king or a moderated misery (even) with him.

Many people nowadays, whether on the left or the right of politics, still credit Hobbes's argument for top-down government. They believe, writes the liberal economist Donald Boudreaux, "that we human beings left undirected by a sovereign power are either inert blobs, capable of achieving nothing [thus say the Dems and Labour, and old John Dewey], or unintelligent and brutal barbarians destined only to rob, rape, plunder, and kill each other [thus say the GOP and the Tories, and old Thomas Hobbes] until and unless a sovereign power restrains us and directs economic energies onto more productive avenues."[2] The people who believe such things are properly called *statists*, such as in recent politics Elizabeth Warren on the left of the conventional spectrum and Donald Trump on the right. The left or right, or middle, wants very much to coerce the blockheads and the barbarians to get organized. Both the progressives and the conservatives, in other words, view ordinary people as children, ignorant or unruly, unable to take care of themselves, and dangerous to others, to be tightly governed. Terrible twos.

We modern liberals don't. We want to persuade you to join us in liberalism in the old and honorable sense—or, if you insist on the word, to join us in a generous version of *libertarianism* (a 1950s coinage we would like to retire). You don't really favor pushing people around with a prison-industrial complex, or with regulations preventing people from braiding hair for a living, or with collateral damage from drone strikes, or with a separation of toddlers from their mothers at the southern US border, do you? We bet not. As one version of the Golden Rule puts it, do unto others as you would have them do unto you. With an open mind and a generous heart, dear reader, we believe you will tilt toward a humane true liberalism. Welcome, then, to a society held together by sweet talk among free adults, rather than by the leviathan's coercion applied to slaves and children.

§

Yet in olden days the Hobbesian, statist, antiliberal case had some plausibility—enough in the minds of its advocates, for example, to justify slavery as getting the enslaved to do something useful, or to hold Indonesians in Dutch apprenticeship for another century, or to keep women properly under the control of their king-like husbands. When the Irish were illiterate and the Italians superstitious and the women confined, a masterful state seemed to make sense. We don't actually think so, but you can at least see why the masters could point to evidence for blobbish or brutal children, whom the masters would so wisely discipline by rod and knout.

But the case looks a lot less plausible in an age in which the Irish and the Irish Americans have among the highest educational attainments in the world, in which women are independent and venturing, and in which the Italians, despite some strange voting recently, are far from barbaric and superstitious. In other words, what fits the modern world is modern liberalism—as we define it here, and not, we repeat for the last time, the way it's been defined for a century in the United States (namely, as the wide subordination of voluntary arrangements to governmental coercion). The vision in our modern liberalism is of educated and venturing adults, able to take pretty good care of themselves and their families and to provision their neighbors in voluntary exchange. We think the liberal vision is better for humans than either the old leftish vision of disorganized proletarians properly led by the Communist Party or the old rightish vision of dim-witted peasants properly led by the aristocracy.

In other words, if ever there was a time to let adult and dignified people have a go, to accept the Bourgeois Deal, it's now. To be more precise and to paraphrase an African proverb, the best time to let adult and dignified people have a go, to accept the Bourgeois Deal, is actually twenty or two hundred or two thousand or two hundred thousand years ago. The second best time is now. People are ready for liberal autonomy. Permitting them to have it has permitted them to grow up. The time for nudging and judging by big governments, or overmastering by lords and husbands and experts, was yesterday, if ever (we say, "never"). Now is the time for what is sometimes called an obsolete-sounding "*classical* liberalism." It's not obsolete, and we want to drop the "classical." The leviathan state, we suggest, is what's obsolete, whether run by former kings or present tyrants, Charles I or Tayyip Erdoğan.

Our point, and the point of the Bourgeois Deal, is that the world can—and after 1800 emphatically did—escape the poverty, nastiness, brutishness, and brevity of life as it was in 1651, without a danger of falling into a war of all against all. We make the case here that

Hobbes was correct in his description of the actual and potential miseries of 1651 but that modern times have belied his belief in the necessity of overmastering governmental power. And the $130 a day, or even the $33 a day, steadily rising, and its spiritual results have belied our friends the moderate statists of the left and of the right. Even more so, the facts have belied our enemies the revolutionaries. The dictatorship of the proletariat or the Thousand Year Reich didn't work for human betterment. The Bourgeois Deal did.

§

Until the 1800s, understand, Hobbes's argument seemed wholly *natural*, in societies of chiefs or kings, Genghis Khan or King Solomon. Tyranny fitted reasonably well an economy of herders, and it fitted very well indeed a society of farmers. The chiefs and kings were happy to take personal advantage of their monopoly of coercion over farmers unable to run away. English history up to the so-called Glorious Revolution of 1688–1689, and world history up to the American and French Revolutions, gave little room for anything but Big Daddy or Big Brother in charge, anywhere.

It had always been so, since humans stopped being hunter-gatherers—which for literally millions of years was an especially liberated if extremely poor condition of humanity. It placed in your genes a taste for liberty.[3] But people are complicated. They imagine at the same time that they dearly want a king, a father of the nation. A knee-slapping passage in the Hebrew Bible recounts how the ancient Israelites, like Argentinians today, and Italians and in truth most every electorate in some moods, wanted *more* of that top-down statism, Bonapartism, the man on the white horse. To be safe and great. In the story, the Israelites appeal to Samuel to give them a king, "like all the nations." Samuel consults with God, who tells him to warn them about getting what they want. "So Samuel spoke all the words of the Lord to the people" (1 Samuel 8:11–18):

> This will be the procedure of the king. . . . He will take your sons
> and place them for himself in his chariots . . . and some to do
> his plowing and to reap his harvest and to make his weapons of

war. ... He will also take your daughters for perfumers and cooks and bakers. He will take the best of your fields and your vineyards and your olive groves. ... He will take a tenth of your seed and of your vineyards and give to his officers and to his servants. ... Then you will cry out ... but the Lord will not answer you in that day.

"Nevertheless, the people refused to listen." Ha, ha.

Yet quite unexpectedly, even in the time of Hobbes, a gathering flood of liberal writings began to challenge the statist assumption. It was such liberal ideas, we argue, that made the modern world, inspiring ordinary people to be free and to venture as adults, and not serve as plowmen and perfumers enslaved like all the nations to kings. From the middle of the seventeenth century the list lengthens of liberal wielders of the pen, from the Levellers in England during the 1640s and the de la Court brothers in Holland during the 1660s. The Englishman John Locke, much influenced by the Dutch during the 1680s while hiding in Holland from King James II, gave liberalism a form that would become influential in the American Revolution a century later. In 1733 the Frenchman Voltaire, who admired the beginnings of liberalism and bourgeois dignity in the Britain of his time—as against the king-worshipping snobbery of rank in his own country—agreed with Locke in praising a free commerce. He wrote sarcastically, "I don't know which is the more useful to the state, a well-powdered lord who knows precisely when the king gets up in the morning . . . or a great merchant who enriches his country, sends orders from his office to Surat or to Cairo, and contributes to the well-being of the world."[4] About forty years later, the conflicted slaveholder Thomas Jefferson wrote famously that all men are created equal and should be permitted to pursue happiness in commerce. In the same year of 1776, our own special hero of liberalism, Adam Smith of Scotland (1723–1790, who shares a birthday, you will be pleased to know, with Carden's daughter), penned into being an ideology of the "obvious and simple system of natural liberty."[5] He published, four months before the Continental Congress approved the final draft of the Declaration of Independence, his *Inquiry Into the Nature and Causes of the Wealth of Nations*. It said what we say: liberty makes for prosperity and does not corrupt the soul.

The liberal idea of course had causes. Smith came from two-and-a-half centuries of accidental preparation, in a northwestern Europe formerly very far from liberal. Think of Henry VIII, no liberal, ruling England with a hard hand from 1509 to 1547. Contra present-day white nationalism and lesser lunacies, Europe was not born exceptional. It was, as late as 1492, a poor, nasty, brutish, and short-lived corner of the world. Then, slowly, slowly, the ideology of leaving people alone, the Bourgeois Deal, came there to be honored. The long Dutch revolt of 1568–1648 against the Habsburg kings, for example, left the middle class, "the middling sort," the "bourgeoisie" (pronounced *boor-zwah-ZEE*), to step into the void in Holland left by a battle-thinned aristocracy. The cities of the Lowlands had anyway long come to be run by the upper bourgeoisie, the great merchants and guildsmen called *regents*. It was a tough governing of the lower classes, who did not have political rights. But it was a little bit liberal, especially in the economy.

Then, starting late in the seventeenth century, inspired by the amazing Dutch economic success, the idea that ordinary people might be left alone without detailed regulation by their masters would gradually emerge in England and Scotland and their colonial offshoots. England first and a little later Scotland came to esteem what they had previously despised—that is, buying low and selling high, by a merchant who enriches his country and contributes to the well-being of the world. Leaving people alone economically came slowly into favor. The great economic historian Eric Jones speaks for example of the decline of guild restrictions in England: "The joker in the pack was the national shift in elite opinion, which the courts partly shared. The judges often declined to support the restrictiveness that the guilds sought to impose. . . . A key case concerned Newbury and Ipswich in 1616 . . . to the effect that 'foreigners,' men from outside a borough, could not be compelled to enroll"—that is, to join the guild and be subject to its restrictions.[6] The British, who were once violent and illiberal worshippers of kings, slowly became, in a phrase of the time, "a polite and commercial people."

Indeed, declared the literary man Samuel Johnson of London in 1775, "There are few ways in which a man can be more innocently employed than in getting money." His interlocutor at the time, his publisher William Strahan, who also lived by commerce, and was a friend of bourgeois Benjamin Franklin, remarked, "The more one thinks of this, the juster it will appear."[7] Looking at Britain from France, Voltaire, who himself made a fortune in speculation with his money earned as a playwright, had written in 1733 that a British nobleman's "brother does not think traffic is beneath him. . . . At the time that the Earl of Orford [that is, the prime minister Robert Walpole] governed Great Britain, his younger brother was no more than a factor [that is, a merchant's representative] in Aleppo."[8] A Swiss traveler in 1727 wrote that "in England commerce is not looked down upon, . . . as it is in France and Germany. [In Britain after 1707] men of good family and even of [aristocratic] rank may become merchants without losing caste."[9] What was previously dishonorable and contemptible—the pursuit of filthy lucre—was celebrated, or at the least not vigorously obstructed by guilds and governments. (We worry, and so should you: Is an illiberal and medieval obstructionism by regulation being reimposed?)

The result of the new liberal idea was that after 1800 or so, a tsunami of betterment rolled over the West and eventually over much of the rest. The betterment is properly called the *Great* Enrichment. Railways. Mass schooling. Skyscrapers. Electricity. Sewage treatment. Universities. Antibiotics. Containerization. Computers. In the places that have experienced it fully, the average Jack or Jill, whose great-great-grandparents were starkly impoverished, lives a life that is connected, wealthy, far from nasty, peaceful, and by historical standards amazingly long. Not Hobbesian. Wow.

2

It's the End of the World as They Knew It, and You Should Feel Pretty Good

Relatively speaking, at any rate. Lord knows there is still plenty wrong among the nations, and nothing we say is meant to imply that the job is finished or that there is no more to do for the remaining poor and tyrannized. By some counts, for example, there are still some forty million bought-and-sold slaves. Out of the seven and a half billion souls nowadays, the economist Paul Collier properly laments a "Bottom Billion," who still live the Hobbesian nightmare— though it should be noted that the Bottom Billion are typically ruled by a leviathan of a government, or an incompetent and corrupt one, sometimes all that and more.[1] North Korea. Chad. But Collier agrees with all informed observers that the *one* billion is an astonishing improvement over the situation as recently as 1960, when about 1.5 of the total then of three billion people on the planet lived lives that were poor, nasty, brutish, and short. They dragged along on that three dollars a day, or less.

Our present lives almost anywhere, in still very poor places, are of course not at all, in Hobbesian terms, anything like "solitary." More than half of the world's population now lives in what the person's nation reckons is an "urban" area, usually a very big one, a share rapidly growing. Fully 90 million Chinese farmers, for example, one fourteenth of the entire population of China, moved to big cities in the seven years from 2012 to 2019. About half of such urbanites worldwide have internet access.[2] Radically cheapened transport and communication—such as the railway, then the telegraph, then the bicycle, the tram, the telephone, the subway, the auto, the radio, the TV, the airplane, capped by the internet—have since 1800 fashioned a global village, the breaking down of local monopolies, and the end of solitude in a cave or desert, or the nasty nonsolitude of a traditional village.

So not at least "solitary." But especially you need to grasp that the world is no longer uniformly "poor." That's the crux, a miracle since 1800, or even since 1960, of enormously increasing world real income per person "in the face of," as it is conventionally put, a world population seven times larger since 1800 and 150 percent more since 1960.

The conventional phrase "in the face of," though, supposes that population growth causes *lower* per person income. It doesn't, not in the modern world. The phrase evokes an old commonplace in a zero-sum world, of too many new mouths outnumbering the hands and backs to grow the food. Thomas Malthus wrote so in 1798. On the contrary, economic science now, and anyway the raw experience of the past couple of centuries, says emphatically that having more people born is good, not bad. Not for Keynesian reasons of demand, but for neoclassical reasons of supply. (It applies to immigration, too. Listen up, you nativists and white nationalists.) More people now mean more opportunities to trade and to innovate, inside a "village" of almost 8 billion souls.

Our ancestors, we said, lived on about $3 a day, expressed in US dollars at 2008 prices. The poorest places were down at $1 a day, the richest as an average in 1800, up at a still pathetic $6. Now the two billion or so people in the very high-income nations earn more like $80 to $150 a day. They are on the sharply rising blade of a hockey stick of the Great Enrichment, after three hundred thousand years bumping along the $3 a day of the handle. The enriching people live in liberal economies in which you can venture on betterments for all, and profit from them—Toyota as against the impoverished Japanese of a century ago; Volvo as against the impoverished Swedes of a century and a half ago.

The great magnitude of the increase is not at all in scientific doubt, ranging from 1,000 to 10,000 percent over the pathetic base, depending on where one measures it or with what technical adjustments for quality improvement. The Nobel laureate in economics William Nordhaus notes that the conventional magnitudes are greatly understated precisely because the quality of goods and services has improved: "If we are to obtain accurate estimates of the growth of real incomes over the last century, we must somehow construct price indexes that account for the vast changes in the quality and range of goods and services that we consume, that somehow compare the services of horse with automobile, of Pony Express with facsimile machine [facsimile machine—how quaint!], of carbon paper with photocopier, of dark and lonely nights with nights spent watching television, and of brain surgery with magnetic resonance imaging."[3] The world's daily bread, along with clothing and shelter and entertainment and lighting and dentistry and air conditioning, has increased by a factor of easily *ten* globally, and much more, thirty to one hundred times, in the high-income nations. Such high income was once a club that Europeans imagined to be exclusively their own. Now places like China and India are knocking at the door. The average, including in the figure even some still wretchedly poor nations like Haiti or Mali, is equal to the average in Brazil, now about $33 a day, which was the US level in 1940. It is well below the present US level of $130 a day, but even $33 is a miraculous leap from $3 or $6. Never before.

Bring it into the terms of your own insanely rich life. Consider the last time you went to your local gourmet coffee shop. You can think of the 0.75 fluid ounce shot of espresso as the wherewithal for premodern daily consumption—and after all, the shot does cost about $3. It's probably not even espresso but rather watery, scorched, church-foyer coffee. But the change since 1800 is not an increase from a 0.75-ounce shot to, say, 1.5 ounces, which was the sort of magnitude seen in previous eras of temporary prosperity. Oh, no. It's an increase in the worldwide average to a heart-stopping 8-ounce cup. And the increase has been much, much larger in countries like the United States and Japan and Norway that have gone up to a full *31* ounces of premium coffee, blended with ice and topped with whipped cream and caramel for good measure. The increase is insanely good by historical standards. And it does not leave the poor behind. It does not come at their expense. It is amazing.

Nor is a modern and rich country Hobbesian "nasty," any way you want to think about it. If ethically, the political scientist John Mueller has pointed out that the popularity of war as an extension of politics has been declining for two centuries.[4] Liberals don't like starting wars. If physically "nasty," look at the pipes that bring you clean water to wash your clothes and dishes and body, and consider the indoor plumbing and refuse collection that whisk away the waste. (We are not forgetting where the waste goes, but that, too, is improving compared with 1800, when people were dumping sewage and garbage into the canal in front of the house, even in relatively rich Amsterdam.) Advances in cleanliness and hygiene have become routine, teeth regularly brushed and bodies washed and abundant clothing changed. Moderns have hot water on command and closets full of clothing, once reserved for dukes and duchesses, and doubtfully even for them. Perfume usually did the job. The Hall of Mirrors at Versailles, where the elite attended in 1700 on the Sun King, had no toilets: the dukes and duchesses relieved themselves in the staircases.

Hobbesian "brutish"? Not remotely, by historical standards. For all the anxiety about crime rates and terrorism now, an anxiety stoked by populists of the right, you are less likely than your ancestors to die at the hands of another person—or for that matter, to be mauled by an animal. As for the terrorists, John Mueller also found that the threat of modern terrorism is grossly overblown.[5] Outside the Middle East, in which nonstate violence in aid of political ends has indeed sharply increased, terrorism has fallen to a tiny percentage of its level during the 1960s and 1970s. You older readers can remember, among other terroristic horrors from Colombia to Kashmir, the weekly bombings in the United States in opposition to the Vietnam War and in favor of radical economic change—radicals tried and failed to bomb the economics department at UCLA in 1968 but succeeded in a building at the University of Wisconsin—or the bombings in the United Kingdom by the Irish Republican Army. Europe in the 1960s and

1970s saw bombings in Spain by Basque separatists, kidnappings for ransom out of their autos of politicians and businesspeople in Italy by the Brigate Rosse and in West Germany by the Baader-Meinhof Gang. The joke in Germany at the time was that BMW autos, high-end and therefore often driven by wealthy businesspeople able to pay large ransoms, amounted to *Baader-Meinhof Wagen.* The chance in the United States of dying at the hands of terrorists, domestic or international, Mueller notes, is close to zero.

As for the animals, until the nineteenth century in Europe, the nature outside the village or town was viewed as a terrifying enemy, not as a romantic prospect or a glorious national park for Bambi the Fawn and Smokey the Bear. In the early nineteenth century, packs of wolves roamed parts of the urbanized Netherlands, and still more recently they were a scourge in eastern Europe. The historian Steven Pyne observes that, until late in the nineteenth century, the Grand Canyon of the Colorado was viewed as a nasty obstacle to travel, a terrifying entrance to hell.[6] The historian Barbara Hanawalt discovered that the murder rate in ye olde villages of medieval England was far higher than in the worst US police precincts.[7] Modernity has given us plenty of imagined and real violence in video games and movies and football, rather like ancient Greek drama or Chinese opera or Roman gladiatorial games. But nowadays they are mostly substitutes for the real and major violence. You and your children are more likely to die of diseases of the very old, in a bed surrounded by loved ones, than in a quarrel in a bar with men routinely armed with daggers and swords, as the playwright Christopher Marlowe did in 1593, or in a battle death, as did a startlingly high percentage of the men of the medieval English nobility.

Nor has life remained, as Hobbes put it, "short." Life expectancy at birth at the height of the Roman Empire was twenty-four years. The Roman cemeteries are crowded with the remains of children. By 1800, it was lower than forty in England and France and other western European countries, and often lower elsewhere. Today it is around eighty in wealthy countries and around sixty even in the poorest. The average is more than seventy years globally, and rising smartly. A baby born in Nigeria today can expect half again as many days as could a baby born in the richest countries in the world in 1800. As the economist and Nobel laureate Angus Deaton put it in 2016, "Today, children in sub-Saharan Africa are more likely to survive to age 5 than were English children born in 1918."[8] That was in *England* a mere century ago—then as now near the top of the world's income tables. And the Nigerian child's life-years will be radically healthier, her literacy higher, her prospects greater than they were for her parents. In the first decade of the twenty-first century, sub-Saharan Africa started to share in world growth, at rates doubling real GDP per person in a single long generation. Ethiopia is booming.

And more. Go to OurWorldInData.org and turn over the attested facts of income, health, education, human rights, and a host of other measures of well-being. It's not 1960 anymore, class, not to speak of 1800, as the great Hans Rosling (1948–2017), a Swedish professor of public health, urged us to realize. He argued that the simplest single measure of welfare is infant mortality, because it reflects the over-burdened lives of poor adult caretakers as much as the poisonous quality of water available to their babies.[9] Infant and child mortality has fallen since 1960 like a stone worldwide. By every measure, the lives of average people—and of the poorest, too—are better than they have ever been and are rapidly getting still better.

The world *is* making poverty history. The poor are *not* always with us.

3
Nostalgia and Pessimism Worsen Poverty

So the world has been enriched. But for whom? *Cui bono?* asked the Romans: "Whose benefit?"

Answer: Yours, and more and more of your fellow humans, with a believable promise that the whole world will presently become rich and free.

Consider *Les Misérables*. One of the novel's and the musical's main characters is Fantine, a single mother in Paris in 1832 living a hard life. In the summer of 2014, the Red Mountain Theatre Company in Birmingham, Alabama, staged the show. An advertisement in the program for the Women's Fund exhorted the audience to "Help Women Like Fantine in Birmingham" and noted, "The median income for a single mother with two children is ["only" implied] $29,390."

We admire the Women's Fund for tying its mission to one of *Les Misérables'* central themes. As Victor Hugo wrote to one his publishers, "Wherever men go in ignorance or despair, wherever women sell themselves for bread, wherever children lack a book to learn from or a warm hearth, *Les Misérables* knocks at the door and says: 'Open up, I am here for you.'"[1] Yet we wonder, in our economists' cold manner: Is the median single mother of two children in Birmingham, Alabama, really "like Fantine"?

Since the mid-twentieth century, economic historians have gathered the evidence to give a decisive answer: No, she is not. Not even close. Around 1832, the annual per capita income of France (in 2014 US dollars) was as low as $1,750 or as high as $2,270, depending on which technical adjustments one makes.[2] For each person in a family, that's $4.79 to $6.22 per day. As members of the Misérables, Fantine and her daughter Cosette would have earned much less than the French average. Compare such an 1832 income per person to the median three-person, single-mother-headed household in Birmingham in 2014. It would be the $29,390 the Women's Fund mentioned divided by three people and then divided by 365, a daily income of $26.84. It is between four and five-and-a-half times higher than the French *average* of 1832, or more like eight to ten times higher than impoverished Fantine. In short, a single mother in Birmingham in 2014 led a vastly more comfortable life, materially speaking, than did someone like Fantine in Paris in 1832. Running water. Health care that works. Literacy. Enough to eat. An apartment instead of a miserable shared room. It isn't heaven, Lord knows, but it wasn't the hell of the poor in France in 1832.

And the difference is underestimated, considering the difficulty of adjusting fully for improvements in the quality of the goods and services available now. Think of medicine in 1832, still bleeding people—a little earlier, a bleeding administered by doctors had killed George Washington. Or think of transport, by foot or a rich man's horse ("If wishes were horses, beggars would ride"). In olden days the heating, education, glass in buildings, and hygiene such as sewers were pathetic by the standards of the nonrich in Birmingham in 2014.

The $26.84 per person per day is pretty close to the present global average we mentioned of $33. Compared with the rest of the world, the single mother in Birmingham with two children in 2014 had a solidly middling income—a real income around what the US average, we have noted, was during the 1930s and 1940s. Not heaven, again, but not hell, either. (McCloskey as a small child was there; pretty good, it seemed—penny candy at the corner store.)

Fantine would choose Birmingham every time. She would be better off in goods and services, with a prospect for improvement. This is not to say that no one even in rich countries such as the United States is unskilled, addicted, badly parented, discriminated against, or simply horribly unlucky. Think back to Florida Man. George

Packer's *The Unwinding: An Inner History of the New America* (2013) and Barbara Ehrenreich's earlier *Nickel and Dimed: On (Not) Getting By in America* (2001) carry on a long and distinguished tradition of telling the bourgeoisie about the poor—one extending back to James Agee and Walker Evans, *Let Us Now Praise Famous Men* (1941), George Orwell, *The Road to Wigan Pier* (1937), Jack London, *The People of the Abyss* (1903), Jacob Riis, *How the Other Half Lives: Studies among the Tenements of New York* (1890), and the fount, Friedrich Engels, *The Condition of the Working Class in England* (1845).

They are not making it up. Anyone who reads such books is wrenched out of a comfortable ignorance about the "other half." In fictional form one is similarly wrenched by John Steinbeck's *The Grapes of Wrath* (1939) or Richard Wright's *Native Son* (1940) or James T. Farrell's *Studs Lonigan* trilogy (1932–1935) or, from earlier in Europe, Émile Zola's *Germinal* (1885) or indeed Hugo's *Les Misérables* (1862). Such books helped form the minds of many socialists (including McCloskey at age sixteen). The wrenching is salutary. It is said that Winston Churchill, scion of the aristocracy, believed that most British poor people lived in rose-covered cottages. He couldn't imagine back-to-backs in Salford, with the outhouse at the end of the row. Wake up, Winston.

But waking up does not imply despairing nor introducing policies that do not in fact help the poor—or proposing the overthrow of "the system," if the system is in fact enriching the poor over the long run, or at any rate is enriching the poor better than those other systems that have been tried from time to time. The children of the sharecropping families in Hale County, Alabama, whom Agee and Evans objectified, to the lasting resentment of the older members, are doing pretty well, holding decent jobs; many of their own children are going to college.[3] That even over the long run there remain some poor people does not mean the system is not working for the poor, so long as their condition is continuing to improve and the poor are getting real help. And the poor in the United States and elsewhere that liberalism has been tried are in fact improving, contrary to the newspaper stories and the pessimistic books. Massive help to the poor is working, if not as well as it would under a more consistent liberalism. The percentage of desperately poor is heading toward zero. That people still sometimes die in hospitals does not mean that medicine should be replaced by witch doctors, so long as death rates are falling. Economically speaking, in the tyrannies of Mao Zedong's China or Hugo Chávez's Venezuela, and even in Bernie Sanders's imagined sweet democratic socialism, the witch doctors are put in charge. Magically, they promise, the poor will be better off. Simple. Cast a spell.

Uh-oh. One wishes that TV producers and newspaper editors would worry about their relentless story line and its statist and magical implication. Look at the dying patients, they cry. Look at the still poor.

§

A Fantine whisked off to modern Birmingham could get the picture by going down to the local library and checking out any number of books documenting long-run economic, political, social, and cultural betterment—the Rosling family's brilliant summarizing book *Factfulness*, for example, which we draw on heavily here.[4] (Highly recommended. Wake up.)

People have, Hans Rosling and his coauthors note, more political liberty now. In 1816, with Fantine's world emerging from a generation of French wars, 1 percent of the world's population lived under democratic institutions. In 2015, 56 percent did. In 1800, slavery was legal in 193 out of 194 countries (the UK was the exception). It had fallen to 3 by 2017. In 1893, only one country out of the 194 considered by Rosling (New Zealand) allowed women to vote. It had risen to 193 by 2017.[5]

"But that's the last two hundred years," you protest. "Things have deteriorated recently." Oh, heavens no, dear (says McCloskey), they have not. You're quite mistaken. You may be cherishing your (as you imagine) sophisticated and good-hearted pessimism more than a scientific factfulness from the Realistic Rosling or historicoeconomic truths from the Mindful McCloskey and the Candid Carden.

McCloskey was born on September 11, 1942, at the height of the

Battle of Stalingrad. During that fateful year, 201 people out of every 100,000 on the planet died in battle, unsurprisingly considering that it was the turning point of World War II. In 2016, the Rosling team reports, only one person out of every 100,000 died in battle. What's mildly surprising is that you hear more about the thousands of them than about the tens of millions in World War II, and therefore you get the impression that war is more prevalent now. It's not.

The fraction of people living in extreme poverty around the world was very high in 1942, and it was still 50 percent in 1966, when Mc-Closkey was a graduate student in economics, as the sixties began to swing. It was 29 percent as late as 1997, when Carden graduated from high school and Princess Diana died. By 2017, it was 9 percent. In 1997, 42 percent of the population of India and China, home to four out of every ten humans, lived in extreme poverty. By 2017 those percentages had fallen to 12 percent in India and 0.7 percent in China. In Latin America, the proportion fell from 14 percent to 4 percent. Access to health care has changed, too. In 1980, when John Lennon was murdered, Carden turned one year old and was among the merely 22 percent of one-year-olds worldwide who got at least one vaccination. The percentage by 2016 had quadrupled, to 88 percent.

We suggest therefore, following the Roslings, that you set aside a hazy nostalgia for the good old days, such as the famous 1950s and 1960s during which McCloskey grew up. (*Oh, Elvis!*) Put the actual facts into the chronology of your own life. In 1950, when the Korean War began, 28 percent of the world's children between the ages of five and fourteen worked full time. By 2012, when Carden's third child was born, that figure had fallen to 10 percent. In 1970, near the beginning of McCloskey's dozen years teaching economics and then also history at the University of Chicago, 28 percent of the people in the world were undernourished. By 2015, the year Carden got tenure at Samford University in Birmingham, 11 percent were. And on and on, year by year—with no recent slowing, not at all. Rather, there has been recently a rapid approach to a worldwide Great Enrichment.

Think about the rights of women and racial and ethnic minorities and LGBTQ folk. Think it possible you see the past like the character Wee Bear in a couple of 2005 panels from the comic strip "Pearls

Before Swine."[6] Wee Bear implores the then-seventy-four-year-old pioneer of African Americans in major-league baseball Willie Mays, as "an icon of a past era that somehow seems better than today," to "go back to centerfield and everything will be okay." Mays declines. Wee Bear persists, exclaiming, "I'm drowning in a sea of Sean Hannitys and James Carvilles and Ann Coulters and Al Frankens. . . . I want to return to 1957 when this was one nation!" Uh-huh. Mays replies, "When I couldn't eat in certain restaurants?" Think it possible that 1957 (Sputnik; troops in Little Rock) was a bad year for most of humanity. Radically less so now.

Yes, we understand. You view pessimism as more honorable than optimism. Pessimism says that you really, really care about the world's poor and *les misérables*, and really, really want to do more, or at least coerce other people to do more. And it says, too, that you are cool and sophisticated, unlike the cockeyed optimists Rosling, Carden, McCloskey, and numerous other demographic and economic scientists. A realist. "So much more remains to be done," the politician declares. Done by giving the politician more power to coerce. "The world has appalling problems remaining," declares the self-appointed planner of your life. Historical facts and economic principles be damned. "Better the precautionary principle," declares the enthusiastic environmentalist. The time is late. Humanity is doomed.

Pessimism sells. For reasons we have never understood, people love to hear that the world is going to hell. They become huffy and scornful when some idiotic optimist intrudes on their pleasure. A cartoon in the *New Yorker* shows a couple who have just passed a bearded man in a prophet's robes holding up a sign saying, "The End Is Near." One of them remarks, "Say, wasn't that Paul Krugman?"[7]

But the evidence is that pessimism has been for a long time deeply mistaken. The evidence lies all around, we have noted, in sober and in silly sources. The economists Steven Horwitz and Stewart Dompe exploit evidence from the long-running TV show *The Simpsons*. In the first season of the show, which debuted in December 1989, at the conclusion of the regular opening sequence, you see the family plopped down in front of an old vacuum-tube TV set topped with a rabbit-ear antenna.[8] ("What's that?" the Generation Z reader asks.) Twenty seasons later, the TV is a flat-screen model. Still later it's falling off the wall and the characters are ignoring it and attending to their laptops and smartphones.

The world is bettering. Let's keep doing it, and not let ourselves be charmed by an unscientific pessimism.

4

Under Liberalism the Formerly Poor Can Flourish Ethically and Spiritually

The world since 1800 has grown richer spiritually, too—in contradiction to fears from both the left and the right that people have exchanged a material for a spiritual poverty. On the contrary, a spiritual great enrichment has accompanied the material. A young American, Timothy Walker of Cincinnati, was host in 1831 to the French aristocrat Alexis de Tocqueville during his American tour. Walker, excusing his country's primitive high culture at the time, declared, "Our doctrine is that men must be released from the bondage of perpetual bodily toil before they can make great spiritual attainments."[1] And so the Americans at length did, compliments of their bourgeois such as Walker. God and Mammon have coexisted for two centuries.

Trade per se is not vulgar, dirty, dishonorable, mean, or selfish. On the contrary, it can easily be honorable, spiritually ennobling, altruistic, and possibility-expanding—when governed, as it regularly is, by a balanced system of the virtues of faith, hope, love, courage, justice, temperance, and prudence. Jeffrey Tucker's brilliant and humane book of 2019, *The Market Loves You: Why You Should Love It Back*, notes that trade among people is an occasion for love. Yes, love. "It's not personal love," he writes, not always, though you personally in fact come to love (or sometimes hate) your office mates and the server who pours your coffee at the local eatery every morning. Tucker quotes C. S. Lewis (he of *The Chronicles of Narnia*), noting that ordinary life depends, after all, on affection, ancient Greek *storgê*: "Affection is responsible for nine-tenths of whatever solid and durable happiness there is in our natural lives." Tucker comments on Lewis's remark that affection in markets is "like structural love, a system-wide devotion to benefaction [Latin for 'good-doing'] based on giving and getting. . . . We need each other. We trust each other. We are lovers" in the market as much as by other paths in the home or office or on the playground.[2]

Oh no, said the philosopher Michael Sandel in a 2012 book entitled *What Money Can't Buy: The Moral Limits of Markets.*[3] Well, of course money shouldn't buy everything, such as much of *storgê*, though in a market. Sandel gives numerous examples of the moral dilemmas in choosing money prices rather than time spent standing in line or racial status or Communist Party membership to allocate things, from selling kidneys to buying baseball players. Surely many things are sold that shouldn't be, such as college term papers or, as we have come to know, college places for phony athletes. We agree with Sandel that the study of markets should be remoralized, in just the way Jeffrey Tucker does. People should know why they believe, morally speaking, that bread should be allocated by a market but children should not. It's not enough to simply sneer from the left or right or middle. Economists, too, need to do the philosophical work. "Markets are not mere mechanisms," Sandel wisely observes. "They embody certain norms."[4] He later adds, "Market reasoning is incomplete without moral reasoning."[5] Yes.

Yet, surprisingly, his moral thoughts are two only, and thin versions even of these: that a state-enforced equality of outcome, beyond a liberal equality of permission, is good; and that the sacred can be corrupted by the profane. Sandel states, "The fairness objection [to what money should buy] asks about the equality [of outcome] that market choices may reflect; the corruption objection asks about the attitude and norms that market relations may damage."[6] That, philosophically speaking, is it. Never mind, it seems, the inequality of time to queue or racial status or Communist Party membership that in the absence of supply-and-demand prices comes to determine who gets what; never mind, it seems, the norms that *non*market relations such as nepotism or political dogma or gender prejudice may damage.

Sandel is a prominent representative of antimarket thinkers who have not paused to do much thinking about what they condemn. His analysis of equality as a moral principle, his "fairness objection," does not get beyond the schoolyard taunt that such-and-such is "not fair." Yet if charging tolls on congested highways is "unfair to commuters of modest means" (in Sandel's repeated formulation of the first principle), what is to stop society from concluding that charging for bread and housing and clothing and cable TV and Fritos is "unfair"?[7] Nothing. The society ends in full-blown statism, a modern leviathan. The unanalyzed dictum that it's "unfair" that Carden does not have his own 5,000-square-foot supersuite at the Bellagio in Las Vegas (he really does find it troubling) would slip down to allocation by state direction by the Communist or Nazi Party for everything. Byelorussia.

One can devise moral principles to stop the slip down the road to serfdom. But Sandel does not offer any, like the majority of our good friends the communitarian and regulatory and soft-socialist critics of markets. In accord with a thoughtless dogma of fairness, Sandel leaves his college class to conclude that unadorned "unfairness" is a moral taunt suitable to discussion among grownups.

His second principle, and a better argument for what money can't buy, and the deep source of anger at an enriched modernity, is that buying with money can sometimes cause the sacred to be spoiled by the profane. Sandel does not actually use the theological words. He would have benefitted from studying theology and would have gotten further in his moral philosophy. But, yes, "we corrupt a good, an activity, or a social practice whenever we treat it according to a lower norm than is appropriate to it."[8] Got it.

Meanwhile, though, his theory remains again at the playground level of an unanalyzed contrast between the two, high versus low. Sandel is persuasive, admittedly, when he goes after the equally shallow moral theories of Prudence Only by many of our fellow economists. Sandel is correct that what is called "agency theory," which since 1980 has taken over American graduate schools of business, is ethically crazy. It declares that all that humans require are incentives, like trained seals. No. Humans require also Lewisian/ Tuckerian *storgê*, affection, and professionalism and judgment and history and norms, as bankers have recently learned.

Yet Sandel offers no philosophical standard for the sacred versus the profane, no guide to his students or the bankers. One can agree that buying grades or honorary degrees or a friend's advice or a husband's sexual services are viewed nowadays as immoral. But why exactly? Once upon a time all such things were for sale—and today still are in some societies and circles. Note again the college admission scandal, by which rich parents can buy their child's admission to Harvard by buying the fencing coach's house at twice what it is worth. It has long been true in Russia. In the European Middle Ages one could buy almost anything—wheat and iron, yes, but also husbands, marketplaces, kingdoms, eternal salvation. Sandel claims repeatedly that "market triumphalism" is new. It's bad history, although it's what most people believe: that in olden days the people were pure and fair but now they are "capitalist" and corrupt. But the actual golden age of allocation by alleged fairness and actual disgust and corrupt politics was not those far olden days but rather 1933–1965, the height of statist experiments. Before 1933 a market logic pretty much ruled, in China and India as much as in England and Italy.

Sandel worries properly that the market can crowd out the sacred. A corporate financing of, say, elementary classrooms might crowd out self-critical teaching about innovism. Yet Sandel does not inform his college students that financing by the state might crowd out self-critical teaching about the bad results of, say, the unthinking patriotism taught to McCloskey as a child in the 1950s or the unthinking obedience to the nanny state taught to Carden in the 1980s, or the unthinking environmentalism taught to Steven Landsburg's daughter in the 1990s that he eviscerated in the last chapter of his fine book *The Armchair Economist.*[9]And what about crowding *in*? A society allocating goods by race or gender or party membership is not obviously superior in moral terms compared with one like Sweden in which market prices rule. Sandel declares that "we must also ask whether market norms will crowd out non-market norms."[10] But he provides no philosophical analysis or historical evidence about how you would answer the opposite crowding, as when nonmarket norms of Jim Crow in the brief Sandelian golden age before 1965 crowded out the market norm that Willie Mays's money is as good at a lunch counter as a white person's. A market society is by no means contemptible ethically, if one looks into the actual ethical effects and thinks about them. The French spoke in the eighteenth century of "sweet commerce," the civilizing effect of markets introduced into societies of status or solitude. That's right.

We agree with Sandel that there are things that are for sale that shouldn't be, such as slaves and college term papers. But we also agree with Sandel's critics Jason Brennan and Peter M. Jaworski—of *Markets Without Limits: Moral Virtues and Commercial Interests*— that it isn't the introduction of exchange that makes these things wrong. Slavery is wrong even if you are giving away the slaves. Plagiarism is wrong even if you get a ghostwritten essay as a gift. It isn't, Brennan and Jaworski argue, the introduction of market exchange that turns something worthy into something wicked. We think their principle—"If you may do it for free, you may do it for money"—is much more defensible.[11]

Brennan and Jaworski offer an answer to Sandel. Sandel recoils at the idea that people can pay to have their wedding toasts written, but Brennan and Jaworski ask us to imagine a Twin Earth with a Twin America in which a Twin Michael Sandel teaches at Twin Harvard and has written a book titled *What Money Can't Buy*. There's a twist, though: in Twin America, it is customary for people to pay extravagantly for wedding toasts written by first-rate wordsmiths and customary for the members of the wedding party to bake the cake. There is, in Twin America, a growing business in making wedding cakes, and Twin Michael Sandel includes the burgeoning market in wedding cakes as an example of how market logic is corrupting the sacred. And yet Real Michael Sandel lets the actually existing market for wedding cakes, wedding planners, catering, and event spaces pass without comment.[12] There are thriving markets in a great many evil and corrupting things. But it isn't that they are traded in markets that makes them evil.

§

Think: Fantine of 1832, if she could pass over magically to 2014 Birmingham, would have more than bread. Frenzied betterment brought about by the Bourgeois Deal multiplied the voices in the artistic and spiritual conversation as much as the food-and-shelter conversation and amplified them. Indeed, the argument for commercially tested betterment in profane markets is the same as the argument for choice-tested betterment in sacred arts and worship. The Mississippi Delta is said to begin in the lobby of Memphis, Tennessee's Peabody Hotel. On December 15, 1977, Congress officially recognized nearby Beale Street in Memphis, now a booze-soaked tourist attraction, as the "Home of the Blues." Playing the blues and succeeding on Beale Street required an entrepreneurial spirit and a creative mind—and the permissions of the Bourgeois Deal.

It also required the modern abundance of musical instruments. As the musician and writer Chris Kjorness has shown, for many of Memphis's musical pioneers in 1908, the instrument was the electric guitar from the Sears, Roebuck & Co. catalog for $1.89 (about $53 in today's prices; two hours' work now, three days' work then).[13] Cheap electric guitars were labor-saving instruments for a creatively destroying innovism. With instructional manuals from Sears, too, black musicians like B. B. King and white musicians like Roy Clark learned their craft.

Sears was not a charity. Commercial innovism literally brought new, previously silenced voices into the musical conversation. By leaving Sears alone to innovate in distribution (compare Amazon today, which has reinvented the Sears-Spiegel-Wards mail-order business for the internet age), commerce made a musical revolution. It has happened repeatedly. Fifth-century Athens, fifteenth-century Florence, the 1950s of New York City were great ages of art and science pouring out of highly commercial societies reaching new peaks of prosperity. Riches in material things led to riches in spiritual things.

True, even the blessed Adam Smith noted that the division of labor could be stupefying, if people became savants in one task and idiots in all others. But it hasn't actually happened. Factory work was no more soul-destroying than the idiocy of rural life. An anti-factory English folk song goes: "A nice young man was William Brown. / He worked for a wage in a northern town. / He worked from 8 to 6 at night / Turning a wheel from left to right." To be sure. But William's grandfather worked from eight to six at night turning a scythe from left to right, on meadows and wheat fields. And after the Great Enrichment, birthed by the factory, William's grandson became a chartered accountant and his granddaughter a ballet dancer.

McCloskey's mother knew how to hang wallpaper and her grandmother knew how to preserve vegetables. McCloskey can't do either. But the diminished portfolio of her homemaking skills is more than offset by the energy she can spend on other and sometimes more spirit-elevating things. (Not that hanging wallpaper has no spiritual reward. McCloskey did try it once for her little daughter's room and couldn't walk past it without a surge of craft pride. She hung a door, too. Once.) True, in Carden's case the other things that specialization frees him to do has sometimes included watching pro wrestling. McCloskey is appalled. On the other hand, she is equally addicted to English cricket matches and Fred Astaire movies, some of them not of the highest artistic quality. Anyway, people after the Great Enrichment have the modern leisure to do spirit-elevating things, if they so choose, such as adventure travel to Antarctica to watch birds or hours of practice on the cello to master a Bach sonata.

"Yes, but innovism means vulgarity, uniformity, homogeneity, and a loss of diversity," you say. False. The economist Tyler Cowen argues, for example, that commercial tests for traditional crafts, such as soapstone carving among First Nations in Canada, save the crafts.[14] True, the big shopping streets in Birmingham and Chicago and Los Angeles and Paris and Taipei have come to look more and more alike as the global economy has integrated. But the range of cultural and culinary offerings within each city has exploded. Back in the 1970s Chicago was a meat-and-potatoes town, save for hot dogs and deep-dish pizza. Not anymore; you can find cuisine from nearly any nationality there now. The opening of Wasabi Juan's in Birmingham meant the people of the Magic City could get sushi burritos without having to go to Los Angeles or even Atlanta. ("Sushi burritos": there's an amazing world-cuisine outcome.) Where a few years ago Birmingham had no Ethiopian restaurants, it recently had two and now has one (and Washington, DC, has thirty). Is the world somehow poorer, culturally, because people in Birmingham can eat sushi burritos or lamb tibs just like people in Los Angeles and Atlanta? Or Tokyo or Addis Ababa?

Cosette growing up in Birmingham in 2014 would have unmatched opportunities for self-authorship and self-definition. Mario Vargas Llosa, a liberal and a Nobel laureate in literature, defended liberty-fueled globalization:

> Globalization extends radically to all citizens of this planet the possibility to construct their individual cultural identities through voluntary action, according to their preferences and intimate motivations. Now, citizens are not always obligated, as in the past and in many places in the present, to respect an identity that traps them in a concentration camp from which there is no escape— the identity that is imposed on them through the language, nation, church, and customs of the place where they were born.[15]

"But doesn't innovism encourage cultural imperialism?" you ask. Maybe. Some noble savages have perhaps been ripped or enticed out of admirable cultures. Tocqueville in 1832 took a side trip by canoe to the Upper Peninsula of the Michigan Territory and down to what is now Wisconsin, in search of the noble savages of Enlightenment imagining. He thought he found a few. But some *ig*noble savages, too, have learned a life free of tribal patriarchy and family violence. Good lives can be and actually are lived on a gigantic scale in the modern, bourgeois town, freed from child penury and the little tyrants of the fields. In Alan Paton's *Cry, the Beloved Country,* John Kumalo, from a village in Natal and now a big man in Johannesburg, says, "I do not say we are free here." A black man under apartheid in South Africa in 1948 could hardly say so. "But at least I am free of the chief. At least I am free of an old and ignorant man."[16]

Tragic? Not in the eyes of Kumalo. People have voted with their feet by the billions to become more free in bourgeois towns. The medieval motto in German was *Stadtluft macht frei*, town air makes one free, as it in fact did in law. If you fled from serfdom and managed to stay in a town for year and a day, your serfdom was over. People nowadays have fled from workers' paradises in Eastern Europe and Cuba and now Venezuela, lining up for the opportunity to be exploited as day laborers in Paris, Texas, or Paris, France. True, there are voluntary exceptions to the embrace of innovism. The Amish, in the United States scattered in little communities along the 42nd meridian from Pennsylvania to Iowa, come to mind. The Amish allow their young people to try out the world of the "English," as they call it, but allow them back, too, and most do come back. Fine: a free choice. We liberals approve.

Fantine and Cosette today, then, would live comprehensively better lives. Would it be because they got help from the Women's Fund? No, not mainly, though such charity is admirable. Would it be because wealth was redistributed by coercive law from the rich to the poor? Not mainly. The riches of the rich aren't enough to greatly enrich the poor. A socialist is supposed to have come to Andrew Carnegie's office at the height of his wealth in the 1890s and argued to him that the wealthy should redistribute their wealth to the poor of the earth. According to the anecdote, Carnegie asked an assistant to go get him a rough estimate of his current wealth and of the population of the earth. The assistant returned shortly with the figures, and Carnegie performed a calculation, then turned to the assistant and said, "Give this gentleman sixteen cents. That's his share of the wealth."[17]

Overwhelmingly the imagined enrichment of Fantine and Cosette transferred to Birmingham in 2014 would come from the Great Enrichment, long in full swing—and swinging to the benefit of Fantine and Cosette and other poor people. Much of it happened well before the welfare state emerged in Europe and its offshoots.

The condition of the poor has been raised much, much more by the Great Enrichment than by charity or regulation or redistribution, a point that Senator Cory Booker made during the primaries for the Democratic nomination of 2020, in arguing against Senator Elizabeth Warren's proposals for taxing the very rich. When he was mayor of Newark, he realized that what the poor really need are jobs and especially entrepreneurial opportunities. As the economic historians Ian Gazeley and Andrew Newell concluded in their 2010 study of "the reduction, almost to elimination, of extreme poverty among working households in Britain between 1904 and 1937": "The elimination of grinding poverty among working families was almost complete by the late thirties, well before the Welfare State."[18] Their chart 2 exhibits weekly income distributions in 1886 prices at 1886, 1906, 1938, and 1960, showing the disappearance of the inflation-adjusted classic line of misery for British workers, the money income of "'round about a £ a week."

Fantine and Cosette in Birmingham would live in a world that has adopted the Bourgeois Deal and does not honor the aristocrat with his nine-hundred-year-old name or the Robert Moses city planner with his ample tools of coercion. It honors the Bangladeshi mother running a knitting machine in a factory to feed her children, and the Tokyo buyers and sellers at the early morning tuna auction, and the Cincinnati accounts-payable manager double-checking his figures, and the Silicon Valley computer programmer looking for a better way to index the world's information.

Giving people what they want, and are in justice willing to pay for when they can, is a good system. "Economics," writes Jeffrey Tucker, "is not just about making money. It's also about a chance to be valuable to others, to yourself."[19] By contrast, giving people what the critics of "capitalism" think they *should* want, or what people do want but want to get magically free of sacrifice of their own efforts for other people, burdening another person for their own gain, is a hideously selfish society. Saint Paul scorned the new Christians in Thessaloniki sitting around waiting for the Second Coming. "We were not idle when we were with you, nor did we eat anyone's food without paying for it . . . so that we would not be a burden to any of you. . . . For even when we were with you, we gave you this rule: 'The one who is unwilling to work shall not eat'" (2 Thess. 3:7–10). Our model society is liberal, and it in fact made people rich and free and self-respecting. The other is statist, whether socialist or fascist or populist, burdening one group to benefit another and in the end burdening everyone. It has made people poor and slavish. The one made for art by Chagall and Matisse, sold in a market. The other made for socialist realist paintings of tractor drivers, ordered up by the commissar of art. Look at them and choose.

Markets in fact provide a voice for the voiceless. Money talks, and the poor man's dollar bill speaks as loudly as the rich man's. In aggregate, ordinary people in rich modern economies speak loudly, lavishing profit on Walmart and Disney and other purveyors of ordinary life. To be sure, profits arising from political favors, such as nowadays in US wind farms and sugar fields and ethanol distilleries and medical doctoring, are not expressions of democratic wants in free society. They arise from the government's monopoly of coercion, expressing the desires of politically connected interests getting a subsidy from you or restricting your entry into their business. US medicine is expensive because it is a great assemblage of monopolies enforced by the government. Senators from a handful of sugar-producing states have ordered up the restrictions that make sugar twice as expensive in the United States as in the rest of the world.

But when people come together in markets, they speak as a free people choosing. Free people will not build pyramids over the grave of the pharaoh (actually, some archaeological evidence suggests that workers on the Egyptian pyramids were not slaves but laborers paid in cash). They will, however, gladly build a fake pyramid on the Las Vegas strip, voting with their willingness to work at its wages and voting with their pay packets on tattooing and the blackjack table.

A nostalgic, haughty, and ill-informed clerisy sneers, undemocratically. Stop it.

5

Consider the Possibility
That Your Doubts
Might Be Mistaken

You will doubt all this, so irritatingly contrary to received opinion. Yet in 1650, Oliver Cromwell wrote one last time to the Scottish presbyters, before crushing their rebellion, "I beseech you, . . . think it possible you are mistaken." We too beseech you.

"But growth has destroyed the environment," you say, doubting our optimism. Think it possible, for all the received opinion one hears repeated of the "existential crisis" for the environment, that you are mistaken. The environmental record has in fact improved, through regulation and commercially tested betterment. The Roslings' data say so.[1] In 1970, the world pumped out from smokestacks and the rest 38 kilograms of sulfur dioxide per person. The amount fell by 2010 to 14 kilograms. In 1970, ozone-depleting substances were emitted at 1,663,000 tons in total. By 2016, such emissions had fallen to 22,000 tons. In 1979, 636,000 tons of oil were spilled from tanker ships, a peak. In 2016, it was 6,000 tons.

In the increasing number of rich countries, the disasters from the environment, too, are less deadly. The Galveston hurricane of 1900, in a place then rich by the standards of the time, if miserably poor by present-day standards, killed about 8,000 people. Disasters killed 971,000 every year in the 1930s. From 2010 to 2016, that annual figure had fallen to 72,000—and the world's population, meanwhile, had more than tripled. If climate change were to lead to a tenfold increase in disaster-related mortality, which we reckon is a crazy overestimate, the death rate would still be far below what it was in the 1930s. Progress.

"But aren't people more socially isolated than before?" you ask. Think it possible you are mistaken. The biggest change in Carden's lifetime has been the revolution of communications. In 1980, 0.0003 percent of the world had mobile phones. It was 65 percent in 2017. No one was using the internet in 1980. In 2017 nearly half of the world's population was. You'll reply, "Aha! Exactly! The cell phone itself has made people into screen watchers!" Well, sure. Mc-Closkey, approached at speed on the sidewalk of Michigan Avenue by a millennial intently scanning his smartphone instead of watching out for knocking down old ladies, gets the point. But the result has been a gigantic rise in the number and strength of "weak ties," as the sociologists call them, at little actual cost in fewer "strong ties." You still have a mother. (And, by the way, why haven't you called her today?) Commercially tested betterment destroys some social connections. McCloskey remembers that when television came in during the 1950s, there was a sharp drop-off in casual visits of an evening to the neighbor's front porch—excepting a rise in visits to watch Archbishop Fulton J. Sheen together on the TV. But it *creatively* destroys them, regularly replacing old connections with new ones, and vastly more of them. In the old days, before the proliferation of big cities, you were cornered in town by a few people who knew the place, and your place. The narrowing old days were not so golden, or for that matter not so very olden—Sherwood Anderson's portrait of late nineteenth-century lives in the little mythical town of Winesburg, Ohio (1919) is not cheering, and in long perspective it was only yesterday.

Rising literacy is crucial to a wider life, such as on the internet. Of reading, in 1816 the working-class poet John Keats wrote, "Much have I traveled in the realms of gold / And many goodly states and kingdoms seen," in imagination. The internet and rock music, among other English-speaking modernities, have made English, in a phrase that must depress French speakers, the lingua franca of the world. People are more attached, not less.

"But the world is not as safe," you say. Again, think it possible you are mistaken. The global village of news makes it appear that crime is rampant, when in fact it is in most places falling. McCloskey has tried to persuade her ninety-seven-year old mother that the great width of coverage is what gives her the impression that the world is much less safe than in her childhood in Saint Joseph, Michigan, in which even a local case of arson might not be reported, if politically sensitive. (Tom Lehrer sang, "He was the village idiot / And though it seems a pity, it was so. / He loved to burn down houses just to watch the glow. / And nothing could be done / Because he was the mayor's son . . . / In my home town.") Now it's "if it bleeds, it leads," worldwide. Look at the tedious coverage by CNN of any commercial plane crash anywhere in the world. Three days' worth is standard. Yet any sensible person knows that such crashes are extremely rare, rarer than being hit by a car as a pedestrian while attending to your smart phone.

The kidnapping of children by strangers in the United States has dramatically fallen since 1960, but from the coverage, which is more and more national and international, you would think it is much worse. It has resulted in hovering parents and an undermining of the maturation of young people.[2] The undermining is an instance of illiberal over-supervision, affecting children as much as adults. McCloskey remembers being told on a Saturday in the 1950s to "go out and play, and come back when the street lights come on." To do so now would trigger a visit by Child Protective Services.

From rumors reverberating in the global village, people hear daily of horrors on the other side of the world and are made fearful—and ripe for populist tyrants. Some 14.5 million crimes were reported in the US in 1990 (when the country's population was just shy of 250 million) but under 9.5 million in 2016 (when the country's population was about 325 million).[3]

"But growth has happened at the expense of finer sensibilities," you protest. Again, drawing on the antipessimistic statistics of Hans Rosling and his coauthors, among others, no, no, no, you are mistaken. The book industry issues 2.3 million new titles every year, 30 percent or so in the lingua franca of English. Most of them are rubbish, admittedly, but after all, precisely 2.3 of them are one-in-a-million masterpieces. (Ha, ha. But no wonder your big Barnes and Noble, which can stock perhaps 200,000 titles at a time, most of them

old, doesn't stock *all* of McCloskey's splendid books. For shame.)
The book trade is one of the older parts of a dizzying outpouring of
novelties in arts and sciences enabled by the Great Enrichment. It
hardly needs to be said that there was not one new music recording
in 1760 to give ordinary people access to the world's very best musicians. There was *one* in 1860. They made do with the local violinist,
not Jascha Heifetz. Nice in one way, but not nice in another. They
got local Shakespearean performance by Huck Finn's friends the
King and the Duke instead of Kenneth Branagh's *Henry V*. There
were 6,201,002 new musical recordings in 2015—late in what has
been called "the age of mechanical reproduction." In 1906, there
was *one* new feature film. Good. There were 11,000 new movies in
2016, pouring out of Hollywood and especially Bollywood. Better.
Science? There were 119 scholarly articles published in 1665, the
Rosling team claims, compared with 2,550,000 in 2016. Making your
own music? In 1962, there were 200 playable guitars in the world
per million people. In 2014, there were 11,000. (McCloskey has one
sitting in the corner that she hasn't played for years, along with her
accordion, pennywhistle, recorder, piano, ukulele, harmonica, and
mandolin, none of which she practices. Carden's guitar re-emerged
due to COVID-19.) Streaming services put an unlimited selection
of classical music, film adaptations of Jane Austen, and other high-
cultural goodies within reach of anyone with an internet connection
and a few dollars a month. Every recorded opera in the Metropolitan
in New York since the 1950s is available online.

"But it has come at the expense of the world's poor," you say.
Crucially, we repeat, and will say to you again and again until you
confess your deep error, and stop repeating it (your error makes
you feel charitable and progressive, though you have not ever served
breakfast to the homeless in the church basement, or given a dime to
the Salvation Army), no, no, no. For one thing, as we argue, the poor
have been the chief beneficiaries of the Great Enrichment, considering that getting enough food to eat is a little more important for
human flourishing than another yacht to a billionaire. For another,
the Enrichment has not at all been limited to Europe and its overseas
extensions, though it started there, and naturally enough is further
along there—in 1960 much further along, but by now giving way.

Even many very poor countries, like Bangladesh, are now bettering at a rapid pace—in Bangladesh recently at 6.25 percent per year in real GDP per person, thanks to a vigorous export of knitwear and the green revolution in crop production (opposed bitterly by progressives). The Rosling team points out that at the time of Bangladesh's independence in 1972, women averaged seven children each, the child survival rate was 80 percent, life expectancy at birth fifty-two years. Now Bangladeshi women have an average of about two children, the child survival rate is 97 percent, and life expectancy at birth is seventy-three.

Like us and every sensible social scientist, Rosling and his coauthors give example after example of ways in which life has improved on account of the lurch up to the Great Enrichment. On health Rosling notes (a natural example from a professor of public health) that the five-year survival rate of youngsters before age twenty diagnosed with cancer was 58 percent in 1975, with best treatment, but 80 percent in 2010. The share of people in the world with water from a clean source in 1980 was 58 percent; in 2015, it was 88 percent. Countries allowing leaded gasoline in 1986 numbered a nearly universal 193, in 2017 merely 3.

And a central betterment in the modern world—literacy—is shooting up. A modern-day Fantine, we have noted, is able to use the library in which she reads *Factfulness* or *Leave Me Alone* or, for that matter, to use the smartphone she likely owns for similarly noble projects. In 1800, only 10 percent of adults worldwide had basic skills of reading and writing. The figure had risen by 2016 to 86 percent. The proportion of girls of primary school age actually enrolled in school rose worldwide from 65 percent in 1970 to 90 percent in 2015. Rosling calls literacy "the secret miracle of human progress."[4] Yes, and it is the route to self-cultivation beyond bread alone—we would say spiritual growth.

§

As the economic historian John Nye asks you to imagine, suppose that in 1200 CE—or, for that matter, 1200 BCE—you are an honored guest at a king's feast.[5] (Fat chance, of course, because you, like the ancestors of Carden, McCloskey, and Nye, would very likely be illiterate, groveling, ground-scratching, scat-smeared peasants. Or dead.) You would get a pretty good selection of meats, though many of them suspect as to freshness, the rot being held off only partially with salt and masked with whatever spices you can get. You would get some seasonal fruits and vegetables, ample bread, some mead or wine, and a few sweets—though in Europe they would be, like the mead, made from honey, not sugar, and not much at that price.

A feast fit for a king, in those swell old days of yore—but laughably inadequate compared with what you can get for dinner at Golden Corral for about fifteen bucks, less if at lunch. Golden Corral's food is cleaner and safer, considering the losses attending a restaurant that poisons its customers in a society with a free press and free entry into the restaurant business—remember the Chipotle scandal in 2015. The cooks and servers at Golden Corral have doubtless washed their hands. The palace kitchen staff in 1200 doubtless not. Golden Corral has air conditioning unavailable to your great-grandparents. The best the king could do in 1200 was to get a lackey to fan him. You pay the fifteen bucks with a credit card (in China with your smartphone), hop into your air-conditioned car (in China onto your electric scooter), and listen to an audiobook of *Bourgeois Equality* (in China censored) while you drive to your clean, air-conditioned, multiroom apartment (in China's big cities five hundred square feet for the equivalent of $2,000 a month). The king after the feast retired to a stone room with no glass in the windows. Before going to bed, you might brush your teeth with an electric toothbrush that Louis XIV couldn't have bought for all the gold in France.

Consider an ample breakfast at home of three eggs in a spinach omelet, a bowl of oatmeal with peanuts and milk, and a banana. We said "ample." It would be a miracle for an ordinary person to have had such a meal in 1900. At Amazon prices for brand-name goods now, the meal comes to about $2 (plus electricity or natural gas and the opportunity cost of time spent in making it). Eating such a big meal three times a day (*not* recommended) would bring in about 2,300 calories for $6. It amounts to $24 to feed a family of four each day, or about three and a half hours at the federal minimum wage, or just over one hour at the US median wage. The minimum wage worker has earned his family's (admittedly unexciting) daily bread before his lunch break. The office worker at the median wage—half above, half below—has earned it before finishing her second cup of coffee.

For a species that has long struggled to get enough calories to keep going, and which often lost the struggle, the present cost of food is miraculous. The historian Graham Robb details the poverty of rural France even in the improving nineteenth century. Over the winter in Burgundy the vineyard men hibernated, and not merely figuratively. An official reported in 1844 that "these vigorous men will now spend their days in bed, packing their bodies tightly together in order to stay warm and to eat less food."[6] "Let them eat cake," Marie Antoinette is supposed to have said when told that the people had no bread. The twenty-first-century problem in Bourgeois-Dealing countries is that people have too much bread—and cake.

"But the pace of life was so much nicer," you say. Your poor ancestors and ours moved more slowly during the "simpler times" for which you yearn, yes. But their slowness commonly arose out of the need to conserve energy in a world of very low agricultural productivity—not out of a taste for pastoral serenity. Robb remarks that in French agriculture in the nineteenth century, "slowness was not an attempt to savor the moment."[7] Economists have long recognized that the world's poorest farmers often run out of caloric energy before they run out of money, the more so when they are afflicted by malaria and sleeping sickness and other debilitating diseases.[8] The plowman homeward plods his weary way. "A plowman who took hours to reach a field," writes Robb, "was not necessarily admiring the effect of morning mist. . . . He was trying to make a small amount of strength last for the working day, like a cartload of manure spread over a large field."[9] In 1879, the French literary historian Hippolyte Taine expressed the point thus: "The people are like a man walking through a pond with water up to his chin."[10] Think of Jean Valjean in *Les Misérables* carrying Marius on his back through the sewers of Paris: one false step and they drown.

It took some time before lives really improved meaningfully. Even in Hans Rosling's Sweden, which grew faster than any non-Japanese economy in the world after it liberalized in the 1860s, slowness was a way of life. The novelist Vilhelm Moberg (*The Immigrants* and many other works) describes his childhood around 1910. He could remember only the summers: "Life in winter was literally shut in: we dozed by the open fire and slept through many hours of the [long Swedish winter] night: it was, for children, a quiet vegetating in the darkness under the low cabin."[11] It wasn't a fun choice of a camping holiday. Adequate clothing to play outside in winter was for poor children too expensive (the Swedes say, "There's no such thing as bad weather, only bad clothing"). The winter was not lit by electricity. The children dozed in the carbon monoxide of the cabin.

Wealth reduces risk for the poor. The citizens of Florence, Italy, in the glorious Renaissance endured famine prices every five years or so.[12] In Florence, Kentucky, or Florence, Alabama, after the First Nations there is yet to be a famine. Being among the Italian Florentine artistic and intellectual elite during the Renaissance would certainly have been exciting, but the chances are that if you were there, you would have been poor, or sick, or dead. The poor people of cities before the time of the automobile were free of having to breathe car exhaust, yes—instead, they breathed bacteria-laden pulverized horse manure.[13]

The poor, we say yet again, have been the big winners. Louis XIV couldn't have written with a laptop or tweeted about what he ate for dinner, in the unlikely event that he would have wanted to, but he could dictate his thoughts to his attending scribes. Electric lighting, as the economist Joseph Schumpeter noted in 1942, was "no great boon" to nobles who had wick trimmers and housemaids to keep expensive candles burning.[14] The Duke of Ferrara could purchase the great pleasure of saying, "That's my last Duchess painted on the wall, / Looking as if she were alive. I call / That piece a wonder, now; / Fra Pandolf's hands / Worked busily a day, and there she stands." Yet now ordinary people can have pretty much the same pleasure, or close substitutes. The Frick Collection at 1220 Fifth Avenue in New York City—don't miss it—is a pretty good substitute, at least for us peasants, for a personally owned fresco of a wife you had recently ordered to be strangled.

6

Pessimism Has Been since 1800 a Rotten Predictor

The columnist Jonah Goldberg begins his 2018 book *Suicide of the West* "with some highly pessimistic assertions":

> Capitalism is unnatural. Democracy is unnatural. Human rights are unnatural. The world we live in today is unnatural, and we stumbled into it more or less by accident. The natural state of mankind is grinding poverty punctuated by horrific violence terminating with an early death. It was like this for a very, very long time.[1]

That last is certainly true, but not liberalism's unnaturalness or its implied precariousness—once the genie is out of the bottle and people realize that the genie can give enrichment. The taste for liberty, we have noted, is very old in the human genome. For much of history, the hunter-gatherers enjoyed it. But agriculture brought kings and bureaucrats. Humans only recently realized they could throw them off. Admittedly, as we have said, they keep forgetting they can, reverting to Israelite demands for a king to take 10 percent or more of their fields and crop, and nowadays 35 percent and higher. Goldberg is giving a counsel of vigilance in defense of the new liberalism, similar to George Orwell's *1984* warning of a boot stamping on a human face, forever. We admire the vigilance but reject the pessimism.

The economic historian Douglass North (1920–2015), our friend and teacher, also tended to be pessimistic, as in his 2005 book *Understanding the Process of Economic Change*:

> Economic history is a depressing tale of miscalculation leading to famine, starvation, defeat in warfare, death, economic stagnation and decline, and indeed the disappearance of entire civilizations. And even the most casual inspection of today's news suggests that this tale is not purely a historical phenomenon. Yet we do get it right sometimes, as the spectacular economic growth of the past few centuries attests. But ongoing success is hardly a foregone conclusion.[2]

Yet the Great Enrichment came, and it looks to go on, unnatural or not. Yes, it's not foregone. The world might mess it up, as it did for a long while after 1914, with various crazes from left and right, "trying socialism" tried once again in Venezuela, or "protecting the nation" from bettering trade and immigration. But if not, it will keep on going.

It will do so, we reckon, against a long list of pessimisms about the inevitability of poverty. After every one of the six biggest financial crises since 1800, the air has been thick with spooky stories about the end of betterment and the corrupting effects of consumerism, exploitation, economic maturity, environmental decay, and inevitable inequality. And every time, the continuing commercially tested betterment has proven them wrong. The historian and British liberal Thomas Babington Macaulay had even in 1830 given the correct response:

> On what principle is it that, when we see nothing but betterment behind us, we are to expect nothing but deterioration before us? If we were to prophesy that in the year 1930 a population of fifty million, better fed, clad, and lodged than the English of our time, will cover these islands, that Sussex and Huntingdonshire will be wealthier than the wealthiest parts of the West Riding of Yorkshire now are, that machines constructed on principles yet

undiscovered will be in every house, many people would think us insane.[3]

"Whiggish" and liberal and bourgeois and progress-minded and vulgarly pro-betterment though Macaulay was, he was in his prediction exactly right, even as to the population of the United Kingdom in 1930. If one includes the Republic of Ireland, which was separated about a century after Macaulay's time, he was off by less than 2 percent.

Even the pessimistic, anti-Whiggish economists who rise up after every crisis—"gloomsters," the headline writers call them—would not deny that humanity has before it fifty or a hundred years in which now middling and poor countries such as South Africa and Brazil and Haiti and Bangladesh will catch up to what is already, in the numerous rich countries, a stunningly successful level of average real income. The Nobelist Edmund Phelps, among the gloomsters, believes that many rich countries have lost dynamism.[4] Yet China and India since the late twentieth century have become radically more free-market than they once were and therefore are quickly catching up, growing with notable dynamism (and considerable variation), at about 6 percent per person per year—and Chinese growth has regularly been greater than 10 percent per year. Average real income per person in the world is rising fast, at about 2 percent per year.[5] It doesn't sound like much, but compound interest is relentless. The result will be a gigantic increase in the number of scientists, designers, writers, musicians, engineers, entrepreneurs, and ordinary businesspeople devising betterments that spill over to the now rich countries allegedly lacking in dynamism. Unless you believe in mercantilist/business-school fashion that a country must "compete" to prosper from world betterment, even the leaky boats of the Phelpsian undynamic countries will rise.

To appreciate fully what has happened in the world's economy since 1800, and what will happen over the next fifty or a hundred years of commercially tested betterment, it's a good idea to pause to hear tell of the "Rule of 72." Every educated person should know it.

The rule is that something, such as real income per person, growing at 1 percent per year will double in about seventy-two years. The fact is not obvious without calculation. It just happens for moderate growth rates to be true. You can confirm it by taking out your calculator and multiplying 1.01 by itself seventy-two times.

The fact implies that if the something grows *twice* as fast, at 2 percent instead of 1 percent, then the something will double in half the time, thirty-six years. (That, as we said, is the pace at which world income per person is doubling, on the most conservative projections.) A runner going twice as fast will arrive at the mile marker in half the time, and thirty-six is half of seventy-two. Similarly, something growing at 3 percent a year will double in a third of the time, which is twenty-four years. Something growing at 4 percent, likewise, will double in a quarter of the time, which is eighteen years. And so forth. The general formula, then, says that something growing at i percent per year doubles in $72/i$ years. The approximation of the Rule of 72 gets less exact for extremely high growth rates—something growing at 72 percent per year obviously won't double in one year. But for the growth rates we're considering here, or 2 or 7 or 12 percent per year, it's good enough.

Now reflect. If you take 9 percent as the combined annual per person growth rate in the 37 percent of world population living in China and India, the rest of the world could have literally *zero* growth per person and yet the world's average growth per year of real income per person would be 0.37 × 9, or 3.3 percent, which is a little faster even than during the great postwar boom of recovery from depression and war of 1950–1972. If the rest of the world were to grow merely at the subdued rates of 1973–2003 (namely, 1.56 percent per person per year conventionally measured, without allowance for improved quality), the world result, factoring in the Chinese and Indian marvels, would be, if the population share held up, (0.37 × 9.0) + (0.63 × 1.56), or 4.3 percent per year, the highest in history.[6]

A rather lower sustained growth rate worldwide of, say, 4 percent per person per year would result in a doubling of the material welfare of the world's average person within a short generation (again, $72/4 = 18$ years), with the economies of scale in world invention kicking up the rate. In two such generations, just thirty-six years, it would mean a quadrupling, which would raise the average real income in the world to the levels attained in 2012 in the United States, a country that for well over a century has sustained the world's highest per person income of any place larger than Norway. Pretty good. And it will be good for solving many if not all of the problems in the environment and in human lives.

If the world doesn't slip permanently into wars or revolutions that kill the golden goose, no limit to fast world growth of per person income is close at hand—not in your lifetime, nor even that of your great-grandchildren. Then, in the year 2120, with everyone twice as rich as US people are now, and hundreds of times more engineers and entrepreneurs working on improvements in nuclear power and carbon dioxide capture and making trash into biodegradable plastic, humanity can reconsider the limits to growth.

§

Apply the Rule of 72 to the facts of the world, in which the Bourgeois Deal is accepted, or not. At the 6 percent growth per person per year in places like China and India—which moved sharply in their policies toward the Bourgeois Deal—income doubles in about twelve years (72 divided by 6 percent is 12). At the 12 percent rate China often achieved before Xi Jinping began crushing dissent, it's a mere six years. One can witness the outcome in the astounding modernity of Chinese cities now. At a six-year doubling, a single generation of, say, twenty-four years witnesses its comforts and capabilities' increase by four of those six-year doublings ($2 \times 2 \times 2 \times 2$, which is to say, fully 16). It happened in China and is happening at only a little slower pace in India—both places thought when McCloskey was a student in the 1960s to be hopeless. Earlier cases of fast catch-up were Sweden and Japan in the late nineteenth century, or Ireland and Taiwan in the mid- to late twentieth century. The Chinese achievement, in other words, though impressive in scale, is not unique. Talk of the "Chinese model" is muddleheaded. But obviously if China and India can do it, any place large or small that decides to adopt liberal economic policies can do it, too. The Bourgeois Deal rules. (We implore the politicians in Brazil and South Africa, say, to listen, really listen, to what the economic history says.)

Even at the modest 4 percent per person per year that the World Bank reckons China will experience out to 2030, the outcome will be a populace almost twice as rich. The specialists on China's economy Dwight Perkins and Thomas Rawski reckoned in 2008 on a 6 to 8 percent annual growth out to 2025, by which time the average Chinese person would have a 1960s-US standard of living. In 2020, actually, it is already not far off.[7] China and India during their illiberal experiments in collectivism of the 1950s through the 1970s were wretchedly managed. No genetic argument, surely, is believable that Chinese or Indians or Africans or Latin Americans should do worse than Europeans permanently. Maoist communism and Gandhian regulation were the opposites of the Bourgeois Deal, a Bolshevik Deal: "Let me, the expert in tyranny, coerce you physically in aid of unprofitable schemes I dreamed up last night, and I'll make you poor." In 1978 in China and in 1991 in India, there was therefore a lot of ground to be made up merely by letting people open shops and factories where and when they wanted to, after suitable bribes to local politicians. It was the Chicago way of the 1880s replayed. As Perkins pointed out as early as 1995, "When China stopped suppressing such activity, . . . shops, restaurants and many other service units popped up everywhere . . . [because] Chinese . . . had not forgotten how to trade or run a small business."[8]

People said yes to the Bourgeois Deal, A Drama in Three Acts: "In the first act you-all leave us, the middle class, and for that matter the working class rising into the middle class, like Edison the paper boy or Carnegie the weaver's son, alone to buy low, sell high, and come up with what we think are better ways to do things. Perhaps we will do a little better than the geniuses in Washington proposing industrial policies. Let us keep the profits if we succeed. We, reluctantly, will accept the loss if we fail. (Gee, it *would* be nice if the public purse bailed us out with industrial planning.) Even more reluctantly, we recognize that in second act some other people will enter the market and compete with us, the rats. (Gee, it would be nice, too, if the gov-

ernment would give us a stable monopoly by patent or regulation.)
But by the time the dust settles in the third act, we will have made
you rich." And massively from 1800 to the present, they did.

We would not be at all pleased if the Bourgeois Deal and the ensu-
ing Great Enrichment had simply made the rich richer and left the
poor in their parlous state. If so, we would join our old socialist pals
on the barricades. Hang the bankers. The poor, however, have been
the biggest winners, as we keep pointing out (*when* will you start
listening?!). The proverbial phrase "The rich get richer and the poor
get poorer" made sense in the zero-sum world before the Great Enrichment. But it's silly now, though fun to say, with a knowing smirk.
In his 1942 classic *Capitalism, Socialism, and Democracy*, Schumpeter
summarized what he calls "the capitalist achievement": "Queen
Elizabeth owned silk stockings. The capitalist achievement does not
typically consist in providing more silk stockings for queens but in
bringing them within the reach of factory girls in return for steadily
decreasing amounts of effort."[9] After which, 1942 to the present, US
income per person increased by a factor of four. It's four times more
silk stockings within the reach of factory girls.

That's what we celebrate. And that's what we seek to explain.

7

Even about the Environment

The environmental limit, for example, worries even the middle of the political spectrum. It once was a conservative worry, by people who loved the forests and swamps formerly used for a bit of hunting by the local lord. They opposed the vulgarly commercial people cutting down forests and draining swamps for houses and farms. But now the worry is largely a leftward one.

Economists, unlike physical scientists, are inclined to use the Rule of 72 as follows. Suppose that climate change (which we have no doubt is caused by carbon emissions from the old technologies of fossil fuels) will reduce world income per person by a shocking 20 percent a century from now. Not good, though to be sure not the end-of-the-world scenarios assumed by noneconomists, who do not credit human creative adjustment and the finding of substitutes. Now suppose, as all the evidence suggests, that meanwhile the world's income per person grows at as low as a 2 percent rate per year. All right, apply the Rule of 72. Real income will double every thirty-six years, or roughly three doublings in a little over the century to come. World income per person now, we have noted, is roughly that of Brazil's, $33 a day. So the arithmetic implies a world income in 2120 of eight times higher ($2 \times 2 \times 2 = 8$), or $264 per person ($33 \times 8$)—twice the present real income in the United States.

You will doubt it. But on what principle? Someone in 1900 looking forward to the present would have doubted that the miserable income even so late in the Great Enrichment would increase by a similar factor. But it did. The American economist John Bates Clark predicted in 1901 that "the typical laborer will increase his wages from one dollar a day to two, from two to four and from four to eight."[1] Expressed in 1901 prices, that's exactly what happened.

All right, what, then, is the loss a century from now from climate change? It would be 20 percent of the $264 per person, which is to say, a deduction of $53. Lamentable. But the world nonetheless goes from $33 to $211. That's a lot of money to spend on abatement, and it transforms the lives of the world's poor.

Climate change is real and needs to be faced. But as you can see, it is not obviously, as many people claim, "existential." It can reasonably be expected to be overcome by serious engineers and entrepreneurs implementing serious technologies, such as carbon capture and growing vegetable "meat" and expanding nuclear power (India in 2014 bought ten nuclear reactors from Russia). Meanwhile, even without such serious efforts, the world will do startlingly well. The real threat to such prosperity is tyranny and its correlate of hopeless poverty—a reversion to the preliberal, zero-sum world implied by populism, whether of left or right. The real threat is not environmental change, the fear of which can itself inspire unwise populist proposals.

And you need to realize that the environmental worry is often based merely on mathematical arguments, free from the world's facts, which is the reason that people assert them with such angry certitude and express indignation at anyone who queries them. They are true by definition and arithmetic, like the Rule of 72. They are scientifically relevant only if, as in our own use just now of the rule, they are clothed in the world's actual, historical, contingent, engineering numbers. It is said, for example, "After all, nothing can grow forever." Uh-huh. But the practical limit is scores of times larger than the present level. To speak of population change, the actual carrying capacity of the earth, as one can judge from such densely populated places as Holland or Java, is almost certainly far, far greater than the ten or eleven billion or so at which it will soon peak and then start falling in response to rising per person income. It is said, too, "After all, resources are finite." Uh-huh. But what a "resource" is, as the economist Julian Simon showed back in the 1990s, is ever changing in response to human ingenuity.[2] Bauxite ore was once useless dirt, but it became valuable for making aluminum, if you have enough electricity, which itself was once a front-parlor experiment in static electricity, not a "resource" with practical use. Rare earths were not economically rare until they came to be used for computer batteries. Helium was a laugh until it showed its economic value for the strictest testing for leaks, as for a space suit. Valuable whale oil became shortly after 1859 almost useless (and for a long time saved the whales) compared with the newly exploited resource from the ground called just "oil." Black rock from the ground called "coal" was rediscovered in Europe many centuries ago, and in London became useful for heating houses and making glass, though it had been known two thousand years earlier in China. Underground water inaccessible with old drilling techniques suddenly became minable. Its large if limited amount is soon to be supplemented, as it already is in some arid places, and on cruise ships, by ingenuity in finding ways to desalinate sea water by reverse osmosis cheaply, as in Western Australia powered by wind and sun.

The environmental limit looks in historical and economic fact to be solved by the ingenuity of liberated people that caused the Great Enrichment in the first place. It will not be solved by some of the stranger antieconomic suggestions, such as "eating local." As a friend of ours put it, "What will be next? 100-mile-sourced medicines? 100-mile-sourced ideas? 100-mile-sourced economic history?"[3] Some of the more unreasonable environmentalists along this line have campaigned against genetically modified bananas delivering vitamin A, a betterment that could save 700,000 children's lives each year and prevent 300,000 cases of blindness.[4]

Yet reasonable environmentalists have for decades in rich countries been solving such problems—for example, the smog caused by coal for heating, or intelligence-reducing emissions from cars using lead-enhanced fuels (how many of these problems, we wonder, would have been solved had the 700,000 children per year not died, or 300,000 not gone blind because of vitamin A deficiency?). They will continue their virtuous labors with the hearty approval of we economists and economic historians and liberal philosophers. After all, the goal is not growth-regardless, in the style of the North Carolina legislature in 2014 requiring science curricula to be revised to make rising ocean levels appear less threatening, or the governor of Florida issuing instructions that the phrase "global warming" be banished from official documents. The goal is *actually bettering* commercially tested betterment, such as making poor people richer, which has in fact happened, or reducing inequality in essentials, which has also happened. Making people dangerously ill with bad air (or, for that matter, denying children lifesaving genetically modified crops) is not ethical, or bettering. Nor, by the way, is it something "the corporations" want. Nike and Toyota, unlike some governments with their tempting local monopolies of physical coercion over their citizens, do not want to sicken or kill their employees or customers. Why, after all, would they? Dead customers don't buy.

The rich countries in the 1980s, for example, decided to take seriously the threat to the ozone layer from air-conditioning fluid and hair spray (hair spray!). They were led in this effort by Margaret Thatcher, the Conservative British prime minister (and a big user of hair spray). Now the ozone gaps at the poles are getting gratifyingly smaller. Waterways, again, which were open sewers until the development of effective waste treatment at the end of the nineteenth century, are in rich countries largely cleaned up. Levels of particulate matter from burning coal for house heating in American cities in the 1930s and 1940s—American income per person then was, as we have noted, about the same as Brazilian income now—were comparable to those in present-day poor countries and fell by the late twentieth century to an eighth of their previous level. McCloskey can remember in 1948 Boston windowsills sooty by evening that her mother had wiped clean in the morning. In 1912–1913 a poor and therefore smoky Chicago was smothered in suspended particulates half again higher in amount per cubic yard of air than those in fifty-eight poor Chinese cities during 1980–1993.[5] Men and woman wore hats for more than keeping warm. The east side of Northern Hemisphere cities, where the prevailing winds dump soot, is the poor area for the same reason. After the use of coal in British cities was banned in 1954 and then more rigorously in 1968, the Royal Courts of Justice in now-rich London have been scrubbed to return to their original white stone facing. Little but rich Denmark spends a good deal of its riches on avoiding carbon-based fuel and is prominent in the world market in windmills. As Steve Chapman, the liberal columnist at the *Chicago Tribune*, reported, "Since 1980, carbon monoxide pollution in America has been cut by 83 percent, lead by 91 percent, and sulfur dioxide by 78 percent. But total economic output per person, adjusted for inflation, has risen by 77 percent. We've gotten greener and healthier as we've gotten richer."[6] If you care about the environment, then, let people become prudently and temperately rich. Then the now richer people can do some good for the environment.

But what about the presently poor countries polluting? Rising real income per person at such heady rates as 7 or 12 percent per year, with the level quadrupling in a generation, is understandably popular with ordinary Chinese and Indian people. But when their incomes went up, the formerly poor, such as the Danes and the British, we just noted, came to value the environment more. Sometimes, true, they have valued it irrationally, as for example by stopping nuclear power, which has made dirty old coal the fastest-growing source of energy worldwide. Yet China, bettering but still very poor, now has a vigorous environmental movement—a movement against coal, not against nuclear power—with numerous riots substituting for actual democracy. In a nervous response to the movement, and maybe even because it's good for people, the Chinese government in January 2014 said it was going to require fifteen thousand factories to report their air and water pollution in real time and to release the results to the public. If they actually do so (don't hold your breath; and when visiting Beijing in the winter, do), the Chinese standard of transparency in controlling pollution will be higher than that of the United States. Also in 2014, China signed an agreement with the Obama administration to work seriously on restraining the release of atmospheric carbon, though Donald Trump took that one down, among others.

China is now at a stage of industrialization similar to England's in the 1870s or the United States' in the 1890s, during which sulfur-laden coal smoke rising from Birmingham, Warwickshire, or from Birmingham, Alabama, was viewed not as an occasion for rioting but for celebration. In the 1940s, when McCloskey's grandparents (born in the 1890s) would drive to Chicago around the southern edge of Lake Michigan, they would note with approval the smoke rising from US Steel plants in Gary, Indiana—an improvement, they implied, over the shuttered mills of the 1930s.

Oil supply, too, has no long-term limit, as the failures of limits-to-growth predictions from the 1960s to the present have shown. The natural scientists making the predictions don't seem to care that the evidence runs against them. Worldwide a "peak oil" has yet to happen, decades after it was confidently predicted by natural scientists ignorant of economic science. The paleontologist Niles Eldridge, for example, as late as 1995 quoted with approval a geologist at Columbia University who had predicted in the 1960s on the basis of "simple measures of the volumes of the great sedimentary basins" that the world would run out of recoverable petroleum in the mid-1990s.[7] Ah, yes, simple measures. In fact, after the 1960s worldwide the proven oil reserves grew—a miracle unless you realize that "proving" is itself an economic activity. World crude-oil production has increased since 1970 by over 50 percent.[8] Fracked gas in Pennsylvania and oil sands in Alberta and deep discoveries in the Falklands/Malvinas seas and in the Australian outback come from geologists working to find more deposits whenever the price of oil rises. And after such revisions upward of carbon-fuel reserves, the price of oil corrected for general inflation falls back. That's how entry works in markets, to the irritation of the original suppliers and to the joy of consumers. (One would expect a paleontologist to understand such a process, so similar to entry into ecological niches; or a geologist to understand it, so similar to water finding its level.) The real price of oil during the 1990s, when oil was supposed to have run out, was the same as in the late 1940s.[9] When episodically the Organization of Petroleum Exporting Countries was able to make its cartel work to drive down pumping, the price was jerked upward, as for example in the late 1970s and after 2003, helped along on the demand side by exploding world economic growth. But the price rises were not from nature's peak oil so easily predicted by simple measures of the volumes of the great sedimentary basins.

Yet a peculiar rhetorical triumph against *nuclear* power has worsened global warming. The Green Party in Germany supports lethal coal over safe nuclear. The rhetoric can be overcome (some reasonable people have argued) by realizing that even the destruction in 1986 of the Chernobyl reactors, incompetently managed by the Soviet Union (thus the environmental record of socialism), resulted in few fatalities—a onetime event of fifty-six direct fatalities and a few thousand shortened lives. Lamentable, but two or three orders of magnitude smaller than the coal-caused deaths in the same region *every year*. The disaster of the ill-placed Fukushima nuclear station, destroyed in 2011 by a tsunami hitting Japan, resulted in still fewer fatalities, and the only big US nuclear problem, in 1979, Three Mile Island, none (unless you believe conspiracy theories on the left). According to economists studying Germany's nuclear phase-out in the wake of the Fukushima reactor, "the social cost of this shift from nuclear to coal [is] approximately 12 billion dollars per year," far greater, they argue, than "the costs associated with nuclear accident risk and waste disposal." Some 70 percent of the cost, they argue, comes from higher mortality risks from fossil fuel–related air pollution.[10]

Society, that is, can return to an improved nuclear power—or, if you are optimistic about coal, and resistant to the actual evidence about nuclear power, and determined to stay spooked about the "one big disaster," which French nuclear engineering has solved—you can wait for clean coal, on which Southern Illinois University is feverishly working.[11] (Go Salukis!) The present engineering is anyway clear. France, with 80 percent nuclear power for its electricity, the cheapest in Europe, has one-fifth the carbon pollution of neighboring, coal-fed-if-green-loving Germany. However you come down on nuclear power, on what principle is it that, when you see nothing but betterment behind you, are you to expect nothing but deterioration before you?

8

In Fact, None of the Seven Old Pessimisms Makes a Lot of Sense

You wouldn't think the world has changed radically for the better from the news you hear or the rows of apocalyptic books of fiction and alleged nonfiction at your local bookstore. Pessimism sells, we have noted, and seven old pessimisms plus three new ones yell "Naaah!!" at optimistic stories like ours.

But the pessimisms are flat-earth versions of economics and economic history, finding their way into newspaper op-eds and blog posts, immune to reason and evidence. For example, Charles Dickens, contrary to popular belief, knew next to nothing about the Industrial Revolution happening far north of the London of his novels, and he cannot be considered a guide to economic history. His vision of poverty was the traditional, nonindustrialized poverty of London. His one novel of northern industry, in 1854, *Hard Times*, was based on a brief, rare visit to the industrializing North of England. It is muddleheaded in its understanding of industry. Dickens's contemporary the historian Thomas Babington Macaulay called the book "sullen Socialism."[1] Yet most people see his novels as trenchant criticisms of "capitalism." The French novelist Honoré de Balzac, likewise, it is said, knew more about French society than any sociologist. We don't think so. Like Dickens (and unlike, say, Jane Austen or Herman Melville or Émile Zola or John Steinbeck or Robert Frost), he did not trouble to know economics or the economy. Some readers, likewise, will seize on the 1848 *Communist Manifesto* of Karl

Marx and Friedrich Engels. But for all its passion and brilliance, it is mainly historical and economic fiction.

The first old pessimism, of 1798 and 1848, said that the poor were fated by Malthusian logic to stay poor. The second pessimism, of 1916, said that only Europeans were genetically capable of getting out of $3-a-day poverty. The third, of 1933, recurring again in the 1970s and 1990s and especially after 2008, said that the "final crisis of capitalism" was at hand. The fourth, of 1945, said that betterment had finished, that stagnation had set in, and that excess saving would pull incomes down. The fifth, of 1968, said that anyway (when humanity got out of the non-final crisis and found that technological stagnation did not in fact happen) a consumerism had corrupted its soul. The sixth, of 1980, said that the enrichment of the "core" countries required an army of the exploited in the Global Southern Periphery. A not-so-old seventh of the 1990s, dating back to the 1890s, said that Old Europe and the United States were doomed to fall down the league tables as other countries caught up to and surpassed them in output per person. They couldn't "compete." They lacked "dynamism."

None of these have been fulfilled. Not one. Not close.

As for the first, that the poor will stay poor on Malthusian grounds, you have seen how poverty around the globe has in fact plummeted.

Growth has also given the lie to the second, the imperial and Eurocentric pessimism. The Great Enrichment since 1916 and especially since 1980 has gone spectacularly global. The success of the Asian Tigers and the Celtic and Icelandic ones, and the burgeoning middle classes in China and India, to say nothing of the success that non-Europeans have regularly enjoyed when they have moved to Europe and its offshoots, refutes the claim that only Europeans are genetically capable of a Great Enrichment. What pessimism and racism predict, experience refutes.

And so it has been with the third—the half dozen or so claimed final crises of capitalism from 1857 to the present. The Great Depression of the 1930s was made worse, not moderated, by governmental cures. After the 1930s, as in every one of the forty or so recessions since 1800, a new historical high in output per person followed. It has been true also of the Great Recession, too, though the recession was much less fearsome than the 1930s. The political hangover in populism and socialism recurs every time. The system is broken. Down with the system.

The steady march of betterment has also given the lie to the fourth pessimism, of *stagnationism*—that betterment is finished and that excess saving would in a Keynesian logic be a drag on income. Give Carden a phone call and he'll comfort you personally about the alleged stagnation—a call made cheap by continuing betterment and by savings implementing non-stagnation in telephoning technology. Perhaps you and he could set up a FaceTime chat, a Skype or Zoom call, or a get-together via Google Hangouts, that would allow you to discuss face-to-face the end of betterment and the uselessness of saving. (Getting the point?)

But aren't people corrupted by "consumerism," as per the fifth pessimism? True, they can use liberty and prosperity to live like pigs. Some people do (remember Carden's disgraceful interest in professional wrestling)—but again, the bad things people do with what they have gained from the Bourgeois Deal is not testimony to the badness of the deal itself. People consumed bad things before it—bear baiting, for example, or dining on songbirds. As we have argued at length, you can if you wish keep up with the Kardashians. But you can also cultivate yourself, as billions do.

"But," you might say, drawing on the sixth pessimism, "wasn't Western prosperity ripped from the mouths of the world's poor? Isn't the West rich because they are poor?" Happily, no. The Great Enrichment occurred because of increased production in (say) Sweden (and Ireland and Japan and the rest), not increased predation in the Third World by Sweden (and Ireland and Japan and the rest). And again, recall that if predation as such could cause a Great Enrichment, it would have happened millennia ago. Predation is an ancient human habit.

McCloskey was a colleague in the 1970s of Milton Friedman at the University of Chicago. Friedman (who, you will surely want to know, shares a birthday with Carden's older son, and with J. K. Rowling and her Harry Potter, and with their copy editor's husband), has been roundly denounced since the mid-1970s for his role in what the left imagines about "globalization" and "neoliberalism." A poster current in 2009 bore Friedman's visage with the caption, "Milton Friedman: Proud Father of Global Misery." Never mind asking why Friedman, who was a wise and honorable man, would *want* global misery. Never mind the astounding economic growth in China—where reformers were in fact inspired by Friedman's *Capitalism and Freedom* (1962)—that has driven humanity's largest-ever, and almost the most rapid, exit from extreme poverty. Some "misery." With enemies like Friedman, do the world's poor need any statist friends?

The seventh pessimism suggests that European and American incomes will fall relative to other societies as the others catch up. But so what? It's good, not bad, that other societies also become rich. In the long run, all societies will achieve about the same real income per person because all will have access to the same recipes in technology and institutions created by free people for making goods and services. The global economy is not the Football Association's league table or the World Cup. British observers in the early nineteenth century, like Americans in the Jazz Age, were startled at the ease with which the country had taken industrial leadership. Britain was the first, yet a few of its clerisy were nervously aware of the oddity of a small island bestriding the world's economy. Fully one-third of world iron production in the 1840s came from Britain. In 1839, early in British success, one James Deacon Hume warned a committee of Parliament that the protectionist British tariffs on imports of wheat would encourage other countries to move away from agriculture and toward industry themselves, breaking Britain's "domination" of world manufacturing: "We place ourselves at the risk of being surpassed by the manufactures in other countries. . . . I can hardly doubt that [when that day arrives] the prosperity of this country will recede much faster than it has gone forward."[2]

Nonsense. It's the rhetoric of "competitiveness," and it has always been nonsense, though a powerful driver of mistaken policies. In the 1840s or the 1990s or nowadays, Britain or the US is made better off, not worse off, by the industrialization of the rest of the world. You would be made better off by moving to a neighborhood of more skilled and healthy people willing to trade with you. British growth has continued from 1840 to the present, making Britons richer and richer. Likewise, Americans are made better off when Japan or China "defeats" us at car making or TV assembling, or by "stealing our intellectual property," because "we"—really, individuals making decisions about what to do, and not the collectivist "we" of nationalist fantasies—then go do something "we" are comparatively good at, say, banking or growing soybeans. "We" let the Japanese and then the Koreans and then the Chinese make the consumer electronics.

It's not a "race" that Britain "lost." The falling British share of world markets was no index of "failure," any more than a father would regard his falling share of the poundage in the house relative to his growing children as a "failure." It was an index of maturity. So too for the United States. The purpose of an economy is not exports (that is, maximum production) but better terms in getting imports (maximum consumption). "Jobs" are not what the society should seek. Goods and services are. In your own life, do you seek to work more? If you could get the same consumption with less trouble, would you? Of course you would. Well, as Adam Smith said, "What is prudence in the conduct of every private family can scarce be folly in that of a great kingdom."[3] "Protecting jobs" is folly.

9

Nor Do the Three
New Ones

The seven old pessimisms, appearing and reappearing among the learned members of the clerisy, only to be refuted again and again by history and economics, have been joined recently by three new ones: that environmental decay is an existential threat, that humanity is being ruined by a new era of inequality, and that technological unemployment from artificial intelligence is the general fate. The new pessimisms are likewise misplaced, on evidence we have sketched earlier. Since 1800, optimism rather than pessimism has been the wise position.

We have told you why worries about the environment are misplaced. A few decades of doomsday prophesying have been countered by Julian Simon's *The Ultimate Resource* (1981, 1996), Matt Ridley's *The Rational Optimist* (2010), and Ronald Bailey's *The End of Doom* (2015) noting that things are in fact getting better, not worse. The solution to environmental problems is not a green repackaging of the central planning beloved of the leftish clerisy. It is to continue private, commercially tested betterment that creates the wealth to address the problems. Get richer so that more people can have the luxury of worrying about the environment instead of their next bowl of rice. Look for ways to encourage markets that signal property values affected by, say, sea-level rise in Miami. Then Miami can do something about it, including voting against governors who deny the rise.

What of inequality? Guaranteeing a material equality, note, requires *political in*equality, in order to seize Peter's goods to pay Paul. It seems unlikely that this one time the politicians will use such powers of coercion in a wise and benevolent fashion. Why would they? The rich are paying them. And material equality is not an ethically relevant goal. What matters is absolute material standards of living, not anger that someone else might be doing better. Obsession with inequality walks with the soul-corroding sin of envy. Envy is insatiable, considering that nearly everyone has something to envy—as Shakespeare put it in his sonnet 29, "wishing me like to one more rich in hope, / Featured like him, like him with friends possessed, / Desiring this man's art, and that man's scope, / With what I most enjoy contented least." It doesn't matter ethically that an NFL quarterback or a celebrity chef makes millions offering services that people are willing to buy voluntarily, for their own good as consumers. Yet it does very much matter ethically that there are still about 10 percent of humans living on less than $1.90 a day. Let's take care of that instead of looking enviously at a billionaire's yacht. Absolute, not relative, income is what matters ethically.[1] It would be a mistake, economically and ethically, to expropriate the NFL quarterback or celebrity chef or CEO for the benefit of the 10 percent of humans living on less than $1.90 a day, because the rich are not the cause of $1.90-a-day poverty. Nor do the rich have enough money to permanently raise up the poor. It is growth, not redistribution, that saves the poor.

In any case, as average incomes rise, money income becomes less and less reliable as a measure of the differences in the relevant goods and services available to the rich and to the poor. Millionaires, and especially billionaires, have limits on how much they can use incomes so very much higher than yours for correspondingly unequal consumption—of, say, trousers, put on one leg at a time. So economic growth, however unequally shared as income, is more egalitarian in its distribution of consumption. Remember John Bates Clark's one dollar rising to eight for a day's work. "Such gains will mean infinitely more to him," Clark noted, "than any possible increase of capital can mean to the rich. . . . This very change will bring with it a continual approach to equality of genuine comfort."[2]

The meaningful differences shrink. Today's Fantine consumes about $25 a day of goods and services. Dwayne "The Rock" Johnson had a 2018 pretax income of $124 million, or $339,726 a day, or over thirteen thousand times Fantine's daily consumption. Does he have thirteen thousand times as much food? Clothing? Shelter? Scope? Happiness? Perhaps he has the world's finest liquor cabinet. Maybe it includes a $600,000+ bottle of very old Macallan scotch. Does it really provide forty thousand times the boozy pleasure Fantine can enjoy by picking up a $15 twelve-pack of Bud Light on the way home from work? (She'll just have one and a half cans herself and invite her girlfriends in.) During the 1950s, Chock full o'Nuts coffee advertised itself as "that Heavenly Coffee—Better coffee Rockefeller's money can't buy." Is the very best and most expensive coffee or chocolate or wine or whatever really *thousands* of times better than what's available to the average Fantine? Not in 2020, in places that have allowed the Bourgeois Deal to work. Or, for that matter, anywhere anytime. And it would be even less of a problem were we to rid ourselves of the barriers to entry that prevent widespread and price-lowering competition and innovation in fine chocolate and fine whisky.

Nor are the spooky fears of technological unemployment warranted. Better techniques make for richer people. It is not "capitalism" that people are complaining about when a machinist is made unemployed by a laser-guided cutter. It's "progress." The progress, we have noted six or seven times (are you listening *now*?), helps mainly the poor.

True, the usual, generous impulse is to give a hand up to people unemployed by progress. If a project hurts someone, help them out. We admire the impulse. Do unto others as you would have them do unto you. But wait. Every human action is a "project." If Henry David Thoreau invents new methods to make high-quality pencils, as he did during the 1840s in his father's business, he harms the less efficient makers. If actual compensation is to be paid to them, as seems only just if it is paid to coal miners in West Virginia and shipbuilders in Le Havre, then every project of every person requires such payment. Something is wrong.

The terrifying phrase "creative destruction" arouses fears and spurs proposals for protection. If you really don't want betterment to happen and don't want poor people to get rich by the 3,000 percent that they have in Japan and Finland and the rest since 1800, then, fine, the society can stick with the old jobs. It can keep in their former employment the elevator operator and the telephone operator, the armies of typists on old mechanical Underwoods, grocery stores with a clerk in an apron handing you the can of beans over the counter. But if betterment is to happen—as it did with Piggly Wiggly in Memphis in September 1916 innovating in self-service grocery stores, or a North Carolina tobacco trucker in 1956 introducing the shipping container—then people, and also the machines and factories owned by the bosses, have to lose their old jobs. Human and physical capital has to reallocate. Of course.

How much? The startling news, according the Department of Labor statistic, is fully 14 percent of jobs per year. In a progressing economy, one out of every seven workers loses a job slot permanently *every year*.[3] Businesses go bankrupt. Factories move to another state. The office gets along on fewer typists. By contrast, the monthly labor reports you hear about on the news give the *net* figure—in a good month 200,000, or 2,400,000 a year, being the net of new jobs in the US gained from moving or betterment minus the old jobs lost from the same creative destruction. That's only 1.5 percent of the labor force, not 14 percent. But the gross figure should be more widely known. A bettering economy requires the workers and the machines to move, to reallocate, to retrain, to shift, to innovate on a massive scale. Of course.

So the practical problem with compensation and protection and schemes of subsidized retraining by government bureaucrats who do not actually know what the new jobs will be in five years is that the nation cannot "afford" to compensate 14 percent of the workforce every year. In a few years half the workforce would be on the dole, or kept in their old jobs at the old pay, or trained in the wrong new jobs. Soon it would be nearly all of the workforce, compensating in tax dollars for every human action. For that matter, the nation would also need to keep physical capital where it began, directing subsidies to factories and neighborhoods rather than letting the people and factories move, as creative destruction requires. And exactly the same moving is required under a perfectly planned socialism as under commercially tested betterment. It's progress, whether ordered by a commissar or tested in a market. Carried out with philosophical consistency, protection would require us to keep shoe manufacturing in Massachusetts as much as coal mining in southern Illinois, economy-wide, forever. As we said, something is wrong, with plans to guarantee jobs or compensate for technological unemployment or keep capital and labor in Youngstown, Ohio.

"But artificial intelligence is different," you say. "Stupid technologies like railways replaced sweat and manual labor. Smart technologies are going to replace problem solving and mind work. My work." But we've been relying on "artificial intelligence" for thousands of years. The bow and arrow is a machine for calculating automatically the accurate throwing of a little spear. The intelligence is in the bow, then in the practice, practice that makes archers at Agincourt act like machines. The safety valve on a steam engine replaced the exercise of human judgment in letting off steam. The adding machine and the slide rule, to say nothing of the pocket calculator, are machines of artificial intelligence. A "computer," as in the Manhattan Project building the A-bomb, was originally a woman who sat in a room adding up long columns of figures. Typists were largely rendered obsolete in the late twentieth century and travel agents in the early twenty-first by the diffusion of the personal computer and its result, the internet. Online travel websites like Expedia and Kayak use "artificial intelligence" to do what non-artificial intelligence used to do. Artificial intelligence has similar creative/destructive potential. As the economic historian Joel Mokyr puts it, "artificial intelligence, the source of much concern that it will replace educated knowledge workers and not just routinized jobs, could become the world's most effective research assistant, even if it will never become the world's best researcher."[4] Yes, we realize that AI is self-learning. But like Mokyr, we think self-learning machines will merely help non-machines called humans to stop having to imitate machines.

Or you can choose to reject improvements in AI. In Berkeley Breathed's "Bloom County" comic strip, the character Steve Dallas speaks of "a special fund-raising concert I'm organizing to benefit a troubled industry." He then pounds the table, exclaiming, "A whole American way of life is disappearing because the govt. won't help out!!"[5] The concert? "Slide-Rule Aid." The world would not be richer had a law saved the slide rule industry from another technology of artificial intelligence. (McCloskey, who was raised on slide rules, however, would have gladly attended Dallas's concert. Slide rules for multiplication, she points out, forced engineers and even economists to attend to the order of magnitude at every step because otherwise they would get the decimal place wrong by a factor of ten or a hundred. Nowadays kids don't think in magnitudes, accepting whatever comes out of a calculator or statistical software package— despite the inherent risk of garbage in, garbage out. Not all progress is entirely progressive.)

10

So to Get Better, the World Had Better Keep Its Ethical Wits about It

To overcome unjustified pessimism, we're saying, it's smart to get the facts straight and then to think about ethics.

If the world does so and embraces the liberal Bourgeois Deal, then an even Greater Enrichment opens up, completing the task of making poverty history. The Bourgeois Era did not thrust aside, as claimed by the leftish American historian Charles G. Sellers rhapsodizing in 1991 about the world we have lost, lives "of enduring human values of family, trust, cooperation, love, and equality."[1] Good lives such as these are lived now. John Kumalo's chief back in the village enforced the traditional society's enduring human values of an oppressive family, narrow trust, coerced cooperation, exclusive love, and enforced equality—and incidentally his own interests and his own arbitrary will.

We are not suggesting that every single thing about the bourgeois world is hunky dory or that everything the bourgeoisie does is Good and Right and Ethical. Many a businessperson is an ethical shell or worse. But the same is true of many a politician or professor or priest or an old and ignorant ruler of a traditional village in South Africa, or the congregation and the planter in Sellers's vision of colonial and early national America.

In a collection of mini essays asking "Does the Free Market Corrode Moral Character?" the political philosopher Michael Walzer replied, "Of course it does." But then he wisely added that *any* social system can corrode one or another virtue. That the Bourgeois Era has tempted people into thinking that greed is good, wrote Walzer, "isn't itself an argument against the free market. Think about the ways democratic politics also corrodes moral character. Competition for political power puts people under great pressure ... to shout lies at public meeting, to make promises they can't keep."[2] Witness the presidential campaigns in the United States in 2016 or 2020. Fallen humans are like that. Or think about the ways even a mild socialism puts people under great pressure to commit the sins of state-enforced envy or class hatred or environmental imprudence. Or think about the ways, before Sellers's alleged "commercial revolution" in the early United States, that his alleged "affective and altruistic relations of social reproduction in traditional societies" put women under great pressure to obey their husbands in all things and encouraged people to hang troublesome Quakers and Anabaptists, and more recently to refuse service to Willie Mays on account of his skin color.

That is to say, any social system, if it is not to dissolve into a Hobbesian war of all against all, needs ethics adopted by its participants. It must have some device—preaching, songs, movies, the press, child raising, or in a pinch the state, as in Prohibition— to slow down the corrosion of moral character, at any rate by the standard the society adopts. The Bourgeois Era has in many ways set a *higher* social standard than others, we have noted, abolishing slavery and giving votes to women and the poor. For further progress, Walzer the communitarian puts his trust in an old conservative argument— namely, an ethical education arising from well-intentioned laws enforced by the police. One might doubt that a state strong enough to enforce such laws would remain uncorrupted for long. Look at the results of Prohibition.

The motto of the Buddenbrooks family in Thomas Mann's 1901 novel about his northern German grain-merchant family was "My son, attend with zeal to thy business by day; but do none that hinders thee from thy sleep at night."[3] It is the bourgeois' pride to be "a fair-dealing merchant," with "quiet, tenacious industry," to "make concessions and show consideration," to have "assured and elegant bearing, . . . tact and winning manners," a "liberal, tolerant strain," with "sociability and ease, and . . . remarkable power of decision at a division" in the town assembly, "a man of action," making "quick decision upon the advantageous course," "a strong and practical-minded man, with definite impulses after power and conquest," but by no evil means.[4] "Men walked the streets proud of their irreproachable reputation as business men."[5] Is it so evil to hope that "one can be a great man, even in a small place; a Caesar even in a little commercial town on the Baltic"? We think not. What is wrong with "the dream of preserving an ancient name, an old family, an old business"?[6] Not much, at any rate by comparison with the blood spilled by aristocrats defending a nine-hundred-year-old name, or the blood spilled by the clerisy-in-charge inspiring and then leading mass slaughters during the twentieth century. On the contrary, preserving by continuous betterment a business of making mutually advantageous trades is good for the rest of us, the Bourgeois Deal.

Contrary to a common opinion since 1848, that is, the arrival of a bourgeois, business-respecting civilization did *not* corrupt the human spirit, despite temptations. Mostly, in fact, it elevated it. Walzer is right to complain in the same essay that "the arrogance of the economic elite these last few decades has been astonishing." So it has. But the arrogance comes from the silly theory that greed is good, not from the moralized economy of exchange that Smith and John Stuart Mill and Milton Friedman saw around them and which continues even now to spread.

Modern Christianity and modern socialism both are mistaken to contrast a rural Eden to a corrupted City of Man. William Cowper, the popular poet of the sentimental revolution in Britain in the late eighteenth century, expressed in 1785 a cliché dating back to ancient Greece: "The town has ting'd the country; and the stain /Appears a spot upon a vestal's robe, / The worse for what it soils."[7] No. The urban, bourgeois world here below is not a utopia. But neither is it, we have argued, anything like the opposite. The specifically bourgeois world should not be judged a hell by a sneering and historically uninformed definition of *bourgeois*. The judgment should depend on factual inquiry and not on ignorant clichés about economics and history, in the illiberal politics of left and right and middle.

Businesspeople, in any case, compare favorably to people in other professions when it comes to, for example, honesty. Obviously, if a businessperson gets caught lying, it costs him or her in customers and colleagues. Compare the low costs to pundits and politicians when they shout lies at public meetings. Lying is hardly unique to business. In other words, the moral failings of the bourgeois are because they are business*people*, not because they are *business*people.[8] Perfect? Never, but as the political scientist we keep mentioning, John Mueller, put it in a pretty good (well . . . very good) book in 1999, it's pretty good, à la Ralph's Pretty Good Grocery in Garrison Keillor's imagined Lake Wobegon, Minnesota.[9] Compare the French baron Montesquieu in 1748, an early liberal, noting, "Commercial laws, it may be said, improve manners for the same reason that they destroy them. They corrupt the *purest* morals. This was the subject of Plato's complaints; and we every day see that they *polish and refine the most barbarous*" (emphasis added).[10] We doubt his "purest," if purity is imagined to be achieved by aristocratic and Homeric slaughter. And we do not recommend Plato's aristocratic sneers against trade and democracy. But yes, markets polish and refine.

§

We are claiming that the Bourgeois Era has not been the worst in ethical practice. And we are recommending carrying on with an ethical market economy—neither an unethical social Darwinism pushing the poor off the road nor an unethical authoritarianism pushing them back along the road to serfdom and poverty. An ethical market economy, we further claim, has been best achieved not by industrial policy from Paris or Washington but by a free society, one with no masters: modern liberalism.

Consider. Ethics has three levels: the good for self, the good for others, and the good for the transcendent purpose of a life. The good for self is the prudence by which you self-cultivate, learning to play the cello, say, or practicing centering prayer. Self-denial is therefore not automatically virtuous. As God's creature, you owe improvement to yourself. (How many self-denying mothers does it take to change a lightbulb? None: I'll just sit here in the dark.) The good for a transcendent purpose—at the top, so to speak, of ethical behavior—is the faith, hope, and love to pursue an answer to the question "So what?" The family, science, art, the football club, and God give the answers that humans seek.

The middle level is attention to the good for others. The late first-century BCE Jewish sage Hillel of Babylon put it negatively: "Do not do unto others what you would not want done unto yourself." It's masculine, a guy-liberalism, a gospel of justice, roughly the so-called Non-Aggression Axiom as articulated by libertarians since the word *libertarian* was redirected in the 1950s to a (then) right-wing liberalism. Matt Kibbe puts it well in the title of his 2014 best seller, *Don't Hurt People and Don't Take Their Stuff: A Libertarian Manifesto*. On the other hand, the early first-century CE Jewish sage Jesus of Nazareth put it positively: "Do unto others as you would have them do unto you." It's gal-liberalism, a gospel of love, placing upon us an ethical responsibility to do more than pass by on the other side. Be a good Samaritan. Be ye kind, one to another.

In treating others, a humane liberalism attends to both Golden Rules. The one corrects a busybody and coercive pushing around. The other corrects an inhumane and soul-destroying selfishness. Together they are the other-ethics of modern liberalism. What the world does *not* need is the social Darwinist or authoritarian version, the old spoof of the Golden Rule—namely, "Those who have the gold, rule." Nor does the world need to follow the Florida football player on the eve of the Florida–Florida State game, "I follow the Good Book: 'Do unto others before they do it unto you.'" Neither is nonaggressive or nice.

The Golden Rule in either formulation, note, is radically egalitarian. In the Abrahamic religions of Judaism, Christianity, and Islam, you are to treat every human soul the way you would wish to be treated. You are to honor your one God and keep God's day holy, but the rest of the Ten Commandments are about treating other humans as you would wish to be treated in matters such as truth telling or adultery. By contrast, in the theism of the Hindus or in the civic religion of the Confucians, you are to treat the Brahman and the emperor as superior souls. An untouchable or a peasant or a woman or a younger son is not to expect equal, reciprocal treatment. Of course, it was not until the bourgeois societies of late eighteenth-century Europe that anyone but an early Christian radical or a late Muslim saint thought to carry out in any large society the sweetly other-regarding theory of Abrahamic egalitarianism. Until Tom Paine or Adam Smith, a duchess was still a duchess, a sultan still a sultan, King Herod still Great.

The double Golden Rules should govern thinking about how to treat others. People should be prudent and just but also prudent and loving. A free economy encourages both. A non-free economy violates one or the other. Consider, for example, the policies of subsidy, protection, prohibition, industrial policy, and a hand up to those unemployed by progress. When they are not merely payoffs to favored interest groups, which is lamentably common, they might satisfy Jesus. But in their seizure of Paul's goods to help Peter, they massively offend Hillel. Not good. Humans need a temperate balance of love and justice, female and male.

The intemperate application of the Jesus principle in economic "protection," we say, violates the Hillel principle. Economically speaking, people are not islands, entire of themselves. Each person is a piece of the continent, a part of the main. That is to say, every person's action to buy or not buy, to offer for sale or not, to enter a trade or not, to invent or not, affects someone else for better or for worse. If "protected," everyone becomes everyone else's slave. As the economist Donald Boudreaux puts it, "What no person is free to do is to oblige others to subsidize his or her choices. I, for example, should be free to work as a poet but not empowered to force you either directly to buy my poetry or to obstruct your freedom to spend your money on mystery novels, movies, and other items that compete with my poetry."[11] If I buy a loaf of bread, someone else cannot have it. Ask: should you be stopped from buying bread because you impose a tort on others in buying it? If yes, everyone should compensate everyone else for everything, for every human action.

Whoops. We will await your payment for *not* buying our book and choosing to do something else instead. Change of any sort, all progress, all benefit to the wretched of the earth, comes to an abrupt end. All exchange stops. And the life of humans becomes solitary, poor, nasty, brutish, and short.

11

And True Liberalism Celebrates a Life *Beyond* Wealth

"But there is more to life than wealth," you will say. Yes, of course. Only a Shallow Hal regards his worth as his income, or his life as the pursuit of toys, though Carden is especially grateful for his income and an even imperfectly functioning price system that made it possible for him to book a quick appointment and get a root canal on the day he was supposed to send the revised, copyedited version of the manuscript back to McCloskey (we wonder: would Michael Sandel and other philosophers of the limits to markets consider this blameworthy line jumping?). Our students in college will declare when asked that their goal in life is a nice apartment and a nice car. Maybe good dental coverage. But they are nineteen years old. Their parents and especially their grandparents have learned better. As parents and grandparents, we try to help the students along in the matter of sensible, so-what-worthy goals for life beyond possessions.

Materialism, true, is a danger to the soul. The economist and demographic historian Richard Easterlin warned in 1974 that "economic growth is a carrier of a material culture of its own that ensures that humankind is forever ensnared in the pursuit of more and more economic goods."[1]

But wait a minute. Admittedly, humans are "ensnared," even enslaved, by toys. Social science in the twentieth century, however, has discovered an important if partial reply: *any* level of income is a "carrier of a material culture," $3 a day as much as $130 a day. As Easterlin said, "forever." The anthropologists and psychologists point out that *any* meal taking or shelter building or tale telling "ensnares" its people, the Bushmen of the Kalahari no less than the floor traders of Wall Street. Humans make themselves with consumption, as the anthropologists observe. The anthropologists Mary Douglas and Baron Isherwood put it so: "Goods that minister to physical needs—food and drink—are no less carriers of meaning than ballet or poetry. Let us put an end to the widespread and misleading distinction between goods that sustain life and health and others that service the mind and heart—spiritual goods."[2] The classic demonstration is Douglas's own article on the symbolic structure of working-class meals in England, but in a sense all of anthropology is in this business.[3] Goods wander across the border of the sacred and the profane—the anthropologist Richard Chalfen, for example, shows how home snapshots and movies do.[4] Or as the anthropologist Marshall Sahlins put it in a new preface to his classic of 1972, *Stone Age Economics*, "economic activity . . . [is] the expression, in a material register, of the values and relations of a particular form of life."[5]

Easterlin urges "us" to resist consumerism and become "masters of growth."[6] One wants to be wary of such urgings that "we" do something, because the "we" is so easily corrupted—for instance, by a rabid nationalism or by the mere snobbery of the rich and educated. But surely in an ethical sense, he is right. "We" need to persuade one another to take advantage of the Great Enrichment for something other than keeping up with the Kardashians and eating more chips and strutting about in a world of status-confirming consumption, gold toilets and all. People are ensnared, admittedly, as all their ancestors were back to the caves. In modern conditions of wide material scope, however, one can hope that the ensnaring would often be worthy of the best versions of humanness, ensnared by Bach or by the celebration of the Mass or (says McCloskey) by a test match for the Ashes at Lord's on a perfect London day in June.

Such advice, to be nobly ensnared, has been a commonplace since the invention of religion and literature, or back to the coyote tales around the Native American campfire. It has nothing much to do with the Great Enrichment and its alleged "consumerism"—except that thanks to the Enrichment a vastly larger percentage of humanity is open to the advice. The clerisy thinks that other people's spending is just awful—even good economists partake in the clerisy's disdain. The cultural historian Daniel Horowitz argued persuasively that "at the heart of most versions of modern moralism is a critique, sometimes radical and always adversarial, of the economy. . . . Denouncing other people for their profligacy and lack of Culture is a way of reaffirming one's own commitment."[7]

The clerisy, that is, dislikes the consumption of the commoners. Especially in the United States, for instance, the clerisy has been saying for a century that the naive commoners are in the grips of a tiny group of advertisers. So the spending on sodas and gas grills and automobiles is the result of hidden persuasion or, to use a favorite word of the clerisy to describe commercial free speech, "manipulation." The peculiarly American attribution of gigantic power to thirty-second television spots is puzzling to an economist. If advertising had the powers attributed to it by the clerisy, then unlimited fortunes could be had for the writing. Yet advertising is less than 2 percent of GDP, much of it uncontroversially informative—such as shop signs and or ads in trade magazines aimed at highly sophisticated buyers.

Easterlin makes another economist's point, that "how people feel they ought to live . . . rises commensurately with income. The result is that while income growth makes it possible for people better to attain their aspirations, they are not happier because their aspirations, too, have risen."[8] Some other economists, especially from the left or center, agree that standards of consumption are social, and so higher income is spent in an arms race to match other people's consumption—expensive leather furniture in one's pied-à-terre in New York City, say—because that is How Good People Live Now.

Well, what of it? More and more humans are richer, and soon all of them. Therefore, they have an expanded idea of how many square feet a livable apartment must be. They have more scope for painting themselves in more comfortable, sometimes elevated, ways. Good. The "happiness" literature among economists is predisposed to find modern levels of consumption vulgar and corrupting, that arms race.[9] It has become one of the scientific legs of the century-old campaign by the clerisy against the "consumerism" to which the nonclerisy is so wretchedly enslaved, as described in the writings of the economists Fred Hirsch or Robert Frank or Tibor Scitovsky, or the sociologist Juliet Schor, or indeed the sociological economist of a century ago, the great Thorstein Veblen.

In her survey of Catholic and radical thinking on consumption, the theologian Christine Firer Hinze worries that such self-makings in consumption might abandon human virtues, especially the virtue of temperance. She recalls Monsignor John A. Ryan's books of economics in the early twentieth century calculating the costs of dignity as against superfluity. Hinze and McCloskey agree with the anti-consumption clerisy that it is possible to make oneself badly— she and McCloskey are Aristotelians and Aquinians, with an idea of the virtuous life. We are not utilitarians refusing to judge consumption. The economists can be properly criticized for such a species of amoralism, which from the 1980s onward corrupted, we have noted, American schools of business. "Structures of sin" are possible in the sociology of consumption. Hinze and McCloskey would urge "a virtue approach to consumer culture," and to much else. But what evidence, really, is there that "the market can neither generate nor guarantee respect for . . . moral foundations"?[10] Doubtless not without ethical effort, yes. But "cannot"?

The proper story, that is, praises the system people refer to when they use the word *capitalism*. The word itself, though, is often used to mean unmitigated greed, profits over people—that is, whatever advances the interests of the owners of capital, sin incarnate. In her 2006 book *The Bourgeois Virtues*, McCloskey defines *capitalism* as "private property and free labor without central planning, regulated by the rule of law and an ethical consensus."[11] But later she realized that the definition is too static and does not embrace a liberal approval of commercially tested betterment. The better ethical system is that of liberal innovism. It turns proper attention to new, mass creativity and the new, mass liberty to devise or relocate, starting in northwestern Europe and now rapidly enriching the world. Liberal innovism should not be silently assumed without evidence to be corrupting. Stop to consider.

The Bourgeois Deal, and the Great Enrichment it made possible, came under revolutionary scrutiny in 1848, initiating a slow turn to socialism. Innovism and liberalism were almost destroyed in the twentieth century, especially during Europe's seventy-five-year-long suicide attempt (1914–1989), during which such antibourgeois notions as nationalism and socialism and (God help us) national socialism "tore the lid off of hell."[12] The Great Enrichment survived. Better keep it, for a dignified and ethical life for humans.

Part Two

ENRICHMENT DIDN'T COME FOR THE REASONS YOU IMAGINE

12

Liberal Ideas, Not European Horrors or Heroism, Explain the Great Enrichment

So what caused it? Our friends on the moderate right of the political spectrum extoll the "Killer Apps," as the Tory historian Niall (pronounced like "Neal") Ferguson calls them. His list is: better property rights, a work ethic, a consumer society, competition, modern medicine, and science.[1]

We agree that any decent society should want more of these. But we disagree that they are the "killer apps" explaining why people in some places are very rich while people in other places are very poor. Property rights are surely necessary. A society without them will not enrich, as Hobbes so eloquently asserted. But good property rights, which by the way do not require a leviathan, have existed in every society—or else it is not a society but a war of all against all. The classic of English legal history by Pollock and Maitland (1895, mainly by Maitland) showed that the English laws of property and contract were largely formed, as the book's title puts it, "before the time of Edward I." That's 1272. The economist Bart Wilson argues persuasively that the first person who made a spear out of a haft and glue and twine and a stone point and called it "mine" made Homo sapiens into a property owner and a trader.[2] Property rights in ancient Rome and medieval China were as good as in eighteenth-century Scotland. Yet the Scots, not the Chinese, made the modern world. Property is not a sufficiency.

Necessary? Sure. But property was commonplace and therefore hardly a candidate for a killer app peculiar to the modern European world. Anyway, as a matter of logic, necessary is not sufficient. To claim, as did Douglass North (Nobel 1993, but not for this), that better property rights *caused* economic development is like saying that oxygen in the atmosphere *caused* the Great Chicago Fire of 1871 or that the English language *caused* the novels of Jane Austen from 1811 to 1818. Necessary? Sure. Sufficient? Of course not.

The other Ferguson apps are likewise not sufficient, merely sometimes necessary, and are decidedly not killer. As to a work ethic and a consumer society, when have poor agriculturists not worked hard, and when have humans not eagerly consumed what they had? Ferguson's "competition" in markets characterized China from the T'ang Dynasty at the latest down to the last emperor, with a large national extent of markets and with light taxation and with centuries of peace—more competition than in the insanely quarrelsome and fragmented Europe since the fall of Rome.

And modern medicine and "science" came *from* enrichment more than causing it. Sewers in enriching countries, based mainly in the nineteenth century on a nonbacterial understanding of the transmission of disease, for example, brought Europe up to the old standard of urban healthiness in China. And high science had little to do with most of modern growth until 1900 or so, and really significantly only after 1945. Penicillin, discovered in the 1930s, was not released for civilian use until after World War II. McCloskey in 1943 spent a month in the hospital after chewing on the business end of an extension cord. The only antibiotic available was a sulfa drug, also a recent scientific discovery, though the correct dosage for an infant was not known. It stopped infection from the lip surgery entailed, for which heartfelt thanks, but damaged the kidneys some. You hear the combination "scienceandtechnology" a good deal, especially from physical and biological scientists wanting more of your money for their noble undertakings. But most of the world's welfare comes from the technology part, not from high-energy physics or space probes to Saturn and the High Frontier.

§

Our friends on the left, by contrast, say that the West waxed rich by stealing from the rest, by enslaving them and building empires. But, as Ferguson correctly notes, imperial exploitation is the *least* original thing the Europeans did after 1492. Slavery and empires have been commonplace yet never produced a Great Enrichment. The slave trade along the *east* coast of Africa, sending black slaves (like the white Slavs of the north, hence "slave") into the markets of Cairo and Constantinople/Istanbul was of longer duration and was on the same scale as that from the west coast, which is supposed to have made the United States rich. Yet the eastern trade didn't make Egypt or the Byzantine or Ottoman Empires rich, not on even close to the scale of the Great Enrichment. Similarly, for some reason Brazil and the Caribbean, with much larger imports of *west* African slaves than the remote United States, did not share in the magically enriching power of slavery.

Nor empire. The economist Lance Davis and the historian Robert Huttenbach showed decisively long ago that even the vaunted British Empire, on which the sun never set, was a drain on British income.[3] Benjamin Disraeli, before his 1872 conversion to imperialism, had in 1852 complained that "these wretched colonies . . . are a millstone around our neck." He was right in 1852 and wrong in 1872. A few British mining fortunes were made, a few viceroys of India educated at Christ Church College, Oxford, got their portraits up on the walls of the Senior Common Room, and quite a few twits from minor public schools got jobs in the empire, with billiards and gin-and-tonics nightly at the club. But the ordinary Scot or Cockney or Yorkshireman got nothing but the great joy of seeing, by jingo, a quarter of the globe painted red. The poor sods paid taxes on beer and tobacco to support the Royal Navy and then died on the Northwest Frontier in 1880 or on the western front in 1916 or in the Burmese jungles in 1943.

No, this or that right-wing app or left-wing exploitation can't do it. Some few of them increased income in Europe and then the world, a little bit. Consider the tea trade with China (but the Opium Wars). Consider organic chemistry (but poison gas). Canals. Savings banks. One-room schoolhouses. But each had by itself a small effect relative to the 3,000 percent per person to be explained, and many of them had been anticipated elsewhere, without the massive effect—in 1492, for example, the Chinese were more literate and had in their past been much more inventive than the Europeans.

§

Deeper tides of explanation are in order. Improvements of 1 or 2 percent in an industry taking 1 percent or even 10 percent of the nation's inputs are nice to have—you would get along just fine with, say, a mere 1/2,300th of US national income ($8.6 billion a year, thank you very much; it is the modern equivalent of what Robert Clive, the British conqueror of India, enjoyed in each of the seven years he lived after his return in 1757).[4] But a great-invention theory of economic history doesn't work even as well as a great-man theory of political history. As many as twenty net 2-percenters—big deals such as the railway or the high school movement—don't add up to the massive 1,000 to 10,000 percent rise over the miserable level of income per person in 1800. Or to put it another way, the tidal wave of ingenious apps after 1800 *does* add up—but then it is the tidal wave, not the steam engine or the internet or agronomical research on hybrid corn, that is the real explanation. It's the wave, not this or that molecule of water.

What, then, caused the tidal wave of ingenuity?

We argue, with solid support in recent research in economics and in history, that the British got rich—and then Westerners and then much of world, and all humans in the next few generations— because of a change in ethics and rhetoric and ideology.

Strange, yes? Mere ideas, not matter. But the more you think about it, the more obvious it becomes. New ideas, understood as human intentions, precede new actions. Routine profit or routine exploitation can't make you or your world rich. It has to be a new idea that raises everyone's game, and there need to be thousands of them. The source of the wave of molecules, we claim, was the new permission to have a go, inspired by the shocking new ethics and rhetoric and ideology of liberalism. Give ordinary folk the right to life, liberty, and the pursuit of happiness—against ancient tyranny (and modern regulation, industrial planning, and occupational licensure)—and they commence thinking up all manner of new ideas. They think up an ice cream store here, a frontier farm there, an iPhone at last.

Then in a liberal economy they have permission to put them into action, the billions of novelties, tiny and titanic, that liberal innovism yielded, 1800 to the present.

Think of the analogy with a mechanical watch. The usual material suspects in the explanation of the Great Enrichment are like the gears of the watch—necessary but not the motive force. The spring in the mechanical watch of modern betterment was ideas, inspired by the master idea of free human equality of permission, liberalism. People started in the new liberalism—imagined during the eighteenth century and slowly and imperfectly implemented thereafter—to talk differently about one another. Equality of standing and of permission and of legal rights became the ruling theory, against the hierarchy in all previous times (and, we worry, the new hierarchy of governmental domination in present times).

The previous rhetoric, echoes of which you still hear, is that of a jailer in southern France during the thirteenth century scorning a rich man's plea for mercy: "Come, Master Arnaud Teisseire, you have wallowed in such opulence! . . . How could you be without sin?"[5] But at length the advanced thinkers such as Adam Smith and Thomas Paine came to believe the Bourgeois Deal.

A bumper sticker version of evolutionary biology is "descent with modification." The Great Enrichment happened because people embraced *dissent* with modification. They started to honor dissenters —or at least stopped hanging and burning them. Samuel Johnson never indulged in the antieconomic, anticonsumerist, antiprofit yammering so common among the later clerisy and common among the aristocracy and the literal clerics of his times. In 1753, he praised *innovation*, well before the very word had gained its modern prestige—"The age is running mad after innovation; all the business of the world is to be done in a new way; men are to be hanged in a new way"—and took an informed interest in new ways of, say, brewing. He defended hopeful projectors:

> That the attempts of such men will often miscarry, we may reasonably expect; yet from such men, and such only, are we to hope for the cultivation of those parts of nature which lie yet waste, and

the invention of those arts which are yet wanting to the felicity of life. . . . Whatever is attempted without previous certainty of success, . . . amongst narrow minds may . . . expose its author to censure and contempt; . . . every man will laugh at what he does not understand, . . . and every great or new design will be censured as a project.[6]

His was a declaration against the enemies of the bourgeois dignity and liberty to improve. Such a declaration would have been nearly impossible in 1620—although Francis Bacon, for all his aristocratic nastiness, was at the time an early robin in that spring. The American projector Benjamin Franklin, about the same time as Johnson, wrote to similar effect, with an uncharacteristic bitterness: the attempts of an improver such as himself "to benefit mankind, . . . however well imagined, if they do not succeed expose him, though very unjustly, to general ridicule and contempt; and if they do succeed, to envy, robbery, and abuse."[7] As the German sociologist Max Weber pointed out in 1904, the arrival of the creative destroyer "was not generally peaceful. A flood of mistrust, sometimes of hatred, above all of moral indignation, regularly opposed itself to the first innovator."[8] But then people began to attribute the trader's profit to ingenuity and alertness beneficial to all, rather than to zero-sum theft or witchcraft ("How could you be without sin?").

13

Liberalism Supported Innovism and the Profit Test

We've been calling the new idea coming out of liberal equality of people *innovism*, which is a scientifically more accurate word than the misleading *capitalism*. *Capitalism* is what the Dutch call a "beggar name"—a name assigned by one's sneering enemies, such as the words *Quaker* or *Tory* or *Whig*, but then adopted proudly by the victims themselves. Thus "*Forbes*: Capitalist Tool."

The word *capitalism* is a Marxist coinage. Karl Marx himself never used the word *Kapitalismus*, but let's not get pedantic. He freely tossed around *capitalist* to describe the bosses who were busily reinvesting surplus value on top of their original accumulation of capital. In older usage, *capitalist* meant merely someone with a lot of money to invest. Marx gave the word its theoretical edge. Like economists and others before and after, Marx claimed that the accumulation of capital was the watch spring of modernity.

And so by using the word, one adopts without realizing it a particular theory of how the world got rich: by accumulation. Which is mistaken. The Marxian sociologist Immanuel Wallerstein, for example, wrote in 1983 that "the word capitalism is derived from capital. It would be legitimate therefore to presume that capital is a key element in capitalism."[1] No, it wouldn't. So, since the first part of the word *astrology* is derived from the Latin for "star," it would be legitimate to presume that stars are a key element in human fate. That people insist on ruminating on something called "capital" does not imply that its accumulation was in fact unique to modernity.

And it was not. Romans and Chinese and all human beings back to the caves have always accumulated capital, abstaining from consumption to get it. Sheer accumulation, without new ideas, runs up against sharply diminishing returns. Without a new idea for a pizza joint—new in its location or new in its product—adding at great expense another to the corner of Polk and Dearborn, crowding into the half dozen already within a couple of blocks, is a stupid project, privately and socially.

What made us rich were good new ideas for investing capital, directing labor, marshalling land, not the investments themselves, necessary though they were. McCloskey got into a little debate about the matter with her liberal friend Mark Skousen. (The debate happened at the amazing FreedomFest conference every August in Las Vegas, which Mark hosts. It's a hoot. Go.) Mark voiced a typical objection to our view that ideas, not capital, were the springs in the watch. "You must have capital to advance the economy," he said to McCloskey. "Entrepreneurs have plenty of great ideas and budding technology to change the world, but unless they get financing, they will remain unfulfilled."

That's right, but as Skousen admitted, the financing is merely a necessary condition, not a sufficient one. The explosion of human ingenuity after 1800, by contrast, was sufficient. The ideas for railways and electric lights and containerization were so good that financing was seldom a problem. (How does "never" work for you?)

What happened after the Great Chicago Fire of 1871 is a decisive test. One-third of the city burned down. But, immediately, the week after, with the embers still warm in the wrecked buildings, entrepreneurs at all levels started rebuilding the city, this time in brick and stone instead of wood. They dumped the rubbish from the fire into the adjacent Lake Michigan, extending the shoreline a quarter mile. They attracted architects from all over and invented steel-frame skyscrapers. In a few years Chicago was back, bragging so much that an out-of-town journalist named it "the Windy City," a beggar name that stuck, to this day misleading people about Chicago weather: the winds off the lake moderate the temperature, warming it in winter and cooling it in summer.

Why did they rebuild so fast and so high and so arrogantly? Because the location of Chicago was an idea superior to Milwaukee or Saint Louis. The idea made reinvestment in the city immensely profitable, instantly. And so for decades Chicago, despite notorious corruption at every level of government, was among the fastest-growing cities in the world, the Shenzhen of America. A site at the lowest portage between the Great Lakes and the Mississippi River system, reinforced by its equally natural but politically assured center of the nation's railway system ("freight handler for the nation"; thank you, Abe Lincoln, attorney for the Illinois Central Railway) caused the investment. The investment did not cause the site. The idea—put a great city here, for heaven's sake—was the spring. The buildings were the gears.

Necessary conditions are endless and mostly not pertinent as sensible accounts of cause. Having liquid water at the usual temperatures, or a reasonably stable government, is necessary for a Great Enrichment, too. But nobody wants to speak of "water-ism" or "stable-ism." China had stability, but no Great Enrichment. For that matter, it had liquid water. Thus too the mistake since Marx of "capital-ism." The pertinent necessary conditions were shared by a great many societies. Yet such societies did not experience anything approaching the Great Enrichment.

Skousen told McCloskey that "the scarcity of investment capital has kept us from advancing as fast as we could." No, it hasn't. Such a notion was popular at the World Bank during the long reign of what the New York University development economist William Easterly calls "capital fundamentalism."[2] Yet the historical and economic evidence tells against such thinking. Pour capital into Ghana, yet it fails. Don't give China a cent, yet it succeeds. The liberating of ingenuity in human minds is what mattered. Foreign aid has a dismal track record. The Bourgeois Deal, on the other hand, leads to a Great Enrichment. Give people liberty and you give them life.

"Capitalism" is a scientific mistake compressed into a single word. It is dramatically misleading coinage by the enemies of liberty—and of the sadly misguided among our friends who think they support liberty, but in their statism hitched to capital fundamentalism end up not so doing. We recommend in its place "commercially tested betterment" enabled by an ideology of "innovism," itself enabled by liberalism.

The innovistic rhetoric honored the dissenter from the old way of brewing beer or making steel or selling shirts or getting people from the bar to their homes in a ride-sharing vehicle instead of a taxi. Especially, innovism embraced a commercial test that distinguished the wise dissents of which people approved—as measured by their willingness to pay with the fruits of their own labors—as against the stupid dissents of which they would not approve, the Edsels and the New Cokes. It's the intrinsic democracy of commerce, more precise and powerful than actual voting, as much as we approve of the human equality of dignity signaled by the right to vote. Traders and innovators and triers-out of novelties learn by swift commercial tests what needs modification: dissent with modification. Every engineered and designed product goes through such a test. After all, profit is not some arbitrary tax imposed by the power of the bosses. It is the vote of the consumers, conveyed *through* the bosses.

A profit is revenue in excess of the value of the next-best item for which the labor, capital, and raw materials could have been used. It signals a social good, a pat on the back from the invisible hand, an "attaboy" or "attagirl" from people voting with their dollars. By contrast, a loss is revenue short of the value of the next-best thing for which the required labor, capital, land, and raw materials could have been used—rather than, say, the Apple Newton, the Microsoft Zune, the Ford Edsel, New Coke, Crystal Pepsi, the McDLT, football leagues like the first XFL, AFL (sort of), WFL, USFL, WLAF, and AAF, the HP TouchPad, World Championship Wrestling, VHS cassette rental after DVDs and DVD rental after Netflix, the Samsung Galaxy Note 7, Google Glass, Trump University, Trump Steaks, Trump Airlines, *Trump* magazine, the Trump Taj Mahal Casino, the Trump Marina Casino, the Trump Plaza Casino, Trump Mortgage, Trump Vodka, Trump: The Game. It is a slap in the face from the invisible hand. It is, if you prefer, a gentle-but-firm hand conveying the message, "You're wasting resources, dear, and should go do something else." The commercial test is to be contrasted with terrifying fairy tales about "corporate power" or "manipulation" by advertising. If big corporations and extensive advertising worked such magic, contrary to the commercial test of profit from consumers, Sears would still be the biggest retailer in the world.

The profit test is crucial. The US long-distance passenger railway, Amtrak, lives on, despite hemorrhaging money, because it can rely on taxpayers. The economist Randal O'Toole calculates that Amtrak's per-passenger-mile operating loss is higher than the airlines' entire per-passenger-mile costs.[3] A Mars rover that costs $2.5 billion and produces $2 billion worth of Mars roving, for a social loss of half a billion, might seem neat, but it's a waste of resources that makes the world poorer in delights. Profits send memos relevant to whether resources are being used well. Governments regularly don't get the memos, or refuse to read them. Politics often has other messages in mind. The Cardinal Amtrak route from Chicago to Washington, DC, has thirty-one stops, of which more than one-third are in tiny West Virginia. Hmm. Does that have anything to do with Robert Byrd, senator from the Mountain State, serving fifty-one years, longer than any other senator in history? Could be. Governments by definition exercise power, the ability we have noted to coerce people to do something they are not willing to do. But Ben & Jerry's ice cream does not have coercion at its disposal, merely persuasion. If it were to venture on Listerine-and-castor-oil ice cream, the loss incurred from day one would send an eloquent memo to the head office.

Profits are not "incentives" to persons in the way that the left imagines we liberals argue. The left notes that Ben Cohen of Ben & Jerry's is a very rich man, and he can hardly be incentivized to significant *new* efforts in devising flavors by the promise of an extra million added to his many millions. But that is not the relevant margin of incentives. The relevant margin is that of sending a memo as to what is a socially desirable activity, of which more should happen. If a captain of industry earns 10 percent on his betterment when the rest are earning 5 percent, the economy is saying to him and the others, "Do more of it."

That is what was disastrously wrong with Senator Elizabeth Warren's harmless-sounding proposal in her campaign for the presidency in 2019–2020 to take each year "only" 2 percent of wealth away from rich people. Income is the return on wealth, and wealth is the ownership of physical or human capital that helps produce things, such as oil or hospitals or professional football games. If the percentage return on a million dollars of wealth invested in oil exploration is 6 percent, it signals by its 1 percentage point advantage over the usual 5 percent that additional investments should be made in oil exploration. The tax of "only" 2 percent cuts the return from 6 to 4 percent per year. An investment that earns more than other investments will after tax earn less. It won't be made, though socially speaking it should be. In the language of economics, Warren's mild-sounding program would radically distort the pattern of investment. The wrong investments would be made, a result intensified by the inability of the government seizing the income, even if it can pin down the billionaires, to use it wisely. All people, and not just the billionaires directing the investment, would be made poorer.

From 1800 to the present, the places that listened to profit made money, yes, but they enriched everybody by it. Leave me alone, to profit, and I'll make *you* rich.

§

Europeans embraced what Adam Smith, the first modern economist, called "the obvious and simple system of natural liberty."[4] Why in turn did this tidal force of liberated people wash over northwestern Europe?

A series of happy accidents, we suggest, beginning early in the 1500s, explains it. The embrace of the obvious and simple system, and the resulting revaluation of commercially tested betterment, depended on four happy Rs:

1. *Reading* spread. (Compare the internet.) The printing press, invented centuries before in a unified China, entered a politically fragmented Europe that made censorship difficult, opening Europe to new ideas. At length books gave northwestern Europe

the very good idea for a non-slave liberalism once thought to be insane.

2. *Reformation*, enabled by the *Reading*, flattened church governance and suggested to people that they could take charge of their economic lives as much as their spiritual lives.

3. *Revolt* in Holland, 1568–1648 against Spain, and

4. *Revolution* in England in the 1640s and again in 1689, in the United States in 1776, and in France in 1789 overthrew old elites and elevated radical political ideas about liberty and equality to a new ideology, the liberalism of Smith and Mary Wollstonecraft and Henry David Thoreau and Mill. Nothing similar was happening at the time in the other great commercial areas of the globe— Japan, China, the Mughal Empire, and the Ottoman Empire. The "right of revolution" in western Europe made people bold. "Whenever any form of government becomes destructive of these ends," Thomas Jefferson wrote in 1776, which by then was a cliché among advanced thinkers, "it is the right of the people to alter or to abolish it, and to institute new government."

Lots of Rs. Yet the liberal happiness could easily have turned unhappy, thus "accidents." Had Spain's Armada in 1588 succeeded in landing the best army in Europe on English soil, for instance, the Radical Reformation or hierarchy-less congregations would have been sorely checked, and later English liberalism would have been stillborn. Had Charles I not faced a brilliant Puritan general, or had James II been as tolerant as his older brother had been of non-Catholics, or had Lord North been less ham-handed, or Louis XVI better advised, the turn to liberalism and then innovism and then the Great Enrichment might have had to await later developments, perhaps in China or Turkey. But by 1776, to take that symbolic year, liberalism in western Europe was on the march. The new equality of dignity inspired the commoners—that's you—to multiply new ideas about cotton spinning and elementary education and steelmaking and votes for women and mail-order shopping and air-conditioning and mobile computing by Wi-Fi. Europe, that is, was not special, merely lucky.

14

The Great Enrichment Did Not Come from Resources or Railways or Property Rights

Coal and coastlines and navigable waterways and fertile farmland have sat for millennia without leading to a Great Enrichment. Said Alexis de Tocqueville in 1835, "Looking at the turn given to the human spirit in England by political life; seeing the Englishman . . . inspired by the sense that he can do anything . . . I am in no hurry to inquire whether nature has scooped out ports for him, or given him coal or iron."[1] "Resources" don't matter until new ideas make them valuable. Red Mountain iron ore, which signs around Birmingham, Alabama, will tell you "formed the basis" for its steel industry, was there for eons.

We're not saying resources didn't matter at all. We're saying they didn't matter much, because they are less significant than you think, and there are commonly substitutes that human ingenuity, when liberated, found again and again. The world would still have had a Great Enrichment without resource X, so long as the Englishman (or the American, or later the Swede or the Japanese), left to venture, was inspired by liberalism to the sense that he can do anything. He finds work-arounds when he encounters obstacles. This or that thing that seems "essential" has a substitute. Remember whale oil. The steamboats on the western US rivers ran on wood long after most of Europe had switched to coal. The same holds for pig iron, for which the United States and wood-rich Sweden used charcoal from wood long after wood-challenged Britain had switched to coke (not the drink but a pre-burned form of coal that gave high temperatures for making iron and steel).

The man in the street thinks that countries become rich because of resources, in which case Japan and Hong Kong would be poor and the Russian Federation and the Democratic Republic of the Congo rich. The man in the street's mistaken economics can have bad consequences. Many Latin American voters have a deep and dangerous conviction that Latin America is rich in resources, and yet the people are poor. The theme has encouraged wave after wave of populist revolutionaries, promising easy redistribution to make everyone rich. Yet in a modern economy, people on farms compose only 1 percent of the population (and even in Iowa only 7.6 percent, many of them with second jobs outside of farming), and those working in mines or fisheries less. The natural resources used now in the US, including urban land, earn 5 percent or less of national income. They do not determine much of its level.[2] So it is in Latin America.

Lots of things, like coal or free trade or better roads or more saving, might explain a few percentage points of the Great Enrichment. But they arrive at nothing like the 900 percent or 2,900 percent or 9,900 percent increase in standards of living to be explained.

§

The surprising smallness of the usual suspects can be shown from a weird trick economists use, called "Harberger Triangles," named for the Nobel-worthy economist Arnold Harberger. It measures a cause's static contribution to an economy. You ask, "How big is the productivity increase in the sector?" Then you ask, "How big is the sector?" Then you multiply the two answers. The product is the increase in national income attributable to the sector. Not so weird, after all: common sense.

The railway is the classic example. The logic of the railway as an engine of growth is seductive because it made shipping cheaper and therefore caused the location of production and consumption to change radically. Iowa, for example, has many rivers but few of them navigable (Cedar *Rapids* is well named). Without the railway, getting Iowa's corn to market would have been a lot more expensive. The railway made land more valuable and increased the demand for steel and coal. Clearly, it was necessary for American industrialization, no?

No. The weird if commonsense trick—which is one way of describing the pathbreaking research for which Robert Fogel shared the 1993 Nobel Prize in economics—tells a different story.[3] By 1890, US costs of transporting freight had fallen on the routes railways traveled by about 50 percent. Big. The transport routes affected by rail, however, were only about 50 percent of total freight traffic. A lot of freight and some passengers still traveled by river or canal or coastal shipping. To this day, a good deal of the corn crop leaves the Midwest by barge. Still, a 50 percent reduction in cost for half of freight traffic has to be a big deal, right?

No. Transportation in 1890 accounted for about 10 percent of the US economy. Put the Harberger trick together. The national percentage gain from the railways was the 50 percent reduction in cost, times the 50 percent of transport that was affected, times the 10 percent of the national product that came from transport. Half of half of a tenth is 2.5 percent. Two-and-a-half percent, one time, is nice to have. But it's not revolutionary. It was about one year's growth in the US economy. The romantic stories about the iron horse are wrong.

True, the coming of the railway shuffled the location of production. Railways explain why Chicago and not Saint Louis became the economic capital of the Midwest. Without railways, the riverine excellence of Saint Louis might have won the prize (though the portage at Chicago, we have noted, still made transshipment by water easy there, giving Chicago double the waterways). But shuffling is not a net gain. Capital and labor went to Chicago instead of Saint Louis. It's not a net gain. The *net* gain to the nation is that 2.5 percent.

In *Bourgeois Dignity* and *Bourgeois Equality*, McCloskey used the method of Harberger Triangles relentlessly to estimate the effects of various betterments. If you think that the static gain to this or that item is *the* cause of the Great Enrichment, you have an appointment with Harberger. Foreign trade? Small. Cotton and cotton textiles?

Small. Thrift? Small. All together, however, as we've noted, betterments like dropped ceilings (Ever thought of that one? In your office, look up!) and containerization and steam engines and McGuffey's Reader and the rest *were* the Great Enrichment. But the ingenuity had to be astonishingly widespread and persistent to overcome the logic of Harberger Triangles. It means that the widespreadness and the persistence are what need explanation. It leads us back to Tocqueville's Englishman, or American, and now Indian or Chinese, inspired by the sense that he or she can do anything.

§

And in any case the timing for each alleged "one big cause" is wrong. Economics aside, history rejects them. Trade, for example, is ancient. People traded obsidian and shells vigorously across great distances many millennia ago. Amber from the shores of the Baltic and lapis lazuli from Afghanistan turn up in Egyptian grave goods. European grain prices moved together by arbitrage in the late Middle Ages.[4] By the early eighteenth century, decades before the Great Enrichment got going, the English-Scottish grain markets were tightly integrated indeed. But they were even more tightly integrated in China at the time. The trade of the Indian Ocean was larger than that of the Atlantic for hundreds of years before the Enrichment, without causing one. Trade was a necessary gear in the watch, but nothing like the spring.

"Not so fast," you say. "Surely, as many students of the matter have argued recently, the enforcement of *property rights* is the spring." Oh, no. It is again necessary, but nothing like sufficient, as we have said. English common law was in place hundreds of years before the Enrichment. The anthropological historian Alan MacFarlane notes that "England was as 'capitalist' in 1250 as it was in 1550 or 1750."[5] It relied on property rights and the rule of law. Buying and selling was secure, usually. True, Henry Tudor's victory at Bosworth Field in 1485 ended at last an economy-wrecking War of the Roses, and with it many decades of baronial disregard for such rights. Yet good property rights characterized for centuries much of Europe, even crazy

England, without yielding modern growth. Until the seventeenth century, the enforcement of loans in the capital markets of Italy was much more advanced than those of northern Europe. And indeed, loaning and borrowing on a large and small scale was commonplace everywhere in world history. "Capitalism"—if it merely means profit-making business and the making of such credit transactions—was for centuries stretching into millennia as vigorous in Shanghai and Mumbai as it was in Sheffield and Manchester. One can study labor and property contracts and long-distance credit and business letters in startlingly modern form from Mesopotamia, now Iraq, inscribed on clay two thousand years before Christ.

In any case, mere sets of laws—the "rules of the game" that North and his followers assert are the cause of our riches—are strikingly insufficient. Gears, not springs; commonplace, not special to north-western Europe in the eighteenth century. The law of the Mongols did not inspire an explosion of betterment. Of an Iceland without kings, *Njàl's Saga* written in the thirteenth century concerning the tenth century declares, *Með lögum skal land byggja,* "With law will the land be built," and so it was.[6] Most societies worldwide, with rare exceptions such as Russia under an all-owning tsar, had in such matters thoroughly matched England in 1689. The ancient Near East had "norms and rules of behavior," writes the Assyriologist Norman Yoffee, and local powers to back them up. Law codes such as that of Hammurabi of Babylon, who had by the early eighteenth century BCE established a wide hegemony, which "his" laws were meant to justify. But they "were not the foundations of order in Mesopo-tamian society," Yoffee argues, because the order already existed, arising from the bottom up, à la Iceland, "but were . . . instruments used to proclaim a [centralized] simplicity that did not exist."[7] For ordinary English people, the laws that mattered most were for cen-turies before the eighteenth century the vigorously enforced local laws of "leet" courts in each village, concerning crop rotations and theft of land and theft of life.

And people can innovate around many black-letter rules. The enterprising eBay seller skirting Missouri's ticket-scalping laws in 2004 could auction a pocket schedule or a baseball cap along with a note that the winner of the auction would also get four tickets to the Cardinals-Dodgers playoff game. A little inefficient, yes. An insurmountable barrier to prosperity, no. If the Great Enrichment had "simply" been a matter of getting the rules (and, therefore, the incentives) right, someone probably would have found a way to do it, considering the enormous free lunch to be picked up. Laws are in part endogenous, as economists would put it: self-generated in response to profit opportunities, for the public good or the public ill. Witness suburban towns working to attract Walmart and Target; and likewise large cities, at the behest of competitors of Walmart, working to keep it out.[8]

Ideologies about a commercial society, and about expert rule, govern the outcome as much as does the social gain from efficiency. In social democratic Europe, the owners of property downtown can pass laws to prevent cheaper commercial strips from developing outside. In the somewhat more economically liberal US they mostly can't. The result in the US is unlovely but efficient. In the expert-driven liberal parts of Europe—in Germany and Estonia, for example—return-free tax filing is routine, saving those maddening days in April to give the IRS information about your income that it already has. In the K-Street-corrupt US, by contrast, TurboTax and H&R Block have bribed members of Congress to keep you enslaved to doing the pointless April job. They might as well have arranged for you to break rocks. Your tax dollars at work.

15

Nor Thrift or "Capitalism"

Nor saving. As economists, we of course *love* saving and investment. Provide, provide, said the poet. You yourself should do more of it because it is an exercise in caring for you and yours—and, if your bank loans out your saving, caring for society as a whole. Ebenezer Scrooge's saving increased England's capital stock. Yes.

And yet more saving, and the resulting pile of machines and bachelor's degrees, does not do the trick, as McCloskey noted in her debate with Mark Skousen described earlier. Consider. The ancestors used the so-called Acheulean hand axes, unchanged in design, for over a million years. It wasn't an "ax," exactly, merely a sharpened stone such as flint fitted to the human hand and useful for cutting, scraping, and throwing at hyenas trying to get to the same antelope carcass that the local humans were cutting up. Archaeological sites contain scores of them, sometimes hundreds. It was capital accumulation. But by piling up the Acheulean hardware, the ancestors did not make themselves thirtyfold richer. Piling up is precisely what saving is by itself, absent new ideas for better axes. More hand axes would have had a use, but with diminishing marginal returns. The hundredth one wouldn't yield much in better fending off hyenas. Think of a hundredth pair of your shoes; and more so a third house, on which you also have to keep up the roof. Merely piling up hand axes or shoes or houses is accumulation without (much) betterment, and isn't what greatly enriched the world. But a new idea manifesting itself in *better* tools, houses, shoes, or procedures is the spring, a human creativity liberated from the conservative rule or law or routine.

Again the historical evidence reinforces the economic logic. Prudent, temperate saving happens in every society, by necessity. In medieval Europe the yields in barley or wheat per unit of seed were pathetically low, four or five. It required adults to ignore the weeping of their hungry children in the spring, and to engage in saving on a very big scale, by broadcasting on plowed ground upwards of a quarter of the grain crop. The problem in the Middle Ages was the absence of new ideas for investment, not the absence of a fund for saving.

Saving rates in enriching England, actually, were *lower* than the European norm. As a share of national income, investment in physical capital was 6 percent in England and 12 percent around Europe in 1760, and 8 percent in England but 12 percent in Europe again in 1800. British investment rose, but the Britons were less thrifty than their backward neighbors.[1] What they had were strikingly new ideas for the use of the saving, for instance the Duke of Bridgewater's river-bridging canals.

Exhortations to thrift are anyway ancient. The Hebrew Bible associates thrift with diligence: "The sluggard will not plough in the autumn by reason of the cold; therefore shall he beg in [the] harvest, and have nothing"; "Seest thou a man diligent in his business? He shall stand before kings" (Proverbs 20:4; 22:29). The Koran (7:31) says, "God does not like the prodigals." Saving is praised in Buddhism, among other non-Abrahamic faiths, as in the "Admonition to Singala" advising

> He should divide
> His money in four parts;
> On one part he should live,
> With two expand his trade,
> And the fourth he should save
> Against a rainy day.[2]

This holy text of South Asia is recommending here a saving rate of 75 percent. If saving did the job, which it didn't, and the South Asians took the hint, then Europe in 1800 would have been a colony of India.

§

So powerful is the conviction in economics since Adam Smith that capital accumulation is the spring of growth that in 1956 even the great Ludwig von Mises, the Austrian economist émigré to the United States whom Carden and McCloskey admire extravagantly, gets it wrong. Mises writes, "Saving, capital accumulation, is the agency that has transformed step-by-step the awkward search for food on the part of savage cave dwellers into the modern ways of industry." No, it isn't. Accumulation was necessary, as were sunlight and the presence of a labor force, but it raised income sharply only when it embodied brilliant new ideas, such as containerization. Mises then drifts into a related error: "The pacemakers of this evolution were the ideas that created the institutional framework within which capital accumulation was rendered safe by the principle of private ownership of the means of production." True, there needed to exist the ancient idea of protections for property. But it had been widespread in human societies, as we have repeatedly noted, from the cave dwellers on down. Then he goes back to accumulation by itself: "Every step forward on the way toward prosperity is the effect of saving." Doubtful. Saving is necessary, yes, yes. But so is an endless list of things necessary. The existence of language. Counting systems. Liquid water. The universe. It then seems to occur to Mises what the actual spring was, though he mentions it only to push it aside: "The most ingenious technological inventions would be practically useless if the capital goods required for their utilization had not been accumulated by saving."[3] He is falling headlong into the logical error of taking necessity as sufficiency. Try substituting "liquid water" for "capital accumulation" and for "capital goods," and "getting liquid water" for "saving." Then proceed to a liquid water theory of economic growth.

Consider 1492 China, which as we have noted had had a century-long peace, excellent property rights, enforcement of law, absence of crushing within-China tariffs (another contrast to Europe), and plenty of capital, able to build the Great Wall and the Grand Canal with ease, exceeding in the use of saving even Roman capital projects. Yet China, from which in the past a majority of the world's technical betterments had come, did not have the astounding explosion of ingenuity tested commercially that finally after 1800 enriched northwestern Europe.

The classical and Marxist idea that capital begets capital, "endlessly," is hard to shake. In 1983 the historical sociologist Immanuel Wallerstein we mentioned back in chapter 13 wrote of "the endless accumulation of capital, a level of waste that may begin to border on the irreparable."[4] The "endless"/"never-ending" expressions, still resonating in all notions of "capitalism," originated twenty-two centuries before Karl Marx in the Greek aristocratic disdain for commerce. People of business (declared aristocratic Plato and aristocrat-tutoring Aristotle) are motivated by *apeiros* (unlimited) greed. Thus Aristotle in the *Ethics*. The "no limit" in Aristotle is about commerce, which is supposed not to exhibit the diminishing returns that, say, agriculture does. In the thirteenth century, Thomas Aquinas, referring to Aristotle (with a little less than his customary enthusiasm for "The Philosopher"), retails the usual complaint against commerce, which depends on "the greed for gain, which knows no limit and tends to infinity."[5] As the political scientist John Danford observes, "The belief that there is something objectionable about ['unlimited' gain] has persisted for more than two thousand years. . . . The enduring legacy . . . was . . . the view that . . . commerce or the acquisition of wealth is not merely low; it is unnatural, a perversion of nature, and unworthy of a decent human being."[6]

§

The spring was not accumulated capital or old institutions or easily mined coal or other alleged necessities, then, but Smith's "liberal plan of equality, liberty, and justice," a Liberalism 1.0 and then 2.0

first applied with vigor in northwestern Europe. Liberating ordinary people turned out to inspire them to extraordinary ideas, which redirected the capital, and the liquid water, and the labor force. Our friend Skousen, we have noted, channels Mises in the contrary error of "capital-ism." The historical and economic evidence tells against the notion. The liberating of ingenuity in human minds is what mattered, as in India after 1991 and in China after 1878 and in the Anglosphere after 1776. Give people liberty, we have said, and you give them life. In the third act, you give them a rich life in every sense.

If the capital fundamentalism of the Wall Street theorists were correct, then their enemies the socialists would be correct, too. The socialists like Wallerstein assume that the key to capitalism is capital and therefore that the big issue is its accumulation and allocation. So do the Wall Street theorists such as Skousen. Both believe that ideas or entrepreneurship or management are easy. Ideas, they say, are a dime a dozen. That's why the Wall Street theorists dote on the TV program *Shark Tank*, in which ideas are easily shot down by deep-pocketed investors, and it's why the socialists think that the government in Paris or Washington can easily order up an appropriate socialization of investment. Both are sure that the future is easy to lay down. Just accumulate. Liberals know that the future depends on unpredictable ideas from free humans.

So, no. Skousen and Smith and Marx and even our modern hero Mises are mistaken. "Capitalism," and the associated idea that accumulating capital is the watch spring of enrichment, needs to be retired.

16

Schooling and Science Were Not the Fairy Dust

We're sorry to be the bearers of more bad news. We love schooling—we loved it so much that we never left. And we love science, especially when it is correctly defined (as in every language aside from quite recent English) as "systematic inquiry" about anything, whether physics or theology or economics. Thus the Germans speak of *Klassischewiisenschaft* (classics, the systematic study of Greek and Latin) and the French *les sciences humaines* (including systematic literary study). We are not fond, that is, of the narrowing definition of the word in English, emerging from certain academic disputes at Oxford and Cambridge a century and a half ago—namely, "science" confined to physical and biological science, alone.[1] No. *All* the sciences, physical and humanistic, together.

So, hurrah for widening of the human spirit by schooling and science. If you can read this book, thank a teacher in your distant past. If you are in fact a scientist, even by the narrowing only-physical definition, swell. We admire you, as we admire, too, poets and athletes and businesspeople and English professors and ordinary people working to get by.

But as sources of the Great Enrichment, the wonderful schooling and glorious science were limited in scope. The Great Enrichment got going without much schooling and without much in the way of "high" science in the new definition in English. Until 1900 or so, neither was very important to the economy. As the economic historian David Mitch, the doyen of historical studies of education in its economic aspect, puts it, "England, during its Industrial Revolution 1780 to 1840 experienced a notable acceleration in economic growth yet displayed little evidence of improvement in the educational attainments of its workforce."[2] The effect of the later mass public education in Britain, according to the economic historian Jason Long, was "surprisingly modest."[3] More schooling certainly would have led Fantine and Cosette to more flourishing lives in spirit. And yes, it would have made them richer, maybe two or three times richer. But that wasn't what lifted the masses of French people out of poverty. You can see the truth of such a proposition from recent studies of how much more a college graduate makes compared with a high school dropout. The college grad will earn two or three times more in lifetime income. Good, and a good reason to stay in school. But one is not dealing with two or three times better but rather thirty times better.

Education is commonly seen as a fairy dust in raising up the poor. In South Africa, for example, the laws prevent very poor people from having any jobs at all. In particular, a high legal minimum wage, coupled with the inability to fire employees who steal, prevents very poor people from competing with members of trade unions. It leaves 50 percent of young people without jobs. Benevolent folk, who have jobs in the government or in the universities, are troubled by the unemployment. But they do not recommend getting rid of the minimum wage and the labor laws that cause it. They do not want poor people to find voluntary agreements to be hired, making everyone better off. No, they recommend that South African schools be radically (and magically) improved, to make the young people productive enough to be worth employing at the high minimum wage. Create unemployment by coercive governmental action. Solve it not by reversing the governmental action that caused it but by adding still more coercive governmental action. If that doesn't work . . . then add still more coercion.

The educational coercion in taxes and schools for fancy jobs is back to front. If South Africans were allowed to work at whatever wage employers were willing to offer, or were allowed to start businesses without onerous governmental licenses, everyone would have a job and an income, and everyone would send their children to school. You do not need to know algebra or English literature to work in retail in Cape Town, or to run a food truck in Chicago, or to work as a messenger in Paris. A Cape Town or Chicago or Paris in which employment is not hampered will come to want education. People will then learn the joys of Geoffrey Chaucer soon enough, for "gladly wolde he lerne and gladly teche."

§

Doesn't Jack's schooling, though, benefit Jill? If the government left education to an unregulated free market, it is said, people wouldn't get enough of it, because they don't account for the good spillovers to others. Schooling is said to be like a flu shot: our flu shots reduce the likelihood that you will get infected. Free markets will supposedly underprovide flu shots. In the same way, people all benefit from living in a society in which most have literacy and numeracy. Because school is hard and expensive and not always fun, people won't get enough, unless the government steps in with its coercion.

Or so it seems to some people. It's clear that there are spillover benefits from other people getting elementary readin', writin', and 'rithmetic. But it's not clear that education beyond, say, eighth grade spills over enough to justify massive subsidies to high schoolers, and especially to university students. Mostly the gain accrues to the high schoolers or university graduates themselves. If so, in justice and in efficiency, they or their parents should pay for it.

What we now consider ordinary arithmetic entered late into the education of even the aristocracy and the clergy and other nonmercantile professions. Samuel Johnson advised a rich woman, "Let your boy learn arithmetic" (note the supposition that the heir to a great fortune would usually fail to do so). "He will not then be a prey to every rascal which this town swarms with: teach him the value of money and how to reckon with it."[4] In 1803 Harvard College required, naturally, fluency in both Latin and Greek for all the boys proposing to attend. Yet only in that year did it also make arithmetic a requirement.

But in fact—and this is the kind of shockingly cynical and conversation-killing view that makes economists such big hits at dinner parties—subsidized schooling beyond a certain point wastes resources by pushing people into school when their time and the other inputs into the education would be better used elsewhere, as judged by a market test. The central case is university education, which in most of the world is provided free (or, rather, "free") to qualified applicants. Economists note that the result is to subsidize the upper middle class, whose children are anyway best prepared for university, by taxing everyone else. Very poor countries give subsidies to university students exceeding by a factor of ten the subsidies to K–8 students. When it is proposed in France to add any university tuition at all, the students riot in the streets. They are mostly middle class, the sons and daughters of lawyers and doctors and businesspeople. In the 1950s the University of California system charged exceptionally low tuitions. It was a subsidy from poor taxpayers to rich children of lawyers. To a lesser degree than in the 1950s, it still is.

And it's not clear that the spillovers from higher schooling are always positive. A non-diverse system of education, provided by a monopoly of church or state, can of course miseducate. The human capital McCloskey acquired early by reading Prince Kropotkin at the Carnegie library and learning socialism Joan-Baez-style over the airwaves, and even in a good deal of her Harvard instruction in Keynesian economics, with its lessons of magic free lunches for all, was a factor of destruction, not a factor of production. The people studying to become better nudgers, meddlers, bureaucrats, administrators, or Keynesian magicians do damage to the rest of us.

And it is possible anyway to overeducate, at any rate in preparation for the work of the world. For many hundreds of years the Chinese system of examinations encouraged humanistic learning, as European universities did only later, and haltingly. The rigorous examinations, initiated by the Han dynasty after 206 BCE and still going strong under the Qing until 1911, yielded about 18,000 degree holders a year. In, say, 1600 the Chinese figure was roughly comparable to the number of graduates of universities in a Europe with roughly the same population then as China (150 million in China and 100 million in Europe). The production of such human capital in China was hugely superior to that in Europe for at least fifteen centuries after it began. It remained better than Europe's into the eighteenth century. Then the university reforms in Europe after 1810 and the explosion of population in China caused a great divergence in graduates proportionate to population. The Chinese 18,000 did not rise, but the number of graduates in Europe did, and notably in chemistry and other physical sciences.

The result in China was not the worst one can imagine, because knowing classical Chinese poetry, which the examinations tested, is a good thing for a human. Consult rock lyrics or country music. But it obviously did not yield bureaucrats who knew, say, calculation or accounts—though in fact China was until 1492 well ahead of the world in calculation, too. And Europe in the education of its rulers was for a long time no more utilitarian. As long as Latin was the lingua franca, allowing Poles and Italians to write to each other, the Latin-based education in grammar schools was helpful to the world's work—though such learning was confined again to the clerisy, and not even much of the gentry or aristocracy until late.

Yet as the historian Jonathan Daly argues, in explaining the stagnation of Chinese inventiveness during the past five centuries, just when Europe was waking up, "One could achieve no higher or more remunerative honor in society. Some brilliant [Chinese] men studied mathematics, astronomy, and law, but they received only scant official encouragement. Some brilliant literati-officials pursued research and reflection in non-literary fields, but without institutional backing. The examination system was thus a unifying force in Chinese culture but at the cost of stifling much creative thinking."[5]

That is, liberal educations and civil service examinations (adopted by Europeans in the nineteenth century in explicit imitation, Daly points out, of the fabled system of China) can be conservative, in both a good sense and a bad. When the great and original economist John Maynard Keynes took the examination for the Civil Service in 1906, his worst grades were in . . . economics.

§

"Well, all right, maybe education was not fairy dust. But science is. Surely the Great Enrichment happened because of the Scientific Revolution, that heady embrace of knowledge that stirs the blood and animates the mind. Surely advances in basic knowledge created the Great Enrichment, no?"

No.

People can innovate even though they believe the sun revolves around the earth or that a minimum wage does not reduce employment of the very poor. Did David Beckham need to study physics to learn how to bend it like Beckham? Does your bartender need a degree in chemistry to mix a good drink? Did Colonel Sanders need higher education to come up with his original recipe of eleven herbs and spices? No, no, and no. Far more betterment happened (and happens) the way people learn to bend it like Beckham—imitation and practice—and the way people learn how to mix good drinks or make good fried chicken: by trial and error, not high science.

The number of crucial betterments that did *not* spring from recent science is considerable: mass-produced concrete, reinforced concrete, air brakes that made mile-long trains possible, the military organization that kept the trains running on schedule and from running into one another (yes, the telegraph was science-dependent, and important in the case), elevators, asset markets, cheap paper, retail logistics, high-inventory-turnover warehouse clubs, craisins (reconstituted cranberry husks), Kingsford charcoal (from leftover wood scraps at the Ford factory), steel, eyeglasses, and a list of other betterments that could go on for whole books. Libraries, even.

Consider too dropped ceilings, plate glass, horse railways, horse trams, plumbing, irrigation, city water pressure, macadamized roads, vulcanized rubber, canning of food, selective breeding (old but pushed harder: dogs, horses, Darwin's pigeons, but then cotton plants, cattle), mass steel, spring-driven clocks and watches, central heating, wire twist-links (though plastic was needed), and on and on. Little before 1800. An explosion after 1800.

You don't believe it? You think "scienceandtechnology" (a combined word much heard) runs the show? Well, consider the list of betterments tested in commerce that were matters of sheer organization, without science or, for that matter, much in the way of complicated technology: divided highways, containerization again, the modern university, hotel chains, restaurant chains, franchises of all

sorts, condominium real estate, registers of property, weather reporting, mail, mail sorting, ship-line and railway timetables, standardized
time zones, standardized measurement, the gold standard, police,
contracts between beekeepers and orchards, highway numbering,
and on and on. Little before 1800. An explosion after 1800.

The West had a Scientific Revolution, late, but much of its science
until the seventeenth century and the use of the European lead in
optics consisted of rediscovering things the Chinese had known for
centuries, or ancient knowledge as in mathematics refined in the
Middle East. Place-value arithmetic, for example, was invented twice
in history, once in south Asia and once in Guatemala, and came to
the West by way of a tardy adoption of Arabic learning. The word
algebra comes from the Arabic *al-jabr*, "the reunion of broken parts."
Chinese and Arab science was far more sophisticated than European.

The science of prisms and planets that Newton at length practiced
did not help much in worldly pursuits. But at length, with the de-
mocratization of an innovism, useful betterments poured forth from
the craft workshops—not mainly the laboratories. The sometimes
amused esteem for the physical scientist—from *The Absent-Minded
Professor* inventing flubber to Doc Emmett Brown inventing the flux
capacitor and sending Marty McFly *Back to the Future* to Rick Mora-
nis's character in *Honey, I Shrunk the Kids* to Rick Sanchez drinking
his way across the multiverse—was a good thing. But the revaluation
of the petit bourgeois tinkering in his stable and at length his garage
was much more consequential until late.

Science borrowed from commerce, most famously the steam
engine inspiring the high science of thermodynamics. One could
argue, as the economic historian Joel Mokyr does, that what mattered for betterment was the change in outlook among a narrow
technical elite.[6] An essay he wrote with the economic historians
Cormac Ó Gráda and Morgan Kelly puts it this way: "What counted
above all was [Britain's] highly skilled mechanics and engineers, who
may not have been a large proportion of the labor force."[7] If one is
speaking of the immediate cause, he's right. Mokyr's heroes are "the
top 3–5 percent of the labor force in terms of skills: engineers, mechanics, millwrights, chemists, clock- and instrument makers, skilled

carpenters and metal workers, wheelwrights, and similar workmen."[8] One could hardly have such a revolutionary machine for the manufacturing in bulk of the wood screw and the nut-and-bolt without men like Henry Maudslay (1771–1831), already educated in making machines. In 1964 a twenty-two-year-old male student of economic history, one "Donald" McCloskey, found hilarious the remark by a historian of the lathe, a Dr. Holtzappel: "Mr. Maudslay effected nearly the entire change from the old imperfect and accidental practice of screw making . . . to the modern exact and scientific mode now generally followed by engineers; and he pursued the subject of the screw with more or less ardor and at an enormous expense until his death in 1831."[9] But Holtzappel was exactly right, and he supports Mokyr's point that a tiny elite mattered, and that making profit was not its entire motive.

Yet where did such a technical elite come from, with its education and ardor and expense? In Holland and Britain and the United States it came from ordinary people freed from ancient suppression of their hopes. Such freeing is the sole way of achieving a sufficient mass of technically skilled folk, oriented not toward rare luxuries or military victories but toward the ordinary goods of peacetime for the bulk of ordinary people—iron bridges, chemical bleaching, weaving of wool cloth by machines powered by falling water. The problem in, say, France in the eighteenth century was that the engineers came from the younger sons of its large nobility, such as Napoleon, educated for military careers. In Britain, by contrast, a promising lad from the working class could become a bourgeois master of new machines and of new institutions, as an engineer or an entrepreneur. Or at least he could do pretty well as a clockmaker or spinning-machine mechanic. In Britain and its offshoots, the career of the enterprising bourgeois or the skilled worker, as in Napoleon's army or Nelson's navy, was open to talent. John Harrison (1693–1776), the inventor of the marine chronometer, which solved by machine the problem in the wideness of the sea of finding longitude—against the arrogantly enforced demand by the elite that it be solved in the heavens by a literally high science of astronomy—was a rural Lincolnshire carpenter. His first clock was made of wood. Similarly, Maudslay of the screw-making machine, two years younger than Napoleon and thirteen years younger than Nelson, began work at the age of twelve filling cartridges at the Royal Arsenal, becoming then a blacksmith, and by age eighteen a locksmith, and more. The British working man carried the baton of a field marshal of industry in his backpack. Poor boys entering on chemical educations were permitted to have a go and produced a veritable idea explosion: for instance, about nitroglycerine, dynamite, gelignite, TNT, and C-4.

Mokyr is taking as given a structure that in fact had a vibrant modern history, a history driven by the new and bizarre ethic of human equality, of liberty in law and of dignity in esteem. The economic historian Karine van der Beek believes she is supporting Mokyr when she concludes with persuasive evidence that "the innovations and technological changes that were taking place in eighteenth-century England increased the demand for these high quality mechanical workmen."[10] But her case is the opposite of Mokyr's, which is that what caused the betterment was the supply.

The entirely new ethical context, we are claiming, made the demand for the engineers and entrepreneurs grow its own supply, when ardor and opportunity made the supply worth having. The opportunities themselves arose from a new equality in law and in society, encouraging new ideas for Dutch wholesale trade or new ideas for English coal mining. The new and liberal, if partial, equality in Holland and Britain and especially in the United States—for all the lingering sins in Britain of class snobbery and in the United States of chattel slavery—allowed many of the ordinary, and extraordinary, to have a go.

True, the world would not have artificial fertilizer and the attendant increases in agricultural productivity were it not for the high science of organic chemistry, and it would not have had the green revolution without genetics and its applications in agronomy. But without the beginnings of the Great Enrichment, the world would not have had the money to apply the natural sciences to technological problems. Like imperialism and trade, high science was more a result of economic growth than a cause. The writer Matt Ridley puts it this way: "When you examine the history of innovation, you find, again and again, that scientific breakthroughs are the effect, not the cause, of [mere] technological change. It is no accident that astronomy blossomed in the wake of the age of exploration [and we would say, the telescope from a Dutch eyeglass maker]. The steam engine owned almost nothing to the science of thermodynamics, but [as we have said] the science of thermodynamics owed almost everything to the steam engine. The discovery of the structure of DNA depended heavily on X-ray crystallography of biological molecules, a technique developed in the wool industry to try to improve textiles."[11]

Mokyr believes that the high science of realizing that air had weight was important early in making possible for people to imagine the very first, and "atmospheric," steam engines (that is, vacuum-driven, sucking the piston in by the outside pressure of the atmosphere as the steam cooled and condensed back into water). True. But if one does the long-term accounting correctly by weighting betterments by their economic importance instead of merely listing a thousand of them and expressing dazzled admiration, science does not show much of an economic impact until after about 1900. Most of our riches until then, and quite a few of them down to the present (mass-produced veneers and polished granite, divided superhighways), are the result of technologists, the anonymous tinkerers and then the engineers, rather than the high scientists.

We have been using the phrase "high science" because we want to discourage you from using another and dangerous word we have mentioned, much on the popular tongue, "scienceandtechnology." It is in effect a German portmanteau, used by biological and especially physical scientists to claim credit for technology, much of which is only remotely connected with their work. High-energy physicists at CERN outside Geneva, who should be embarrassed that high-energy physics has stagnated for some fifty years (and who therefore are led to call most of matter and energy "dark"), use scienceandtechnology to keep the billions flowing. (We do not exempt our own beloved science of economics from such characterization, though the amount spent on it is three orders of magnitude below what is spent on physics and astronomy; if we spent one order of magnitude more on economics, we would have such a superior understanding of the causes of economic growth that we could easily save out of the resulting growth even more money for elementary particles and manned voyages to Mars). The so-called STEM fields of science, technology, engineering, and mathematics are much in vogue nowadays. The Japanese minister of education proposed closing all public university departments *except* STEM fields, on the barbaric assumption that only they were of use. Yet STEM includes the M of the mathematicians chiefly interested in Greek-style proofs in number theory or algebraic topology, which have epsilon applications to technology. That is, almost none. Much of the S in science, likewise, will never economically benefit any human—for example cosmology, as noble as is its purpose of illuminating our place in the universe. Theology and poetry, though, and most of painting and rock music, have on that subject more to say.

Not science.

17

It Wasn't Imperialism

Nor was it successful violence of any stripe that made the West rich. Most obviously, it wasn't warfare. As it turns out, aggressions that encourage the killing of your people and their suppliers and demanders are not really very good for you. War, like plague, might have kept wages high by keeping the amount of labor low relative to the available land, but where war flourished most—the German lands during the Thirty Years' War (1618–1648), for instance, killing a third of their population—prosperity did not. Slavery, colonialism, and imperialism don't explain why Walmart cashiers in the United States make so much more than their counterparts elsewhere in the world.

To be clear, we are not suggesting that the evils of war, slavery, imperialism, and colonialism were justified, or anything other than evil. True, it was only bourgeois places, we have noted, that began to end the evil. Until England in the late eighteenth century, war was the usual hobby of kings, imperialism seemed blameless, and hardly anyone objected to the system of slavery. And, true, "everyone" does it: African empires, like ancient Rome's and Athens's and Israel's, were slave societies, and after their hobby wars the African imperialists sold people to the Europeans or Arabs waiting off the coast. The Sioux native Americans were tyrants of other native Americans. Yet such "what-about" does not excuse evil.

Or in these cases stupidity. We *are* saying, to be precise, that war, slavery, imperialism, and colonialism were on the whole economically stupid. Suppose killing people, taking their stuff, and establishing empire could create an "original accumulation of capital" that would jump-start the "capitalist mode of production" and thereby create a Great Enrichment. If so, as we have argued repeatedly, it would have happened a long time ago and not in northwestern Europe. Imperialism isn't a new idea. The French liberal Jean-Baptiste Say remarked in 1803, before imperialism became fashionable among the clerisy, "Dominion by land or sea will appear equally destitute of attraction, when it comes to be generally understood that all its advantages rest with the rulers, and that the [home] subjects at large derive no benefit whatever."[1] In 1923, in the aftermath of World War I, a later liberal, the Italian economist and future president of Italy Luigi Einaudi wrote, "Before the [First World] war it was a favorite doctrine with nationalists that new, rising nations . . . were called to high destinies, to conquer territories, to become world Powers. . . . The war of new and rising nations against old and stationary . . . was erroneous both historically and economically."[2]

Alas, others disagreed, such as the American Theodore Roosevelt, or the Japanese prime minister Hideki Tojo. "Our nation," declared Tojo, "stands at a crossroads, one road leading to glory and the other to decline."[3] One still hears such guff. In 1997 the geographer Jared Diamond wrote a brilliant book, *Guns, Germs, and Steel: The Fates of Human Societies*, which was meant to answer the question of a New Guinea highlander of his acquaintance: "Why do you have so much cargo?" He was asking about the Japanese and Europeans fighting over New Guinea during the Second World War, who had abundant goods brought in by cargo planes. The first half of Diamond's book is an illuminating exposition of the importance of the east-west orientation of the Eurasian land mass, by contrast with the north-south orientation of Africa and the New World. If chickens were domesticated in China, as they were, it was easy for people farther west, such as eventually the Spaniards at the other end of the land mass, to adopt them. The weather was pretty much the same in China and Spain. By contrast, corn domesticated in Central America never made it south to Peru, and potatoes domesticated in the Peru of the Incas never made it to the Toltec and Mayan civilizations of Central America. Therefore it was the civilizations of the Eurasian land mass that had the widest array of domestications of wheat and horses and the rest, and the best chance of having a Great Enrichment leading to the cargo-laden airplanes of Japanese and American and Australian invaders of New Guinea.

But then Diamond goes off the rails. Big-time. The second half of his book deals with the promise of his silly title, explaining what we already know—that guns and steel in armor and swords, and germs such as measles and smallpox, made the conquest of the New World easy. He loses track of what he was trying to explain and starts supposing against the evidence that conquest is what pushes societies over into real enrichment. It doesn't, as his very case shows: Portugal and Spain, the first overseas imperialists, with colonies from Mexico to Macao, were on the eve of the Great Enrichment the poorest countries in western Europe, and they did not fully embrace the modern economy until the end of the twentieth century.

Empire, in any event, is expensive. As the British Foreign Office kept warning during the scramble for Africa, guns are expensive in housing and education forgone. The British trade in materials and minerals and tea and spices grew, and a few merchants grew rich, but such profits were tiny compared with British national income. Trade with the "periphery" such as Poland was small relative to the trade of western Europeans with one another. And anyway their foreign trade was minuscule relative to their internal trade with themselves (e.g., French people with French people). In 1790, only about 4 percent of European output was exported. The share was smaller in 1590. And countries like Sweden with trivial overseas colonies and Austria with no such colonies got rich, too, and were able to eat bananas for breakfast—because they traded, not because they raided. For European economic growth, the trade with the periphery was, well, peripheral. The terms on which the British exchanged railway locomotives for jute with India would have been about the same had India been independent—unlikely, considering the disorganization of the Mughal Empire—or, more likely it might have become a French colony. In any case, Britain's exports to India were about a fifth of its exports to the United States and Europe. The collections at the British Museum would now be different, doubtless. But a Britain tending liberal anyway would have waxed rich without seizing an empire.

And so for other imperialisms. Leopold II of Belgium slaughtered his way through the Congo, growing rich on rubber suddenly valuable for boots and bicycles. No other Belgian benefited. Germany's dabbling in overseas empire was utterly pointless, and the genocide against the Herero people in Namibia is still vividly remembered a century on. The Spanish and Portuguese people at home were impoverished, not enriched, by their three centuries of empire. Italian imperialism in Libya and the Horn of Africa might be seen as merely comical, if the butcher's bill in Africans and Italians killed were not added to the balance.

18
Nor Slavery

Everybody most everywhere enslaved the Other. Slavery is a common if horrible human institution. If slavery led to Great Enrichment, it would have happened in the slave societies of Greece or Rome. It didn't. It would have happened in Asia, where "slavery was likewise common," Thomas Sowell observes, or China specifically, where "there [are] records of slavery going back to 1800 B.C."[1] It would have happened in Portuguese-speaking Brazil, which received, we have noted, many more African slaves than North America did. Or it would have happened along the Barbary coast of Africa and in the Middle East more generally, where more *Europeans* were sold into slavery between 1500 and 1800 than Africans transported to North America—and where Sowell reports that "14 million African slaves were taken across the Sahara Desert or shipped through the Persian Gulf and other waterways to the nations of North Africa and the Middle East," compared with some 11 million Africans shipped across the Atlantic.[2] The slave markets of Algiers were every bit as competitive and "capitalist" as the slave markets of Charleston and New Orleans.

It is said that there were large profits to be had in the slave *trade*. After all, as Karl Marx put it, "Liverpool waxed fat on the slave-trade." Indeed. But slave trading did not have barriers to entry. It is such barriers that make for supernormal profit. A ship is a ship, mobile of course between uses in Dublin or Dakar. It earns what a ship earns, regardless of what it carries—a normal, and modest, return, if some of the cargoes were abnormal and prideful.

And the earnings of slave traders from Newport, Rhode Island, or Bristol, England, were trivial sources of investment for industrialization.[3] If the profits, such as they were, of the trade are judged crucial, why not the profits from, say, the pottery industry, of similar magnitude, or from retail trade, much larger? What makes shameful profits more efficacious for the Great Enrichment than honorable ones? (The reason seems to be the desire to see "capitalism" anyway as born in sin.)

It is right to note that, for example, higher demand for cotton textiles meant higher demand for raw cotton and, therefore, higher demand for slaves to pick it. Similarly, to take an interesting case studied by two leftish historians, higher demand for twine to bale American wheat straw meant that Mayans and Yaqui Indians in the Yucatan were forced to harvest cactus to make the twine.[4] But it does not follow that the exploitation was caused by the betterments in cotton and twine. The existing structure of power that allowed slavery or other exploitations in the first place is the salient cause, not the use to which the exploited people were put. At length the liberal theory that no one should be a slave to anyone, and the Great Enrichment following, shook the structures of power. That is what the left should be celebrating and thinking of ways to encourage. Instead it stops at blaming "capitalism" for slavery and patriarchy and other tyrannies, which were in fact relieved by liberalism.

The African American poet Langston Hughes we have quoted sang in the same poem about an imagined America, "Let it be that great strong land of love / Where never kings connive nor tyrants scheme / That any man be crushed by one above." That slavery crushed from above and stole unrequited toil cannot be doubted. That's what being a slave means. Yet the system was accepted on all sides until liberalism and Great Enrichment. Being a slave was viewed as a personal misfortune, of course. The Europeans such as Robinson Crusoe seized by Barbary pirates could tell you about it, as could the Frenchmen sentenced to the galleys for importing calico cloth. But no one, from Aristotle to Daniel Defoe, regarded forced labor as an evil system. Labor enforced by the lash was commonplace anyway among nominally free European laborers before the nineteenth century. Wives and apprentices and children and sailors and the unemployed were routinely beaten. After all, how are we going to get our candles lit and our fireplaces tended in the big house, or get the cotton crop in, without slaves? The answer comes now, as Matt Ridley puts it, by "enslaving" coal and oil and electricity. The metaphorical enslavement depended on human ideas for commercially tested betterment—that is, on innovism. Not coercion.

§

Yet the contrary case appeals. Listen to the Poet President, and weep for the decline of political eloquence. In his second inaugural address, carved now into the north wall of the memorial, Abraham Lincoln declared that "if God wills that [the Civil War] continue until all the wealth piled by the bondsman's two hundred and fifty years of unrequited toil shall be sunk, . . . as was said three thousand years ago, so still it must be said 'the judgments of the Lord are true and righteous altogether.'"

It is a noble sentiment, exhibiting how closely Lincoln read the Bible as boy and man. He is quoting Psalms 19:9, not an especially famous verse. But his sentiment about the role of slavery in American wealth after 1619 is unwisely if widely credited as literally true economic history. Beyond the soaring theology, Lincoln's words have been accepted as economics—that American wealth depended on slavery. The website of Teach US History.org reports as fact that "northern finance made the Cotton Kingdom possible, [and] northern factories required that cotton," and so "we can understand [Lincoln's theme of] the War as retribution." Both North and South, it says, were entangled in the sin of slavery. Both are said to have mightily profited from it, and the blood judgments against both are righteous altogether.

The belief has been reanimated recently in books widely admired on the left, constituting a King Cotton school of US history: Walter Johnson's *River of Dark Dreams* (2013), Sven Beckert's *Empire of Cotton: A Global History* (2014), and especially Edward Baptist's *The Half Has Never Been Told: Slavery in the Making of American Capitalism* (2014). The rise of "capitalism" depended, they claim, on the making of cotton cloth in Manchester, England, and Manchester, New Hampshire, and the making depended on raw cotton raised in the South. And the growing of Southern cotton, they claim, depended on slavery. Conclusion, as our good friends on the left have been saying all these years: "Capitalism" was conceived in sin. The King Cotton historians are offering an analysis of original sin alternative to Marx's claim of the original accumulation from piracy, or Friedrich Engels's of the exploitation of the English working class, or Eric Williams's of the profits from the international slave trade, or the still fashionable claim, first made by John Hobson and Vladimir Lenin a century ago, of the profits from imperialism. On the left the game is Spot the Original Sin.

But each step in the King Cotton school's story is mistaken. In place of economic sense, the story substitutes a warm indignation against the peculiar institution. Needless to say, along with other bourgeois liberals, we join the school in its indignation. But its economics is plain silly. The enrichment of the modern world did not depend on cotton textiles. The cotton mills of the United States and of Europe, true, pioneered certain industrial techniques, but so did other sectors, such as, among fabrics themselves, wool, linen, silk, and jute. And an economy is not a fabric mill. Widespread ingenuity—Yankee clock making and British iron making and French porcelain making—was the ticket to modernity.

And making cotton cloth did not depend on Southern supplies of cotton. During the cotton famine of the Civil War, supplies from Egypt started to replace the South's. Had the war continued until all the wealth said to be piled up by the bondsman's labor was sunk, Egypt and India and Jamaica could have supplied the cotton with ease. Only in the short run is an existing region of supply "necessary." The King Cotton historians depend on the supply-chain fallacy, that if a supply chain is ever interrupted, the game is up—there are no possible substitutes. All links are claimed to be necessary. Such non-economic economics inspired, for example, the strategic bombing in World War II and then in Vietnam. It was ethically repulsive, and it didn't work on German industry any better than on the Ho Chi Minh Trail. Such quasi logic doesn't forge a chain of necessity from slave-grown cotton to modern industry because there are substitutes everywhere.

Furthermore, growing cotton did not depend on slavery. The historical facts are conclusive on the point. Before the Civil War, both whites and the few free blacks grew cotton. By 1870 whites and former slaves, despite a massive withdrawal of freed women from field work, grew as much cotton as the South had before the bombing of Fort Sumter. To be sure, sugar, historically speaking, *was* a slave crop wherever it was grown, in Syria, Cyprus, the Canaries, and the New World. But cotton never was chiefly a slave crop, in India, for instance, or in southwest China, where it was grown in bulk from ancient times.

Baptist and the other King Cottoners are mostly innocent of economics and economic history. That would not be blameworthy if slavery were not an economic institution, as it was, and if a large historical literature had not grown up in the mid- to late twentieth century, as it did, setting the economic record straight. Among others, Robert Fogel and Stanley Engerman wrote *Time on the Cross* in 1974 and follow-up books and articles aplenty. From the King Cotton texts and bibliographies, one would hardly know it. The King Cottoners think, for example, that owning a slave constituted "cheap labor." But as Fogel and Engerman, Richard Sutch, and all the economists and some historians such as Kenneth Stampp noted, the productivity was capitalized into the market price of a slave. If you owned a slave, you faced the opportunity cost of the alternative use of the labor, net of maintenance costs. No supernormal profits accrued to people who bought slaves, so to speak, secondhand, or raised them expensively from babies. What profits that didn't dissipate accrued to the firsthanders, chiefly within Africa.[5]

The King Cotton school has been devastated in detail by two economic historians, Alan Olmstead and Paul Rhode. Their revelations are startling.[6] They point out that the share of slaves in US wealth is grossly exaggerated by the inequality maven Thomas Piketty, whose pseudoestimates are used by Baptist to put slavery into the center of the country's economic history. And Olmstead and Rhode, in line with their own research on the cotton economy of the South, note that the locus of improvement driving up the price of slaves was not more extreme abuse of slaves but an astonishing rise in the productivity of the cotton plant, achieved by selective breeding. Slavery was extraordinarily evil, we now all agree. But slavery was not extraordinarily profitable.

Abolition, and the end of routine beating, came from people like the Quaker abolitionist John Newton, a former slave-trading captain and author of the hymn "Amazing Grace"; and William Wilberforce, son and grandson of prosperous merchants of Hull; and Julia Ward Howe, author of "The Battle Hymn of the Republic" and the daughter of a stockbroker. See the pattern? "Capitalists" and their offspring ended slavery.

Yet again we say: ingenuity, not exploitation, is the story of the modern world. It would be a good idea to stop using, for present-day politics against "capitalism," a faux history of slavery, whether by a hard left in many distinguished departments of history nowadays or a generously soft left and middle piously persuaded by the harder folk. Slavery was bad enough without ornamenting it with bad history and bad economics.

19

Nor Wage Slavery Ended by Unions and Regulation

You may say, "Surely it was the labor movement that ended or at least sharply curtailed the capitalists' ruthless exploitation of the industrial proletariat."

No, not at all. And more generally, the distributive struggles don't do the explanatory job. They are zero-sum explanations for the largest positive-sum change in economic history. And the *negative*-sum possibilities from the labor struggle are well illustrated by British labor relations during the 1970s.

Real wages and working conditions for workers rose because labor became much more productive, on account of commercially tested betterments in field and factory, not because laborers extracted concessions from the bosses. Labor histories and their splendid songs are filled with accounts of literal violence between miners and scabs or, from the other side, the copper bosses framing and executing Joe Hill. Yet the economics is clear. The bosses have resisted unionization, often fruitlessly. Walmart resisted it and incurred the enmity of the left, but competitive labor markets in retail meant they had to adjust the wages and working conditions they offered because they were competing with other unionized retailers. If they didn't, the workers would walk. On the other side, a union's "fight" and "struggle" for a larger share of the economic pie, if successful, damages nonunion labor, which has been in the United States a larger group. If unions meant higher wages and better working conditions for coal miners, then necessarily, unless magic intervenes, it meant higher prices for coal users. Unions in steel and autos and government and trucking do the same. McCloskey's uncle Joe, a union electrician in Michigan, gladly paid union wages because, as he said, he could pass the expense on to his customers. But who pays the higher building costs? You.

And in any case, the gain to unionized workers has been small. The economist H. Gregg Lewis in careful studies over many decades found that the *most* successful unions raised wages perhaps 15 percent.[1] That's not 3,000 percent. And a multi-industrial union like the Teamsters (McCloskey belonged happily to a professors' union, part of the Teamsters' assemblage) has much smaller effects on wages, a few percentage points, regularly offset by worsened conditions of employment. Truck drivers get a tiny boost in pay but drive more hours at a stretch.

It was the point that Adam Smith made long ago about the sum of wages plus the money value of conditions. For the same level of skill in the worker, the sum has to be roughly the same in all parts of the economy. Otherwise the workers in a disfavored part move away to the favored part, until the samensss is reestablished. They walk. Thus African Americans moved north in the Great Migration. Thus you yourself leave a well-paying job with too-long hours. A taxi driver earns less than a coal miner because the conditions in coal mining are worse—more dirty and exhausting and dangerous—conditions for which the coal miner gets compensated in cash. It's not because it's just but because it is a natural equilibrium if people are free to move. Wages and conditions, like water, find their own level, not mysteriously but by the most ordinary behavior of people. In an argument typical of economic thinking, Smith noted that people will crowd into the good wage-and-conditions occupation, driving down wages there, until the equality of wages-plus-conditions is reestablished. Economists use the financial word to describe the point: *arbitrage*. It's why professors, whose technology has not changed since Socrates, nonetheless earn about the same as airline pilots, whose technology compared with ancient Greek ship pilots is thousands of times more productive of travel. A prospective professor who didn't like the pay and conditions could go to flight school instead of grad school. Enough slide from occupation to occupation to keep the water roughly at its own level.

Smith's theorem implies that the Democratic Party's pressure to improve working conditions, or the Republican Party's resistance, is lacking in point. The sum of wages and the money value of working conditions is determined by the supply of and demand for labor, in the same way that rent of lettuce-growing land close to or far from the city is determined by the crop yield net of the cost of transporting the lettuce to the city. And so it is for any "factor" of production, as economists call them: labor in mining and cab driving, or land in farming and suburban housing, or physical capital in factories and houses and machines. Their total compensation, economists have realized since the 1870s—and have shown factually in thousands of studies—depends on the output of the last unit of labor, land, or capital applied, known as the "marginal product." Not bargaining strength.

The contrary theory, inspiring politics left and right, is that the bosses have a pile of gold in the back room that can be extracted endlessly by struggles on the picket line or in Congress, which will make workers better off on net, both in pay and in conditions. If true, it would be wonderful. Pass a law, and make workers vastly better off. Carden and McCloskey would be delighted.

But extraction from fairy gold is not how workers have become better off by 3,000 percent. Skillful bargaining might raise the wage of workers in a tire factory in Ohio by 5 or even 10 percent above what it would have been. One and done. But marginal productivity governs the 1,000 to 3,000 to 10,000 percent to be explained. Clearly, there isn't enough profit in the economy—10 to 15 percent of national income—to even double wages by way of expropriating the gold of the expropriators, much less to increase wages by a factor of thirty. And in any case the gold-in-the-back-room theory assumes against all likelihood that the expropriated bosses will stand there and continue to invest in the factory, though they get less profit in return. The shareholders forced to accept a trim today will not wait to get another next year. Fool me once, shame on you. Fool me twice, shame on me.

Consider coal mining, in the old country tune sung by Johnny Cash, Willie Nelson, and others, "Where it's dark as a dungeon and damp as the dew, / Where the dangers are double and the pleasures are few." In isolated coal mining towns the miners were said to owe their souls to the company store. It's said to be a classic example of the Peabody Coal Company using market power, both as demander of labor and as supplier of housing and groceries. The company could skimp on wages *and* working conditions. So it is said. But it's mistaken. The wages of miners in Appalachia in fact compared favorably to what could be earned in hardscrabble agriculture there. That's why men went down the mine. Prices were higher at company stores than at independent stores, but the company store offered better credit, better selection, and better delivery. Consistent with Smith's theorem, there was a trade-off between wages and working conditions, with more dangerous jobs in more dangerous mines paying more.[2]

§

As to the left's claim that *any* employment, slave or "free," simply *is* exploitation, the other Marx—the comedian Groucho Marx— had something to say. At the height of his success in movies in the 1930s, an old Communist friend of his came by and said, "Groucho, I desperately need a job. You have contacts." Groucho, whose sense of humor was often cruel, replied, "Harry, I can't. You're my dear Communist friend. I don't want to 'exploit' you." And sent him away.

The leftish usage and its politics echo down to the present, as in *The Concise Oxford Dictionary*. It defines *wage slave* coolly as "a person who is wholly dependent on income from employment," with the notation "informal"—but not "jocular" or, better, "economically illiterate." Thus Judy Pearsall, the editor of the 1999 edition of the *Concise Oxford*, who lived, it may be, in a nice semidetached in London NW6 and drove an old Peugeot, was a "slave." You yourself are probably a slave. Carden and McCloskey certainly are. All paid workers are slaves—though all are paid in proportion to the traded value of the goods and services they help produce for others, and none of them owes unpaid, coerced service to anyone. The alternative job may be wretched, but the "wage slave" does have the alternative, as a real slave does not. No boss in a labor market in a free country can use coercion to keep a worker from walking. So it is in any free economy—with the large exception, as Robert Higgs and Carden and McCloskey and many other liberals observe, of slavery to the government, through taxation or draft. That *is* a literal slavery. Try not paying your taxes. Try evading a military draft. Yet slavery by the government is admired by most of the left and by much of the right, in terms that echo defensive Southern rhetoric in favor of slavery in 1860: "The slaves need our guidance, and we make them work by coercion. For the good of the slaves, you understand."

The labor songs are glorious. "They say in Harlan Country / There are no neutrals there. / You either are a union man / Or a scab for J. H. Blair." McCloskey claims to know more such songs than any of her socialist or labor-union friends. She taught them to her colleagues on the picket line of the Union of Faculty at the University of Illinois at Chicago. But the history and the economics of the songs, with their claim that struggle is what enriched the workers, are mistaken. We do really wish that laws and strikes could raise the real wage to the startling degree that commercially tested betterment has. But they haven't.

Part Three

IT CAME BECAUSE IDEAS, ETHICS, RHETORIC, AND IDEOLOGY CHANGED

20

The Talk and the Deals Changed in Northwestern Europe

Enough already of nots.

What did it? Why, of all sad places, did the Great Enrichment start in the dysfunctional backwater of northwestern Europe rather than in the cultivated Italian peninsula, or the treasure-rich Iberian peninsula, or the innovative caliphates of the Islamic Middle East, or the commercial empires of South and East Asia or Africa or the Americas?

Answer: A combination of happy accidents, we have said, beginning in 1517 led ordinary people and their rulers in northwestern Europe to revalue the bourgeoisie and embrace dissent with modification. The bourgeoisie itself did not become greedier, or thriftier, or more hardworking, or more law-abiding. The "bourgeois virtue" in the title of McCloskey's 2006 treatise does claim, as we have said, that the bourgeoisie is not especially evil. But it did *not* say—as, for example, the great German sociologist Max Weber did say in 1905 about the same history—that a psychological or ethical change came over the bourgeoisie that made for enrichment. No.

What happened, rather, was the coming, as in the title of McCloskey's 2010 volume on the matter, of a "bourgeois dignity." In the eyes of the rest of the society, businesspeople acquired a new dignity. And in the eighteenth century the dignity began a long career, in the new liberalism, of application to *all* commoners, the "third estate" beyond aristocrats and priests—everyone from manservant to manufacturer. The outcome was, as the title of McCloskey's 2016 volume puts it, "bourgeois equality" for all. An enrichment of all, in matter and in soul, rapidly came, and will come—as we have said many times now, and given evidence of, and as is argued in McCloskey's political book of 2019, *Why Liberalism Works*.

Little "efflorescences," as the historical sociologist Jack Goldstone has called them, had long come from little flashes of pro-bourgeois ideology, in the northern Italian cities of Venice, Florence, and Genoa, for example, or seventeenth-century Osaka, Japan, or Carthage two centuries before Christ, or ancient "Tyre, the city of battlements, whose merchants were princes, and her traders the most honored men on earth" (Isaiah 23:8).[1] But they burned out quickly. The four Rs—reading, reformation, revolt, and revolution—assured that after 1700 or so, a pro-bourgeois ideology more than flashed in northwestern Europe, and especially in formerly pro-aristocratic England.

Innovism, we have noted, led to great enrichment of the commoners. Competition in the third act erodes profits. The social gain from creativity ends up in the hands of customers, to the tune of 98 percent. The 98 percent, and the 2 percent left in the third act to the innovators, are rough estimates by the economist William Nordhaus (winner of a Nobel Prize in 2018).[2] To be sure, 2 percent of the value of changes to how people make and buy and sell is quite a lot, as you can see in the $143.1 billion net worth of Amazon's Jeff Bezos and the combined net worth of almost $175 billion of Sam Walton's heirs. But even if one supposes that Nordhaus's estimate of the share left to the innovators as against the rest of us is off by a factor of ten, and the customers only get 80 percent of the value Bezos created by revolutionizing online shopping and that Walton created by revolutionizing brick-and-mortar shopping, 80 percent of the betterment is still an enormous sum coming to ordinary people out of commercially tested betterment. Furthermore, Bezos and Walton got their fortunes by dealing rather than stealing, in contrast to the fortunes accumulated by anointed kings or modern tyrants. The Castros in Cuba and Vladimir Putin in Russia and the families of Hugo Chavez and Nicolas Maduro in Venezuela became very,

very rich, but by stealing, not dealing, by taking from others, not by making them better off.

Bezos and Walton are not sinless. We as economists object to Amazon having a patent monopoly on the very idea of one-click shopping. And we object when Walmart gets a sweetheart deal from local politicians eager to attract sales-tax revenue for the uses of the politicians. That is, we liberal economists don't like overlong patents ("intellectual property" is regarded by us as mostly an antisocial confidence game run by patent lawyers). And we don't like most political as against commercial allocations of rights. But we invite all you people without sin to cast the first stone, and then to open a "discount city" cheapo store in Rogers, Arkansas, in 1962, or an online bookstore in 1994 in Bellevue, Washington.

Most criticism of Walmart and Amazon comes because they are commercially successful—a criticism fed also by an irrational and specifically American objection to well-earned bigness per se. The animus does not come because they are politically successful. We doubt therefore that the criticism would change much if Amazon did *not* have a patent on one-click shopping or if Walmart did *not* sometimes get special treatment in local taxes. (Walmart actually, and somewhat imprudently, didn't develop a Washington presence until the government threatened the free international trade on which its business success has been built. The corruption originated from Washington, DC, not from Bentonville, Arkansas.)

§

The Bourgeois Deal has competed during the past couple of centuries with four other Deals for organizing society. The other four substitute coercion for cooperation, the government for the market, the visible hand for the invisible hand, top-down for bottom-up: the Blue-Blood Deal, the Bolshevik Deal, the Bismarckian Deal, and the Bureaucratic Deal. Although often popular at the outset, the four have regularly consigned humans to poverty and slaughter (Blue-Blood and Bolshevik) or to weights around the ankles of innovators and illusory promises of security (Bureaucratic and Bismarckian).

The Blue-Blood Deal, or what McCloskey calls in her 2016 book the Aristocratic Deal, honors the blood of noble birth. It says, "In the first act and in the second, pay your land rents promptly, and curtsey or bow low as I ride by. And go to war to die in battle for my glory and my gain. By the third act, I at least will not have slaughtered you." True, after a noble property is established, the use of it will be efficient if the property is exchangeable. So much does economics affirm, contrary to the labor-input justification of property in John Locke's writings. But in deep origin the Blue-Blood Deal is of course a protection racket. When in 1969 the great economist John Hicks wrote on the basis of slender reading *A Theory of Economic History*, arguing that the aristocrats were "protecting" their serfs, the great economic historian Alexander Gerschenkron observed that "the possibility that the main, if not the only, danger against which the peasant very frequently was in need of protection was the very lord is not mentioned."[3] The Blue-Blood Deal claims to reject mere commercial betterment tested by vulgar profit and loss—though very willing to seize the profit. It embraces betterment only in machines of war tested in noble bloodshed. The nobility was protected for centuries from swords and arrows by steel plate armor and was at last creatively destroyed by the crossbow and longbow and at length the matchlock.

The Bolshevik Deal, like the Blue-Blood Deal, makes the bourgeoisie an offer it can't refuse. The surface motto, stemming from Karl Marx, is "from each according to his ability, to each according to his need." Sounds nice: note again the imitation of a family's ethic, to be applied, as Lenin once said, to a great national factory. As George Orwell's masterful pigs said in *Animal Farm*, all animals are equal, but some animals are more equal than others: "Do your assigned task, turn over the fruits of your labor for distribution by the Communist Party, and above all do not criticize the party. We will make all economic decisions for you. Do not ask for equality with high-level party functionaries. Obey in the first act and also in the second, and by the third act we will at least not have liquidated you."

An anti-Bolshevik alternative to the Bourgeois Deal is the Bismarckian Deal, which was inaugurated in 1881 under the Iron Chancellor, Otto von Bismarck, and triumphant after 1889, the first year of old-age pensions in the German Empire. Ludwig von Mises put Bismarck "among the nineteenth century statesmen the foremost foe of liberty."[4] The Bismarckian Deal was a buyoff, bribing the poor to behave themselves. Bismarck's explicit plan was to steal the thunder of his enemies—that is, of the soon-to-be-literally Bolshevik Dealers, and of the left generally, and of the liberals, too. The Bismarckian Deal is the modern welfare state. In Britain it dates from 1911, with compulsory unemployment insurance. In the United States it dates from 1933 and the New Deal. The Bismarckian Deal says, "In acts one and two you should come to view the present government as your noble and benevolent lord, forsaking family and the institutions of civil society that so imperfectly and inefficiently provide for old-age care and emergency medical care. By the third act we will at least have protected you from the Bolsheviks and the bourgeoisie."

The Bismarckian Deal has worked splendidly as propaganda, if not so well in practice. Private contributions to British universities, for example, largely dried up after the government took over the universities after World War I.[5] On the eve of the British National (Unemployment) Insurance Act of 1911, of the 12 million then to be covered by the act, fully 9 million already had voluntary arrangements, especially through "friendly societies."[6] The same was true in the United States, where voluntary provision of health insurance was robust.[7] (Note the parallels in today's debate in the US about health insurance.) Bismarck's welfare state crowded out private saving for old age, higher education, health care, and other private projects of free adults.[8] The Bismarckian Deal asks (or more exactly compels) people to forsake the animation of a free adult life and become children of the government—and reliable voters for the Bismarckians. In the US it has yielded a powerful voting block of elderly pensioners promising reprisals to any politician who dares touch Medicare or Social Security. (McCloskey gives earnest thanks to younger people for paying her health care—two hip replacements, fixing a burst ulcer, removal of her gallbladder. She gets Social Security, too. Thanks again, and remember that she votes.)

The fourth alternative to our liberal Bourgeois Deal is the Bureaucratic Deal, which sits alongside elements of each of the others. It embraces the private property of the Bourgeois Deal and rejects the mass murder of the Bolshevik Deal. So far, so good. It is the Deal offered by the administrative state—betterment by permission, in contrast to the permissionless betterment of the Bourgeois Deal.[9] In a brilliant book on the US history of administering of the airwaves, from wireless Guglielmo Marconi to wireless Steve Jobs, the economist Thomas W. Hazlett labels the Federal Communications Commission's administrative rule, "Mother, may I innovate?"[10] It rules over the benighted commoners and bourgeoisie through an aristocracy of experts—who, as Hazlett demonstrates in detail, do not actually know what they are doing when denying or accepting the request of Mother-may-I. The outcome was decades-long stagnation in technology, as for example in FM radio. McCloskey recently met a young entrepreneur in an industry dependent on computer technology who told her that the way he escaped the Bureaucratic Deal was to stay ahead of the bureaucrats in computer technology, explaining, "If they don't understand what you're doing, you can do it." For the massive benefit of customers in retail stores.

The Bureaucratic Deal, which is notoriously loquacious in its rulemaking, says, "Fine, sell tacos out of a truck. But before you do that, make sure you have the right answers to all our Mother-may-I questions. Do you have the right permissions from the taxing authorities? Do you have the appropriate licenses for your truck? Will you be within five hundred feet of a brick-and-mortar restaurant? Do you and the people who will do the cooking for you have all the right cards, green and others, granting them our gracious permission to be gainfully employed? Does the local Taco Vendor Licensing Board—staffed, of course, by representatives from expert and already-existing taco vendors—agree that our city needs another place to buy tacos? Are your methods acceptably environmentally friendly, as judged by us experts? Are you thinking of serving soft drinks in 24-ounce cups? Or giving your customers plastic straws? Or cooking with trans fats? Or handing people larger orders in plastic bags? All of this, of course, is for the protection of the consumers and workers you are shamelessly trying to poison or exploit."

The three-act drama of the Bureaucratic Deal, reprised in tens of thousands of pages of regulations it adds each year, continues so: "Honor me, an expert by possession of a master's degree, and give me the power to tax and regulate you in the first act, and also in the second, and all subsequent acts. I forbid you under penalty of the laws (which we experts write) from seeking a better deal, such as moving your factory to Mexico, shifting your money to the Cayman Islands, operating your business without a governmental license (which I give out), or working for less than a decreed minimum (which I determine). If you follow my orders and keep paying your taxes, then by the third and subsequent acts I will at least not have jailed you." We told you this Deal was loquacious.

§

The Bourgeois Deal replies to the Blue-Bloods and Bolsheviks and Bismarckians and Bureaucrats: "Mind your own business." Or as Ayn Rand's character John Galt says in *Atlas Shrugged* when asked for a plan to get the economy going, "Get the hell out of my way!" The Bourgeois Deal says that the taco truck entrepreneur is accountable to the bankers who finance her venture, the employees and suppliers who help her do it, and the customers who vote with dollars for or against her tacos, earned as the fruits of their own labors for still other people. The bureaucratic regulation that claims to protect consumers (but regularly protects traditional interests from competition, as in Germany does prohibition of Uber in favor of traditional taxis) is in fact much worse at consumer protection than is an aroused public opinion in a free society. A restaurant that in 1997 was ground zero for a shigella outbreak in Tuscaloosa, Alabama, did not last long. Carden still associates the name of another restaurant—which he has never patronized—with an E. coli outbreak that originated there when he was in the sixth grade. On mentioning the example to an audience of high schoolers, Carden was brought up to date about still another restaurant that had a similar outbreak—and where the Cardens are now unlikely to dine. A notification from the Nextdoor app tells a neighbor's story about a company not to use because it did shoddy work. An episode of *South Park* lampoons the importance of Yelp reviewers. They are examples of the market working in a society with free speech—imperfectly, but working, and regularly better than the inspectors of the Bureaucratic Deal can deliver.

The common honesty of a society of merchants in fact goes beyond what would be strictly self-interested in a society of rats, as one can see in that much-maligned model of the mercantile society, the small midwestern city. A reputation for fair dealing is necessary for a roofer whose trade is limited to a city of fifty thousand. A professor at the University of Iowa refused to tell at a cocktail party the name of a roofer in Iowa City who had at first done a bad job for her (he redid the job free, at his own instigation) because the roofer would be finished in town if his name got out in such a connection. The professor's behavior itself shows that ethical habits can harden into ethical convictions, the way a child grows from fear of punishment toward consulting an impartial spectator within the breast. An unethical person would have told the name of the roofer to spice up the story. After all, the professor's own reputation in business was not at stake.

No society embodies one or another Deal to the exclusion of all the others. McCloskey's Sweet Home Chicago and Carden's Sweet Home Alabama mix Bourgeois-Dealing innovism and Bolshevik(-ish)-Dealing of socialized control of the means of educational production under the auspices of a Bureaucratic-Dealing license raj, a Bismarckian-Dealing welfare state, and Blue-Blood-Dealing political machines. Life is imperfect. But since 1800, it has managed to get enough of the Bourgeois Deal to produce a Great Enrichment.

21

That Is, Ethics and Rhetoric Changed

We are left, after eliminating the other candidates on offer, with the one explanation, the only one that fits the timeline and fits the geography and fits the human lives involved. In short, people changed their ideas about what is lovely in economic life.

To put it economically, they reduced what Don Boudreaux calls the "dishonor tax" on merchants.[1] The world went from love of battle and courts and cathedrals, and contempt for the bourgeoisie and the market, to airing Milton Friedman's liberal documentary *Free to Choose* on PBS and recommending that students major only in STEM—science, technology, engineering, or mathematics—or business. (We don't: to major in English or history also serves a full life, beyond that first job, about which parents worry; and anyway, most of M and S belong, we have noted, in the humanities, elevating the human soul, not the T and E, feeding the human body.)

People gradually stopped attributing this man's riches or that woman's poverty to fate or politics or witchcraft—at any rate, enough to stop the throttling of what the Nobel-worthy economist William Baumol in 2002 called *The Free Market Innovation Machine* and what the Nobel-winning economist Edmund Phelps (2013) called "the imaginarium"; namely, the Bourgeois Deal and its result in betterment.[2] Against the interests of the purveyors of traditional ideas and traditional paths, the northwestern Europeans of Joel Mokyr's "Industrial Enlightenment" declared for innovism, which resulted in Stephen Davies's "wealth explosion."[3]

Elite talk about betterment, profit, and commercial tests changed from around 1300 to 1600 in parts of northern Italy, the southern Low Countries, and the Hanseatic towns. It changed more decisively down to about 1648 in Holland, and then after 1689 in England, and then after 1707 in Scotland, and before 1776 in Britain's North American colonies, and still more broadly down to 1848 all over northwestern Europe and its neighbors and offshoots. In England the change occurred during a concentrated, and startling, period from 1690 to 1720. The rhetorical and ideological change in western Europe was such that the article on government in the French *Encyclopedia* of 1751–1766 declared that "the good of the people must be the great purpose of government."[4] It was a sharp alteration from the honor-seeking or frankly extractive justifications of earlier governments, in which the glory of the king ruled and the great purpose was far from the good of the mere people. King "Harry" of England in act 3, scene 1 of Shakespeare's 1599 play *Henry V* urged on his troops before Harfleur in 1415 with "Cry 'God for Harry, England, and Saint George!'" Not "Cry God for the economic good of the people in GDP per head!"

Talk, the habits of the lip, mattered, and does still. In England between 1690 and 1720, and still more so down to 1848, ideas and talk about trade, statistics, betterment, and bourgeois life changed. The four so-called pagan virtues of courage, justice, temperance, and prudence and the three so-called Christian virtues of faith, hope, and love, as McCloskey argued at length in *The Bourgeois Virtues*, apply with suitable modification to a bourgeois as much as to an aristocratic or religious society. They appeared in a rhetoric of *prudent* calculation of costs and benefits, and a *hopeful* attitude toward industrial novelties tested by commerce, and a *just*, nonenvious, acceptance of ethically acquired profits. Honor always matters to humans (that "faith"), but what was honorable changed.

Outside northwestern Europe the Revaluation happened much later. Right down to the Meiji Restoration of 1868, after which the rhetoric in Japan changed startlingly quickly, elite opinion scorned the merchant. (And yet a samurai conception of honor came back a half century later in Japanese militarism.) In Japanese Confucianism the ranking from top to bottom had been the emperor (recovering his position in 1868), the shogun (1603–1868), the daimyos, the samurai, the peasants, the craftsmen, *the merchants*, the night-soil men, and last of all Koreans. A merchant in East Asia was not a "gentleman," to use the European word, and had no honor. He might have periods of comparative liberty, as in the lightening of legal restrictions during the Song dynasty of China (860–1279). But he did not have the dignity of the landlord and the general and the imperial official. So too England in 1689. But not for much longer.

Ethics, not laws, are fundamental. We agree again with Alexis de Tocqueville: "I accord institutions [he meant laws] only a secondary influence on the destiny of men. . . . Political societies are not what the laws make them, but what sentiments, beliefs, ideas, habits of the heart [in his famous phrase from *Democracy in America*], and the spirit of the men who form them prepare them in advance to be. . . . The sentiments, the ideas, the mores [French *les mœurs*], alone can lead to public prosperity and liberty."[5] The practical politician Lincoln put it this way, in the first of the Lincoln-Douglas debates of 1858: "With public sentiment, nothing can fail; without it nothing can succeed. Consequently he who molds public sentiment goes deeper than he who enacts statutes or pronounces decisions. He makes statutes and decisions possible or impossible to be executed."[6]

Think about the person sitting next to you on the bus or plane. The codes of conduct to which she adheres are not simply matters of prudence, what she can get away with. She doesn't cheat her customers, and not merely because she would be punished for it. She doesn't fake her scientific results, and not merely because doing so would damage her reputation. She does go rescue children from a burning building, and not merely because she'll get her face on TV.

She does what she does, and doesn't do what she doesn't do, because as an adult and a professional woman, she has formed by upbringing and self-criticism and the influences of her culture an ethical identity, a faith, what Adam Smith called the "impartial spectator within the breast." Institutions absent such an ethic, however clever their laws, don't work: "Political societies are not what the laws make them." The neo-institutionalists Daron Acemoglu and

James Robinson report on an attempt in India to curb absentee-ism among hospital nurses by introducing the institution of time clocks. The economists in charge of the attempt were sure that the bare incentives of law, the "right institution," would work. It didn't. The nurses conspired with their bosses in the hospitals to share their salaries, and they continued not showing up for work. Acemoglu and Robinson draw a moral that "the institutional structure that creates market failures" is what went wrong. But the continuing absenteeism was not about institutions or incentives or laws. A new institution with the right incentives had been confidently applied by the econo-mists out of the tool kit of orthodoxy of the World Bank, and had failed. Acemoglu and Robinson do not see that what failed was the prudence-only theory of the economics profession: add institutions and stir. "The root cause of the problem," they assert, was "extractive institutions."[7] No, it wasn't. The failure was rather about the lack of an ethics of self-respecting professionalism among the nurses, of a sort that, say, Filipino nurses do have, which is why they are in demand worldwide.

Contrary to what is commonly believed, ethical convictions can and do change quickly. Consider the women's movement and the resulting change in labor force participation during the 1960s.[8] Con-sider the changing attitudes about the propriety of gay marriage, denied by the leading presidential candidates as late as 2008. To make such a denial in the 2020 election would be fatal to any cam-paign, even by most Republicans: You go, Mayor Pete. During the Progressive Era around 1900, much of labor law and regulation on mining and other industries simply codified what firms and workers were already doing.[9] It certainly codified a new public sentiment, à la Lincoln. Most home recyclers don't do so because of externally imposed constraints. There are no police standing in their kitchens. They recycle because they believe it is what good people do.

§

There's a bit of useful technical philosophy about all this. Facts are supposed to be incontestable. An incontestable *objective* fact about reality is supposed to be "two hydrogen atoms and one oxygen atom make water" (but what about heavy water?), and an incontestable *subjective* fact is supposed to be "my favorite color is green" (but what about cultural variation in what is called green?). These so-called facts are said to be not up for debate, or not much.

In a 1994 book, McCloskey coined the word "conjective" to describe, however, the numerous facts that are accepted socially but are neither objective nor subjective in the philosophically naive sense that people usually employ.[10] The conjective describes the extremely large area between what is objectively true and what is subjectively true. It is, for example, where the scientific action is, on the frontiers. $F = ma$ might be seen as objective (but what about at the speed of light?). The present (lack of) understanding of dark matter and dark energy is not.

Social consensus is at the heart of the conjective, in science as much as in courts of law or in family gatherings at Thanksgiving. A person, a thing, or an entity does its linguistic job by virtue of a social agreement. The philosopher John Searle has called it by the somewhat odd phrase a "status function": "X is treated as Y in context C."[11] A piece of paper is called a $20 bill when it is issued by the Federal Reserve Bank. Language creates the meanings of X, Y, and C, and these are up for negotiation. Conjective.

For instance, people have through trial and error created a game called soccer. Consider: when a specific part of the soccer ball "crosses" a specific line in the context of a soccer game, it is called a "goal." Similarly, an attacker is "offside" if she is between the last defender and the goalie just as the ball is kicked to her. These are facts, but facts by social consensus as to what the context "soccer" entails. If enough people are unhappy with the rules promulgated by the Fédération Internationale de Football, they can form their own association with their own rules and change the conversation about what "soccer" is.

Sports rules and their evolution are particularly obvious examples of conjective facts, changed by way of dissent with modification. Dissenters from the way basketball was played in the National Basketball Association started the American Basketball Association and introduced the three-point shot, which was ultimately adopted by the NBA itself after the two leagues merged. Farther back, rugby emerged at Rugby School in England when someone decided that soccer might be more interesting if you could pick up the ball and run with it, as was in fact the rule in the lethal intervillage games of the Middle Ages from which all the kicking-and-running ball games descend. Other dissenters modified the medieval or Rugby rules and created Gaelic, Canadian, Australian, and American versions of football. Is an offensive player allowed to run toward the line of scrimmage before the ball is snapped? The answer is yes if the context is "Canadian football" and no if the context is American football. Objective? No, conjective, by consensus.

And that is the world in which we find ourselves, a world in which consensus and conversation are massively determinative of what we do, and can change, as they did about the economy in England after 1689. The brain scientist Raymond Tallis described it this way:

> We belong to a boundless, infinitely elaborated community of minds that has been forged out of a trillion cognitive handshakes over hundreds of thousands of years. This community is the theater of our daily existence. It separates life in the jungle from life in the office, and because it is a community of minds, it cannot be inspected by looking at the activity of the solitary brain.[12]

22

"Honest" Shows
the Change

The perpetual conversations happening within the community of minds, each resulting in a new cognitive handshake, are where the conjective is formed and re-formed. And so it did to make the modern world.

If you merely ask people whether they have revalued the bourgeoisie or not, they'll probably deny it. Buying low and selling high? Yuck. Better aristocratic bloodshed on the battlefield or bureaucratic rule-writing in the halls of the Food and Drug Administration. Yet you can hear what they won't explicitly say if you hear how their words changed over time. For major examples among many of the changes in the conjective, consider how the words *honest, true, innovation,* and *novelty* exhibit the revaluation of the bourgeoisie in English from 1600 to 1800.

§

The word *honest* shifted from aristocratic to bourgeois honor. The sorts of deals people could countenance changed. The shift in the word provides powerful evidence of a change in social ethics, a change in a decidedly bourgeois direction. To call a man "dishonest" in an aristocratic context required a duel with swords the next morning. To call a man "dishonest" in a bourgeois context requires a suit for libel, or more likely an exit from dealing with him.

Honest in its older uses did not chiefly mean "telling the truth" or "paying one's debts" or even "upright in dealing," as it does today. It meant "noble, aristocratic," or sometimes "dignified" in a society in which only the aristocracy were truly dignified. What real aristocrat, after all, would bother with merely propositional truth or merely procedural uprightness when one had to look after style, gesture, heroism, dignity, loyalty to persons, and social position? For Harry, England, and Saint George.

Honest comes by way of Norman French from Latin *honos,* yielding *honestus,* which in classical Latin never meant "telling the truth" or "keeping one's word." That was *sincerus.* The *honestiores* (against the *humiliores*) of the Roman Republic mattered because they were rich and noble and honorable, not because they were in the habit of telling the truth. In 1430, an English lady—the word *lady* then indicated high social standing, not "any adult female," as it does now in democratic usage—asked for a loan to pay for "honest bedding, without which mine husband's honesty and mine may not be saved."[1] *Honest* here meant "dignified and suitable to rank," and the honesty was a matter of social standing.

A couple of centuries later, no change. Charles I declared from the scaffold in 1649 that he was "an honest man and a good king, and a good Christian." He did not mean that he kept to his business bargains or told the truth, which notoriously he did not. He meant that he was noble, aristocratic, and worthy of honor "by virtue," as one says, of his birth and position, an anointed king. The modern use of *honest* as "truth-telling and keeping one's word" does appear in English as early as 1500, but the meaning "honorable by virtue of high social standing" dominates its usage until the eighteenth century.

Shakespeare, for example, uses "honest" in four distinct ways, yet never in its modern, bourgeois, "truth-telling" sense.[2] The closest Shakespeare gets is "genuine," as in the 'umble servant Davy's appeal in act 5, scene 1 of *Henry IV, Part 2* for an occasional indulgence toward knaves: "If I cannot once or twice in a quarter [three months] bear out [be allowed to favor] a knave against an honest [high-status] man, I have but a very little credit with your worship. The knave is mine honest [genuine] friend, sir; therefore, I beseech your worship, let him be countenanced." The other three Shakespearean definitions emphasize only knightly honor, as in *Othello, The Moor of Venice*. "Honest Iago," a phrase common in the play, is being described as a high-ranking soldier by profession who was "honest" in that he was "honorable, noble, warlike, aristocratic." His motiveless malignity toward Othello leads him to violate what we call truth. Yet he is "honest," a bit of dramatic irony playing on all the meanings of the word.

Consider too the old phrase "an honest woman." *Othello*'s Desdemona is so styled, repeatedly, an ironic commentary on her husband's suspicions of unfaithfulness, encouraged by honest Iago. It preserves in jocular talk nowadays the original meaning of the word "honest," with adjustments for a woman's place in a male-dominated culture of honor. Anne Boleyn, Elizabeth I's mother, refused Henry VIII's advances unless he married her, asserting that "I would rather lose my life than my honesty," yet in the end losing both.

In act 4, scene 3 of Shakespeare's lesser known play *Cymbeline*, Pisanio, the loyal servant, says to himself that he must dissemble to remain true to a wider truth: "Wherein I am false, I am honest [honorable and genuine]; not true, to be true" [not truth-telling, yet faithful]. Note the play on *true*, which these days means chiefly "in accord with the facts, propositionally accurate." But it had originally meant "loyal to a person," a meaning that President Trump favors. The *Oxford English Dictionary on Historical Principles*, which we are using here and elsewhere, gives the first and oldest meaning of *true* as "steadfast to a commander or friend, . . . to one's promises." The meaning is labeled "somewhat archaic." In older English, for example, one might "pledge [one's] troth," cognate with *truth* and *truce*. All of Shakespeare's plays turn on genuineness and its lack, as in Hamlet's agonizing or Portia's appeal (in the guise of a male lawyer) for mercy—a double deception since women's parts at the time were played by boys. In none of his plays is bourgeois "honesty" honored.

A century and a half later, the honest man in Adam Smith, by contrast, was not the aristocrat, noble by blood. Smith's honest man was the promise keeper and truth teller constrained by the man within: "There is no commonly honest man who does not more dread the inward disgrace."[3] No one else will know your perfidy—but you will, and you will disapprove, unless your impartial spectator within is poorly developed (consider again Donald Trump). In Shakespeare "commonly honest" would have been a silly contradiction. Commoners cannot be "honest." They are good for comedy in prose, not for noble speech in blank verse, five beats to the poetic line: "I better brook the loss of brittle life / than these proud titles thou hast won of me."

By the eighteenth century the word had changed, signaling a wide social change. *Honest* appears four times in Henry Fielding's novel *Tom Jones* (1749). Every time, Fielding means "upright, sincere" applied to commoners. Samuel Johnson's 1755 *Dictionary of the English Language* gives three senses of the word *honest*: "Upright, true, sincere"; "Chaste"; and "Just, righteous, giving every man his due." Every man. None of his definitions is "aristocratic." In Henry Mackenzie's 1771 *The Man of Feeling*, it appears thirteen times—twice meaning "genuine," twice meaning "not cheating," and nine times meaning "upright."

In the very early nineteenth century, Jane Austen used *honest* thirty-one times, a third of the time to mean "upright," as in "an honest man," but never as in "a person of high rank." A third of the time she used it to mean "genuine," as in "a real, honest, old-fashioned boarding school," and a third of the time to mean "truth-telling" and "sincere." By the 1934 edition of the *Webster's New International Dictionary*, the word *honesty* in the sense of bestowing *honor* was labeled obsolete.

And it wasn't only in English. What is extraordinary, suggesting a deeper social tide, is that an identical change happened in other European languages of commerce at the same embourgeoisfying time.[4] English got its word *honest* from French, we noted, compliments of the Norman Conquest. In both French and Italian after the seventeenth century, the descendants of the Latin word *honos* turned bourgeois, just as they did in English.

What is still more extraordinary is that an identical evolution happened to an entirely different root in Germanic languages, meaning also "aristocratic." In Dutch, for example, the word *eer* (pronounced "air," like the first syllable of the word in German, *Ehre*) means "honor." In former times it meant, as in Shakespeare's English, "aristocratic," but it came as *eerlijk* to mean commercial honesty.

§

Innovation in the use of the word *innovation* tells the same story. The *Oxford English Dictionary* attributes the first use of *innovation* in its commercial sense, "introducing a new product into the market," to Joseph Schumpeter in 1939.[5] The date, we reckon, is a little too late (a tendency in the *OED* arising from its method before texts were digitized), but anyway in "innovation" Schumpeter included, as economists do, all sorts of betterments—in making products, financing them, trading them, inventing them, using them, and so forth. A good thing. By contrast, in earlier times the word was almost always used censoriously. The English translation in 1561 of John Calvin's *Institutes of the Christian Religion* declares, "It is the duty of private men to obey, and not to make innovations of states after their own will." Innovations violated the Great Chain of Being, in which everyone had a master to whom he pledged his troth. Note the illiberal rule that everyone has a master, broken in liberalism. Edward VI issued in 1548 an act "To stay innovations or new rites." In 1597 the Anglican theologian Richard Hooker wrote about "suspicious innovations." The High Church Archbishop Laud's proceedings in 1641 were said to be notorious "in bringing innovations into the Church." As late as 1796 Edmund Burke was annoyed about a "revolt of innovation," which results in "the very elements of society" [being] "confounded and dissipated." No Great Chain of Being, a conservative beloved.

But Samuel Johnson, just a few decades earlier, we have noted, had written that "the age is running mad after innovation," of which he with a certain ironic distance approved. In 1817, Jeremy Bentham would praise "a proposition so daring, so innovational." By 1862 Henry Buckle, the optimistic English materialist, sneered at people for whom "every betterment is a dangerous innovation"—but even then he was playing off the conservative use of the word to attack change. Only in the past century or so has the word graduated to full-throated praise for bourgeois betterment.

§

Novelty, too, long had a negative connotation. Wycliffe's Bible circa 1385 discussed "cursed novelties of voices," from the Latin *profanes vocum novitates* in the Vulgate form he translated—in the original Greek, more accurately, "profane babbling"—that is, heresies that were already evident to Saint Paul. *Novelty* nearly always connotes something verging on silly and trivial: think about its use now to describe what you can get from ice cream trucks and "novelty" stores. It began to acquire favorable connotations, though, in the twentieth century, when, for example, critics of painting and literature began to complain of the absence of novelty.[6]

§

Ideas changed, and the words show the change. In medieval and mercantilist times, patents had to declare that the new idea would increase employment. But in 1742 the goldsmith John Tuite said boldly that his innovation in Thomas Newcomen's engine would *save* labor—that is, put people out of work, which was forbidden in an earlier politics (and now revised in the irrational fear of massive technological unemployment). Two years later, Jean Desaguliers (British, but of French origin) was the first person to emphasize in print that steam engines did indeed save labor.[7] Previously the British government would have obstructed damned innovations and novelties, such as Elizabeth I forbidding the use of the knitting machine. At length, betterment tested by commerce, and bourgeois speech work in support of it, came to be regarded as, of all crazy things, honest, true, innovative, novel, and saving of human labor.

And that, not "creating jobs" or "protecting" one group against another, is what innovism born of liberalism gave to England, and then the world.

23

And "Happiness" Itself Changed

Europeans in the eighteenth century changed how they thought about happiness. On a long view, understand, it's only recently that people have been guiltlessly obsessed with either pleasure or happiness. In secular traditions such as those of the Greeks or Chinese, a pleasuring version of happiness is downplayed, at any rate in high theory, in favor of political or philosophical wisdom. A Chinese sage said of some goldfish in a pond, "See how happy they are!" A smart-aleck disciple asked, "Master, how do you know they are happy?" To which the sage replied, "How do you know I don't know?" Ah. In Christianity for most of its history, the treasure, not pleasure, was to be stored up in heaven, not down here where thieves break in. After all, as a pre-eighteenth-century theologian would put it—or as a modern and mathematical economist would, too—an infinite afterlife was infinitely to be preferred to any finite pleasures attainable in earthly life.

The unhappiness doctrine made it seem pointless to attempt to abolish poverty or slavery or wife beating. A coin given to the beggar gave the giver a leg up to heaven, a *mitzvah*, a *hasanaat*. But the ancient praise for charity in Christianity or Islam or Buddhism or whatever implied no plan to adopt welfare programs or to grant rights of personal liberty or to contemplate the national product. A life of sitting by the West Gate with a bowl to beg was, after all, an infinitesimally small share of one's life to come. Get used to it. For now, and for the rest of your life down here, such is your place chosen by God in the Great Chain of Being. Take up your cross. Quit whining. What does it matter how miserable you are in this life if you'll get that pie in the sky when you die?

Such fatalism in many faiths—God willing, *deo volente, mertsishem, insh'Allah*—precluded idle talk of earthly happiness. Said Job in his travail, "If I have put my trust in gold, or said to pure gold, 'You are my security,' . . . then these also would be sins to be judged, for I would have been unfaithful to God on high" (Job 31:24). "I am the Lord thy God; thou shalt have no other gods before me." The judgments of the Lord are true and righteous altogether.

Then in the eighteenth century our earthly happiness became high fashion. By 1776, "life, liberty, and the pursuit of happiness" was what we all chiefly wanted. Jefferson's formula was by then wholly unoriginal. John Locke in 1677 wrote that "the business of men [is] to be happy in this world by the enjoyment of the things of nature subservient to life, health, ease, and pleasure," though he added piously, "and by the comfortable [that is, comforting] hopes of another life when this is ended."[1] By 1738, Mirabeau the Elder wrote to a friend recommending "what should be our only goal: happiness."[2] Only.

To see how strange such a remark is, consider whether it could have been uttered by a leader of opinion in 1538. Martin Luther? Michelangelo? Charles V? No. They sought heavenly, artistic, or political glory—not something so domestic as happiness. Yet in the late seventeenth century, Anglican priests commenced preaching that God wanted us to be happy as much as holy. They called it "eudaimonism," from the Greek for "happiness," which meant literally "good-guiding-spirit-ism." Think of Clarence the apprentice angel in *It's a Wonderful Life*. Anglicans and, astonishingly, some New England Congregationalists, turned against the old, harsh, Augustinian-Calvinist line. We are not, declared the eudaimonists, mere sinners in the hands of an angry God, worms unworthy of grace. No, we are God's adopted children and heirs (Romans 8:14–17).

Earthly happiness, heaven *here*, took on a new importance. The fourth epistle of Alexander Pope's long poem *An Essay on Man* (published in 1733–1734) opens: "Oh happiness! Our being's end and aim! / Good, pleasure, ease, content! Whate'er thy name: / That something still which prompts th' eternal sigh, / For which we bear to live, or dare to die." Pope was no liberal, but he did emphasize an invisible hand leading to temporal happiness: "Self-love thus push'd to social, to divine, / Gives thee to make thy neighbor's blessing thine." He closes stirringly: "That reason, passion, answer one great aim; / That true self-love and social are the same; / That virtue only makes our bliss below, / And all our knowledge is ourselves to know."[3] It's a poetic foreshadowing of Adam Smith, though uncomfortably close to the amoralism of Bernard Mandeville, which Smith detested.

Earlier generations had touched the transcendent by setting their minds on the things above and anticipating bliss in the hereafter. The eighteenth-century novelty, then, is the talk about happiness here below. As one of its more charming conservative enemies of modernity, William Butler Yeats, put it, "Locke sank into a swoon; / The Garden died; / God took the spinning-jenny / Out of his side."[4]

The eudaemonic turn, we affirm, was a very good thing, resulting in fresh projects to better our stay here on earth, some of the projects remarkably successful. Democracy, for example, was one, because if you followed the fashion for universal happiness, it became impossible to go on and on insisting that what really mattered was the pleasure of the duke or the lord bishop. Enlightened despots of the era such as Catherine the Great claimed to seek the good of all. Frederick, also the Great, claimed to be merely "the first servant of the state." Ha, ha. Such altruistic propaganda paradoxically gave hoi polloi the idea that maybe they themselves could take care of it, thanks, sans tyrant. Alexis de Tocqueville wrote in 1835 that "all the English colonies [in North America] at the time of their birth. . . . seemed destined to present the development of . . . the bourgeois and democratic liberty of which the history of the world did not yet offer a complete model."[5] "Bourgeois and democratic"—that is, liberalism.

§

In the turbulent seventeenth century, especially in England, the theory of happiness started its transformation. In her history of

Quakerism, Rosemary Moore notes that during the English Civil War, "Ideas could flourish unchecked, and the parliamentary armies provided a means for their discussion and dissemination."[6] Radicals began to ask, as the "Digger" Gerrard Winstanley (1609–1676) did, "Why may not we have our heaven *here* . . . and heaven hereafter, too?"[7]

The intellectual historian David Wootton, who has written much on the Levellers, shows that in England between 1658 and 1832 the high theory about what motivated people was transformed. Historically speaking, Wootton explains, "Pleasure and profit were often coupled together." But never, he claims, until 1658—bizarrely in the publication of William Percey's *The Compleat Swimmer*—"were they claimed to be the *only* motivations, to the exclusion of all others, such as honor, virtue, and piety. [It was] a new account of what it is to be a human being."[8] The English political philosopher Thomas Hobbes at the time expressed it in extensively theorized form, and in Wootton's reckoning the new account of pleasure and profit as motivators climaxed a century and a half later in the theory of "utility" proposed by the Jeremy Bentham (1748–1832). Bentham's was a crude version of pleasure and profit, without honor. Wootton would (as we would, too) label him "Bentham the Bad." Bentham declared, among numerous other strange remarks, that the only way he could distinguish poetry from prose was by noting that poetry did not fill the line to the right margin, or, with more consequence, that the idea of justice in legal theory was "nonsense on stilts."

Bentham's heirs among modern economists leap with gusto into such voluntary madness. Carden and McCloskey are both of the Econ tribe, yet we agree with Wootton that the maximizing of utility under constraints, as the so-called Samuelsonian economists put it, does not yield a complete plan of life. "The presumption that we are all, as it were, in business as individuals," Wootton writes, supposes "that the ties which bind us to family, friends, community, nation are purely instrumental arrangements of convenience."[9] So Hobbes had argued. The late Nobel laureate of Chicago, Gary Becker, for example, wrote in 1973 a pioneering paper on the economics of marriage. He insisted on calling male and female humans M and F, who meet in the forest and agree to exchange skill in cooking for skill in auto repair. In the few places in the paper where Becker mentions love, he puts it in disparaging scare quotes, 'love.' It reminds us of an old joke. A beautiful woman offers a lawyer to have sex with him. He responds suspiciously, utilitarian-style, "Yeah, but what's in it for me?"

Yet Wootton claims that such utilitarian reasoning is the heart of the liberalism we so adore here. Liberalism "cuts through traditional assumptions about status, rank, and honor. . . . Those who were most prominent in attacking the old moral codes were also, almost without exception, egalitarians," he asserts.[10] True enough. He correctly observes that Hobbes's suggestion that "people . . . are all fundamentally alike" may be said to mark the beginning of the Enlightenment.[11] But the merger of such an "Enlightenment paradigm" with liberalism inspires Wootton's criticism of what has been labeled (in a historical claim we regard as a fairy tale) the rise of "possessive individualism." In a word, there arose an allegedly new *selfishness*.

Wootton, that is, reduces liberalism, the watch spring of the modern world, to a vulgar utilitarianism of Bentham's sort. Wootton stops the story of liberalism's development with Bentham the Bad, the better to slam the modern economists he detests, the bourgeoisie he detests even more, and the liberalism that he detests most of all. Wootton joins the left and the right in the conventional antibourgeois clamor among the clerisy, as in a letter by Gustave Flaubert to George Sand in 1867: "Axiom: hatred of the bourgeois is the beginning of virtue."

Ah, yes, the familiar hatred of the bourgeoisie. Bentham 1.0 is surely a bad thing as a life plan, though useful for designing highway off-ramps and deciding which car to buy and other projects of cost and benefit. But stopping at Bentham and then rushing on to the most vulgar of the economists is an error. A liberalism under attack even in 1848 from theorists like Karl Marx and Thomas Carlyle bore its social and economic fruit a long time afterward. Wootton attacks the notion that it could have anything good to do with the modern world, though it was bourgeois Europe that created and benefited from a liberalism that led to all our joy, of ordinary people allowed for the first time to have a go—Wootton's grandfathers and his mother, for example.

Wootton's axiom is that Bentham is really all there is to liberalism. Yet he himself quotes Mill after his conversion from Benthamism to liberalism 2.0. If Wootton had made Mill the stopping point for his narrative instead of Bentham, it would have been much harder to reduce liberalism to a desiccated 1.0 calculus of pleasure and pain. Mill is the very essence of mature 2.0. As Mill wrote in a memorial essay, Bentham "was a boy to the last," a suitable ancestor to boyish economists. "No one who . . . ever attempted to give a rule to all human conduct, set out with a more limited conception either of the agencies by which human conduct is, or of those by which it should be, influenced."[12] Which is Wootton's theme precisely.

In fact, liberalism 2.0 characterized the very first generation of liberals, such as the blessed Adam Smith, whose understanding of humans was richer than the much younger Bentham, and whose liberalism Wootton treats most unkindly; or the second generation, Mill in England and, surprisingly, Henry David Thoreau in New England. Yet the Benthamite version of liberalism remains the conventional target of Catholic conservatives such as Patrick Deneen of Notre Dame or left Democrats such as Michael Sandel of Harvard. Deneen, Sandel, and Wootton make their attack on liberalism easy by reducing liberalism to Bentham 1.0 and the portions of Machiavelli, Hobbes, and Smith that seem to fit selfishness.

In reality, people act often enough for reasons irreducible to a business plan of utility. The liberal ideology that Wootton attacks—both crude and sophisticated—can still inspire good politics. But like its doppelganger the modern novel, it's not our full and contradictory selves. Yes, we have modern theories of selfishness. No, we do not follow them. Yes, Bentham was silly. No, liberalism is not.

24

The Change in Valuation Showed in English Plays, Poems, and Novels

The Revaluation would have made great reality TV—*Keeping Up with the Bourgeoisie*. As it was, the drama was performed at first especially in Holland, and only after 1700 or so in England. The portrayal of financial markets on the English stage, for example, spread its technical language to the common tongue.[1] The *Spectator* (1711–1712, merely) of Richard Steele and Joseph Addison was the voice of the bourgeoisie introduced to polite society. It spawned numerous imitators, for instance in Holland and Spain. Addison in particular was, as Basil Willey noted, "the first lay preacher to reach the ear of the middle-classes."[2] In his 1713 play *Cato: A Tragedy*, an inspiration long afterward to the American revolutionaries, the project was to tame the "barbarous" (that is, aristocratic) pursuit of war and loot by preaching sociable virtues. In the 1720s, John Trenchard and Thomas Gordon would use "Cato" as a pseudonym in their advocacy of Locke-inspired freedom of speech and of religion. The cat of liberalism was creeping out of the bag.

The Revaluation in the decades around 1700 shows vividly in the contrast between two plays, each in its era very popular, one from the time of Shakespeare and the other, recording the Revaluation, from the time of Addison, Steele, Trenchard, and Gordon. Thomas Dekker's *The Shoemaker's Holiday* (1599) looks on its face "bourgeois" but in fact celebrates the conventional, antibourgeois hierarchy. One hundred and thirty years later, George Lillo's *The London Merchant* (1731) gives the bourgeoisie its voice—and even honor.

The Shoemaker's Holiday tells of Simon Eyre, a mere shoemaker (based on a historical figure of that name, a draper-mayor in 1445), who ascends to the lordly rank of Lord Mayor of London. Ah, a story of bourgeois enterprise, Horatio Alger–like? No, nothing of the sort, not at all. (For that matter, neither are the Horatio Alger stories.)

From start to finish, Eyre declares that he is a "professor of the *gentle* craft" of shoemaking. It's a joke, because "gentle" meant "upper class," and a shoemaker is not. He says repeatedly, "Prince am I none, yet am nobly born," a joke line taken from a contemporary novel about this Eyre. His name, *Eyre*, is the English version of the Dutch *eer* (Dekker was of Dutch extraction) and the German *Ehre*, meant in this context as aristocratically "noble." Eyre rises through the ranks of alderman, sheriff, and finally Lord Mayor by accident, not by enterprise, and certainly not by right of gentle birth. Dekker has him speak always in prose, not the blank verse that was reserved in the drama of the time for gentle characters. Again, ha, ha. Dekker's audience would laugh out loud at a prose-bound hero born with the name "noble" who in fact made shoes for a living.

"The honor of the Gentle Craft"? "Gentlemen Shoemakers"? "Courageous Cordwainers?" Dekker is sneering at the bourgeoisie, not honoring it. The play's romantic lead, the aristocratic Rowland Lacy, seeks the hand of the somewhat lower-born Rose, daughter of Sir Roger Oatley, the previous Lord Mayor. Rowland disguises himself as Hans, a Dutch shoemaker: "It is no shame for Rowland Lacy, then, / To clothe his cunning with the Gentle Craft, / That, thus disguised, I may unknown possess, / The only happy presence of my Rose."[3] Working among the shoemakers, though, he speaks in prose. When it's revealed at the comic close of the play that "Hans" is actually the very noble and gentle nephew of an earl, it's back to aristocratic blank verse and to his real identity, and the marriage.

All the characters speak as befitted the Great Chain of Being. Through military service, Eyre's journeyman, Ralph Damport, "gentles his condition" (as said Shakespeare's *Henry V* to the commoners at the siege of Harfleur) and speaks briefly in blank verse. But when he returns from the wars a comical cripple—we are not in a liberal age of respect for people with disabilities—it's back to lower-class prose. Eyre and his wife in speaking to journeyman shoemakers use the familiar "thou" (compare French *tu*) but use the formal "you" (*vous*) when speaking to their betters. In every way *The Shoemaker's Holiday* enforces traditional hierarchy. No bourgeois liberalism of equals dealing in markets here. The stage direction "Giving money" is second only to "Enter." Well. Does it make the play bourgeois and disruptive through money in the sense that Adam Smith or Karl Marx or Joseph Schumpeter would understand, or now as a phalanx of Silicon Valley "disrupters" and "influencers" would? No. The payments are almost entirely from a superior to an inferior. They are hierarchy-expressing tips, not the dealing between equals in a market. "Giving money" is not ordinary business, much less the financing of creative destruction. It speaks of a zero-sum world in which one person's loss is another's gain, and therefore it is nobly greathearted to give to one's inferiors.

Eyre gets his lofty position not because of bourgeois enterprise but because of sheer good luck, by happening upon a wrecked Dutch ship and, at the goading of his wife, selling its cargo. As the literary historian Laura Stevenson notes, "by attributing all the innovation to Mistress Eyre, [the story] can celebrate Eyre's later achievements as a wise, just, and charitable rich man without having to portray him at first as an entrepreneur who has sullied himself by conjuring up a questionably honest business deal."[4] Likewise the 110 Horatio Alger stories from 1867 onward are commonly said to represent the essence of innovism. They don't. The attractive boys are helped to their good luck by attentive older men, every time. Innovism has nothing to do with it. So too in *The Shoemaker's Holiday*. Like *The Merchant of Venice*, it dishonors trade, profit, interest, enterprise.

§

In 1731, by contrast, George Lillo's *The London Merchant* inaugurated the "bourgeois tragedy"—a phrase like "gentle craft" absurd by earlier dramatic standards.[5] Tragedies were about gentlemen and gentlewomen (the more gentle, the better), not tradespeople. Right at the outset of *The London Merchant*, the older Thorowgood (names indicating character were conventional stagecraft, like Charles Dickens's Mr. Gradgrind running a school) declares proudly to his apprentice, one Trueman, "Honest merchants, as such, may sometimes contribute to the safety of their country, as they do at all times to its happiness." Note the new definitions of *honest* and *happiness* implied. He speaks of "the dignity of our profession," which would have evoked laughter in Shakespeare's England, and concludes with a defensive flourish in the class language of the time: "As the name of merchant never degrades the gentleman, so by no means does it ever exclude him; only take heed not to purchase the character of complaisant at the expense of your sincerity." *Sincerus* here, modern "honesty."

The play erases the distinction between the noble and the middling. All the characters speak in prose rather than in verse. *The London Merchant* is embarrassingly amateurish when placed alongside a work by Christopher Marlowe or William Shakespeare. But it was extremely successful. In the first three-quarters of the eighteenth century, it was a frequently produced play in England, performed annually for the benefit of the young bourgeois of London, invariably at Christmas, down to 1818 and often also on the Lord Mayor's Day in November.

Thorowgood praises his apprentice Trueman as thoroughly bourgeois: "I have examined your accounts. They are not only just, as I have always found them, but regularly kept and fairly entered. I commend your diligence." The bad apprentice George Barnwell, tempted by a prostitute to evil (though a feminist reading of the play can see her as a symbol of female autonomy), is disastrously deficient, though he had once been promising in bourgeois virtues. He defrauds and then kills his uncle in a shocking affront to the sensibilities of Lillo's day. Of Barnwell, the goody-goody Trueman says that "never was life more regular than his: understanding uncommon at his years; and open, generous manliness of temper; his manners easy, unaffected, and engaging." He remarks sadly on his wayward colleague that "few men recover reputation lost—a merchant, never."

A supplement to a later edition of the play tells of a physician treating a patient suffering from a guilty conscience. The patient had mismanaged some of his father's funds to pay for "an improper acquaintance with a kept mistress of a captain of an Indiaman, then abroad." Upon seeing *The London Merchant*, he had experienced a crisis. But at the doctor's suggestion he was reconciled with his father, and the doctor told the actor who played the miscreant Barnwell, "You have done some good in your profession, more, perhaps, than many a clergyman who preached last Sunday." A preface to an early edition praises the preacherly tale of Barnwell's descent: "No lesson can be more necessary to inculcate among that valuable body of youths who are trained to mercantile business, so essential in a commercial country . . . than this warning how impossible it will be to avoid the snares of ruin, if they suffer themselves to be drawn into the paths of the harlot, . . . and plunge them headlong into vice, infamy, and ruin."

§

The Revaluation shows, at least around the edges, in Miguel de Cervantes's 1605 novel about pseudoaristocratic Don Quixote. The noble, if insane, Don just *does* things, impervious to reason or the complaints of his proto-bourgeois companion Sancho Panza. As the historian Joyce Appleby puts it, "Don Quixote . . . epitomizes the qualities that spelled economic failure for the Spanish. Perhaps his mistaking a windmill for a mighty opponent was Cervantes' way of saying that Spanish gentlemen, mired in the past, couldn't even cognize this benign source of energy for productive work."[6] It was not until very late in the eighteenth century that you find any such praise for bourgeois life as *The London Merchant* employed in Spain's gigantically popular and voluminous drama.

A century after *Don Quixote* and a century before Spain introduces a few liberal characters into its drama, and a liberal constitution for the nation, by contrast, the early island scenes of Daniel Defoe's *Robinson Crusoe* (1719) are filled with bourgeois calculation. Crusoe's problem of choice under scarcity on the island stands against stories of shipwrecks in the *Odyssey* and the *Aeneid* and the Bible, in which

God or gods stand ready to perform miracles of abundance. Crusoe has to make painful choices as to what to take from the disintegrating wreck of his ship. It's the economist's choice under scarcity. In the novel the mundanities of scarcity became art. W. A. Speck writes that it "can be read as a paean of praise to business activity."[7]

And so to dear Jane Austen (1775–1817), in a thoroughly bourgeois Britain. Marriage was the literal business of young women of the gentry, a truth universally acknowledged. The absurdly undignified and unbalanced prudence of many of the minor characters in such a business is contrasted in Austen with the dignified and self-conscious ethical development by the major one—at any rate, when they abandon their folly. The minor Reverend Collins in Austen's 1813 novel *Pride and Prejudice* proposes to the heroine Elizabeth Bennet with idiotic prudence:

> My reasons for marrying are, first, that I think it a right thing for every clergyman in easy circumstances (like myself) to set the example of matrimony in his parish. Secondly, that I am very persuaded it will add very greatly to my happiness; and thirdly— which perhaps I ought to have mentioned earlier, that it is the particular advice of the very noble lady whom I have the honor of calling patroness.[8]

Austen's major characters never speak this way, not after they've grown up. Like Adam Smith before her, Jane Austen is, above all, an *ethical* writer, focusing on the coming to maturity of a free person. Not much happens in the novels except ethical growth. Though she was lower gentry, the daughter of an Anglican priest, and not herself a member of the urban bourgeoisie, she was amiable (a favorite word) toward such folk. One brother became a banker in London. She exhibited none of the antibourgeois snobbery that lasted into recent times among the better sort in Britain, and is characteristic of the modern clerisy.

Beyond her novels, Austen was bourgeois in the sensible concern she had for money. In a letter to her niece Fanny Knight, an heiress, Austen explained that *Mansfield Park* had sold out its first edition, noting that "I am very greedy and want to make the most of it; but you are much above caring about money. I shall not plague you with any particulars."[9] In November 1812 she wrote to a friend that she had sold *Pride and Prejudice* to a publisher for £110, noting that she would have preferred £150 but "we could not both be pleased."[10] The literary critic Marilyn Butler explains that Austen, who was thrilled to have made as much as £400 in total from her novels (twenty times the average annual income of a working family and only a bit below what the Austen household lived on annually), and felt in her last six years (1811–1817) that she was an Author—because she was making money at it.[11] Jane Austen, of all surprising examples, embodied the Bourgeois Revaluation.

Ideology often leads the economy, we say. In India the best Bollywood films changed their heroes from the 1950s to the 1980s from bureaucrats to businesspeople, and their villains from factory owners to policemen, in parallel with a shift in the ratio of praise for market-tested betterment in the editorial pages of the *Times of India*.[12] The people of India are now enriching by doing the same as the English did two centuries before, improving in the most significant ways the poor and the middle class.

For which we say, hip, hip, hooray!

Part Four

THE CAUSES OF THE CAUSES
WERE NOT RACIAL OR ANCIENT

25

Happy Accidents Led to the Revaluation

No one expected the Bourgeois Revaluation and its liberalism, and their enriching fruit. Even if someone had, a sane person in 1492 betting on where there would be a Great Enrichment would have bet the farm on China or the Middle East, regions which then far surpassed Europe in trade, science, technology, property rights, and political stability. Yet betterment in the end flourished in the dysfunctional northwest of Europe.

The Great Enrichment didn't occur because of anything historically deep about Europeans, such as (to mention some of the loonier, if ever popular, hypotheses) melanin-challenged skin, or ancient Germanic liberties, or the highly selective democracy of ancient Athens (populated chiefly by the unfree: slaves, women, and metics), or a Christianity which for some reason waited nearly two thousand years to pay off in mundane equality.

Liberalism and its innovism, and then the Great Enrichment, occurred instead because of a cluster of happy accidents between 1517 and 1789, embodied in the four Rs we mentioned in chapter 20—reading, reformation, revolt, and revolution. They led to the fifth R, a revaluation of commerce and betterment, plain in literature and political thought, we have shown, of England and Scotland, culminating in the Bourgeois Deal. The Deal was slowly expanded to all classes and was partially protected from the other B-Deals by liberalism and the success of the innovism among commoners that it inspired. You know our argument.

Consider reading. The shared language of Latin unified the European elite in high culture, though Europe, as we have observed, was politically fragmented. Once the printing press was reinvented in Germany out of China, the unity-within-fragmentation made it hard to suppress ideas from circulating. After a fierce "battle of ancients and moderns," European elites came to believe in the possibility and desirability of progress.[1] Some other scholars claim that European elites embraced the notion that progress was an obligation entailed by God's gift of reason.[2] It was definitely *not*, however, a fruit of the Renaissance, which was an elite accomplishment hostile to commerce and to equality of permission and favorable to conservation of the high culture of the ancients; nor was it a fruit of the elite portions of the Enlightenment.

What was crucial in the reading of books, though, was reading by ordinary people, inspired by their library cards, so to speak—the Benjamin Franklins inspired by, say, Daniel Defoe's *An Essay Upon Projects* (1697) to leap into extraordinary lives. The presses slowly enabled reading to extend far beyond a Latin-fluent elite. Books came off the presses in all the languages of Europe—this in contrast to effective censorship farther east, in the Ottoman Empire and in China and Japan.

The political elites tried to make censorship work, which then as now was the best way to stop destabilizing innovations, as nowadays in the censorship of the internet in China, Iran, and the Russian Federation. In sixteenth-century Spain, for example, the crown restricted travel and banned many books.[3] In 1675, England's King Charles II issued *A Proclamation for the Suppression of Coffee Houses*, the coffeehouses being a fashionable craze (then as now) where men gathered to hear the news and to study the price currents. Sweden prohibited coffee imports five times between 1756 and 1817.[4] When at length newspapers emerged, the elite turned to capturing them. In 1792, in a supposedly free England, the government secretly owned half the newspapers.[5]

But political competition checked the censors, besides creating safe havens for political refugees such as John Locke, or for that matter Thomas Hobbes. In merely three years after 1517, the printing presses of Germany could spread fully 300,000 copies of Martin Luther's radical works across Europe. In a week in August 1520, Luther could publish 4,000 copies of *To the Christian Nobility of the German Nation*, what he called a "broadside to [the emperor] Charles and the nobility of Germany against the tyranny and baseness of the Roman curia." The next week the press issued 4,000 more of a longer version of his anti-Roman blast.[6] The pope could no more suppress the works of Luther than George Lucas could suppress bootleg copies of the 1978 *Star Wars Holiday Special*.

So it went, across the European edge of Eurasia, with rulers playing a game of whack-a-mole they couldn't win. The allies of the deposed Stuarts of England, such as again Hobbes, could find refuge in France. The allies of the deposed Bourbons of France could find refuge in England. The Dutch printers soon overtook the Venetians as the big publishers of pornography and sermons and political pamphlets, issuing in the 1690s radical Locke's work in English and radical Pierre Bayle's in French. Voltaire's *Philosophical Letters* were publicly burned in 1733, after which many of the philosophes felt the hand of state and church. But no matter: their works circulated, and they undermined the ancien régime. Montesquieu's *Spirit of the Laws* was published anonymously in his old age in 1748 in Switzerland and smuggled into France. After 1832 King Louis Philippe enacted laws against cartoons making fun of his pear-like visage and the corruptions of his régime. The French instead purchased their cartoons abroad, continuing to make merry of the so-called Bourgeois Monarch, and at length toppled his throne.

§

Or consider among the Rs the Reformation. An explosion of such reading material made it possible—that, and Luther's eloquent pen and his political luck. The Bible was translated into ordinary European languages accessible to people who couldn't read Latin, at first a daring act, as when Luther did it in German. In 1401, a translation had gotten the Englishman John Wycliffe denounced as a heretic, posthumously, and in 1536, it got another Englishman, William

Tyndale, executed. By then, however, sixteen thousand copies of Tyndale's translation of the New Testament, or one for every two thousand English people, were circulating. Tyndale's last words were, "Lord! Open the King of England's eyes!"[7] The Lord did: two years later the newly Protestant Henry VIII ordered a translation based on Tyndale's be placed in every parish church. By 1611, the English could read a version of the Bible, ordered and authorized by King James I, or have it read to them in the lessons of the Anglian mass. It justified Tyndale's angry boast to an orthodox opponent, "If God spare my life ere many years [to finish the translation], I will cause a boy that driveth the plough shall know more of the scripture than thou dost."[8]

The priesthood of all believers, and behind it the individualism of the Abrahamic religions generally, mattered to the beginnings of the shocking notion that a plowman has in right as much to say on public affairs as a prince. Yet Luther, appalled by the Peasants' Revolt in southern Germany of 1624–1625, was nothing like a radical in politics and wished the plowmen would stick to their plows, declaring, "A worldly kingdom cannot stand unless there is in it an inequality of persons, some being free, some imprisoned, some lords, some subjects."[9] Not liberal.

On the contrary, what made men and women bold in politics and the economy was not Luther's Magisterial Reformation (from *magister*, master) in Germany and Scandinavia, and also among Anglicans, but the so-called Radical Reformation, ranging from some Calvinists to all Anabaptists and Quakers, and then even Anglicans in the form of Methodism, and finally a liberal Protestantism and even a liberal Catholicism supporting ordinary people having a go. In the first wave of the Radical Reformation in the Netherlands, ordinary people—combmakers, bakers, cobblers, and others without inherited *eerlijheid*, "honesty"—questioned whether the communion host was the body of Christ, and suggested in heretical jest that if the Virgin was holy, then the donkey on which she rode was a holy ass, and compared that same Queen of Heaven to the local madwoman.

The rhetoric of the priesthood of all believers congealed around the notions of progress and dignity of ordinary people, not pie in the sky. The French liberal Turgot lectured on progress in 1750 from a *theological* chair. Robert Nisbet called it "the first . . . secular . . . statement of the 'modern' idea of progress."[10] It took a long time for the "obvious and simple system of natural liberty" of Adam Smith to become the default logic of even the elite. But it did take hold, enough to be revolutionary.

The inspiriting cause of economic change was not, contrary to what Max Weber argued in 1905, anxiety over predestined election. What made people bold in practicing frenetic betterment—not merely, as Weber thought, defensive saving and hard work—was rather the participation of ordinary people in religious congregations with weak or no governance from above. The Radical Reformation, as against the more hierarchical one of Luther or Zwingli or Henry VIII, in other words, was a delivery room for a democratic theory long aborning. In particular, radical Protestant governance of congregations gave standing to any member—thus the governance-by-resistance-to-the-king's-bishops among German Pietists and English Methodists; and governance-by-elders among Scottish Presbyterians and Moravian Hutterites; and governance-by-local-community among Anabaptists (called now Mennonites), Independents (called now Congregationalists), and Baptists (called now Baptists); and, after a while, governance-by-no-one-in-particular among, say, Quakers. John Wesley, for example, emphasized congregational consensus, nonordained preachers, independence from state interference, and sometimes even pacifism and tax resistance in the face of the state's proud projects.

The Protestants discarded fifteen hundred years of church history to return to what they believed was the faith of the first and second century. Political argument shifted away from disputes between popes and emperors and toward disputes between governments and individual consciences. In places like Switzerland, church officials came to be accountable to their congregants rather than to kings and bishops. The wars of religion, though they were nothing like politically liberal in the modern sense, strengthened the conviction that a man's a man, for a' that.

Ideas did it.

26

And Then Old Adam Smith Revealed / The Virtues of the Bourgeois Deal

Adam Smith pushed along the Revaluation, and he was its most noble and persuasive advocate. He is the hero of our book. Though he wrote two and a half centuries ago, he is fresher than today's newspaper.

In particular, the Scottish professor of moral philosophy and father of modern economics never, ever said that "greed is good." Nor did he, unlike his friend David Hume (1711–1776), lead towards a Benthamite notion (before Jeremy Bentham) that "utility" from benefit minus cost runs the human drama. On the contrary, Smith practiced "humanomics," an economics with the humans and their ethics left in.[1] After all, grass is utilitarian, seeking water and sunshine optimally. Rats (except in the movie *Ratatouille*) act for benefit minus cost selfishly in their ratty little schemes. But humans, said Smith, also seek love and justice and courage and the rest of the peculiarly human virtues—and the humans fail, too, with peculiarly human vices, such as envy and hatred and pride.

Most people have not gotten the memo about our hero and his humanomics. The 2001 movie *A Beautiful Mind* is based on a popular biography by Sylvia Nasar about the prominent mathematician John Nash—who surprisingly got in 1984 the Nobel memorial prize in *economics*. The young John (played brilliantly, as usual, by Russell Crowe) is in a bar surrounded by some male Princeton University classmates. A blonde walks in with four brown-haired friends. The young men discuss who should win her, and how. One of Nash's classmates says, "Recall the lesson of Adam Smith: in competition, individual ambition" . . . and everyone except Nash joins him in unison, with smiles all around: "serves the common good!" Nash, who always thinks for himself, to the point of a sweetly Smith-like Asperger's syndrome, has a lightbulb moment, and declares, "No. The only way we *all* get laid" is by *cooperating* rather than competing. He dashes out, presumably to write it down in mathematics, announcing dramatically as he leaves, "Adam Smith . . . is *wrong.*"

Well, no. About Adam Smith, Nash and his classmate were mistaken, and so are the many proud economists and calculators who have not actually read a page of his books. (There are only two: what are you waiting for?) Smith *never* said that "in competition, individual ambition serves the common good." The ambitions of Macbeth or Faust or Stalin, for example, did not serve any good, common or other.

True, Smith in a famous but routinely misunderstood passage in 1776 spoke of appealing to the self-love of others, rather than appealing to their lordly charity or their slavish obedience: "It is not from the benevolence [or the compelled obedience] of the butcher, the brewer, or the baker that we expect our dinner [and from your mother, dear Adam, with whom you lived, and who cooked it], but from their regard [as free people] to their own interest." He is saying that you should be properly democratic in the theater of the marketplace—not expecting by lordly right to take without recompense, or by a beggarly lack of dignity to receive without recompense. You and the baker and butcher are equals in Smith's view. To pay your way is to respect their equal dignity.

Like his contemporary the German philosopher Immanuel Kant, Smith emphasizes in a liberal way that people are not merely means to others' ends, to be used up in one-sided coercing or begging. He is affirming that they are humans with dignity and liberty, with the right equal to yours to reply to a freely given offer, "No thank you." One must give, in a just and democratic humility, to receive without lordship or slavery. Smith, an egalitarian respecter of persons, would have been appalled by the young men in the Princeton bar seeing the young woman as sexual meat, to be chewed from all sides without regard to *her* interest, in a "competition." Smith's ethical and economic point was that an equal right to say no leads to a massive social cooperation, and one's dinner.

Smith, that is, was above all an ethical thinker. He wrote the two books, *The Theory of Moral Sentiments* (1759, finishing the much-amended sixth edition just before he died, in 1790) and *An Inquiry into the Nature and Causes of the Wealth of Nations* (1776, with its own sixth edition, slightly amended, appearing in 1791). Such a meager output would make him a borderline case for tenure nowadays in many universities, and a sure-fire no in most departments of economics. "Good Lord," the economists would say after a hurried look at his academic credentials, "he didn't publish *any* articles in the *American Economic Review* reporting statistical tests or field experiments or mathematical proofs of existence!"[2]

The Theory of Moral Sentiments is routinely ignored by economists (though since the 1990s the academic philosophers, if not the economists, have started to pay the book serious attention). Many practitioners of our beloved economic science don't know that Smith wrote anything other than the *Wealth of Nations*, which anyway few have read. We ourselves are not exceptions. Carden didn't read *The Theory of Moral Sentiments* until the summer after he finished graduate school, and only then because he was recruited to the Liberty Fund's "Adam Smith Boot Camp." McCloskey didn't read it until she *taught* it in a course on economic ethics in 1996 at Erasmus University of Rotterdam, in the Netherlands—when she was fifty-three years old. Her graduate program, in one of Harvard's numerous contributions to the decivilizing of economists, had dropped the history of economic thought as a requirement in 1963, the year before she started her PhD. Shame on us, and on our teachers.

Ignoring *The Theory of Moral Sentiments* (or *TMS*, as sophisticates call it) is a big mistake, supporting the crazy picture of Smith as the theorist of "greed is good," in line with the bright boys in the Princeton bar. Many have supposed that there is a mystery that Smith wrote in 1759 on "sentiments," which they mistakenly take in its modern meaning as love, and in 1776 on prudence, which they mistakenly take in its modern meaning as the opposite of love, selfishness. Which is it, Mr. Smith, they ask, love or selfishness? Long ago, German scholars named the supposed inconsistency *Das Adam Smith Problem*.[3]

On the contrary, Smith's great project in all his writing was to develop a full and temperate ethic for a commercial society—*not* to reduce all behavior to a selfishness suited to grass and rats. In *TMS*, in a rare instance of intemperance in this most temperate of scholars, he gets wound up against the chief greed-is-good theorist of the age we have mentioned, Bernard Mandeville. In a doggerel poem in 1705, Mandeville had embraced vice as good for business. His is the core idea in the conservative theory of trickle down combined with the socialist theory of trickle up. Spend, spend, spend. Break windows to give jobs to glazers. "Such is the system of Dr. Mandeville," wrote Smith, "which once made so much noise in the world, and which, though, perhaps, it never gave occasion to more vice than would have been without it, at least taught that vice, which arose from other causes, to appear with more effrontery, and to avow the corruption of its motives with a profligate audaciousness which had never been heard of before."[4] Thus his blast against "competition" viewed as the Princeton boys' scrum.

Smith's theorizing protected bourgeois betterments—like opening a new trade in pepper or devising a new waterwheel— from the attacks by other businesspeople "competing" by erecting government-sponsored monopolies against the betterments; or by aristocrats intent on "competing" the same way to keep things as they so pleasantly are; or by peasants or proletarians "competing" to seize some of the stuff by tip or gift or theft or graft from the riches of the merchant or aristocrat. By contrast, the bourgeois innovator gets profit, and his dinner, by respecting the dignity of others. He works not by coercing others in violent "competition," but by making an offer to a customer that she may accept or reject. The seller with a worse offer, naturally, regards himself as suffering from "violence" (thus regular taxi driver as against the better offer from ride-sharing company drivers) but he is not to be encouraged in the belief. As the great liberal Mill put it in 1859, "Society admits no right, either legal or moral, in the disappointed competitors, to immunity from this kind of suffering; and feels called on to interfere, only when means of success have been employed which it is contrary to the general interest to permit—namely, fraud or treachery, and force."[5]

The alternative to respecting individual dignity is deciding economic matters collectively, through the government, a government seized by political "competition." After all, there are only two ways to get other people to do what you would like them to do, such as providing your dinner. You can coerce them, by private or public violence; get the government to do it. Or you can persuade them, by persuasion or offers of money. As the modern-day liberal philosopher David Boaz put it, "In a sense, there have always been but two political philosophies: liberty and power."[6]

The eighteenth-century French political philosopher Jean-Jacques Rousseau opted for power, as Thomas Hobbes had, and initiated an antiliberal tradition that eventuated in socialism and fascism. He met Smith, with whom he angrily quarreled, as he did with everyone he met. (Rousseau sent his children to the orphanage to give himself more quiet time to write a treatise telling people how to raise their children. Not a nice fellow.) He imagined that the right of a free and dignified individual to say no should be trumped by a mysterious "general will," which Rousseau and similarly placed experts or Communist Party officials could so easily discern, and impose on others by coercive measures. (About raising children, for example.) For the past century or so many good people of a sort that would formerly have been of a liberal tendency have swallowed Rousseau's notion that the government is therefore a good protector of, say, the poor. Let's do it by power, the absence of a liberty to say no, not by persuasion, having such a liberty. The editorial board of the *Washington Post* declared that "obviously, the market economy's legitimacy depends on equal opportunity, actual and perceived, which is why, contrary to small-government bromides of the political right, government must intervene to protect less-advantaged participants in the marketplace."[7] You bet. Can a government with such powers be trusted not to use them for the "protection" of the *more*-advantaged? When have the rich and powerful, such as doctors protecting their monopoly or farmers protecting their crop insurance or steelmakers protecting their domestic market, not used governmental power for their own benefit? The evidence seems pretty plain, outside of small islands of rectitude such as Denmark and New Zealand. And even there, as Danes and New Zealanders can tell you, governmental intervention to protect less-advantaged participants in the marketplace tends to be clumsy and counterproductive.

The politics of power leads to endless proposals for coercive policies that are less than productive. For example: Let's protect people by government policies of antitrust. The idea of a government as a protector of the people against private monopoly, or as a protector of the poor instead of letting the poor work free of coercion, would have struck an eighteenth-century Scot such as Smith as hilarious. Europeans of Smith's day saw the government as a monopoly-*making* instrument of special interests, especially the interests of the lords in charge—and nothing like a disinterested body discerning a benevolent general will, as though such a thing was plausible on its face.

To say that Smith invented an ethic for a commercial age is not the same thing as saying he admired everything the bourgeoisie did. Smith warned, for example, that the interests of merchants and manufacturers are "always in some respects different from, and even opposite to, that of the public."[8] He was warning against the monopoly-making of a government seized by special interests. Politically, he certainly did not recommend unfettered rule by the bourgeoisie, what we now call crony capitalism. The economist Thomas Sowell used to offer an A in his courses to students who could find any passage in Smith in which he said something nice about businesspeople. That is, Smith was an enthusiast for free markets, but he was no friend of businesspeople using government to "compete" by erecting protective monopolies, such as taxes on foreign businesspeople, paid in the end by domestic consumers.

§

That is, Smith was not naive. The philosopher James Otteson identifies three arguments underlying Smith's defense of a commercial society: (1) the economizer argument, (2) the local-knowledge argument, and (3) the invisible-hand argument.[9]

Regarding the economizer argument, Smith observes that "every individual is continually exerting himself to find the most advantageous employment for whatever capital he can command."[10] That's not greed, merely ordinary prudence, such as you exercise when you go shopping. "Capital" can be taken in a wide sense to mean any useful input (such as labor or land, too) that has some alternate use. Or the money in your purse.

How can you accomplish the most advantageous employment among the alternatives, Plan A or Plan B? Well, you choose by your own lights according to what the plans yield for you. Of course. But note: it is by "your own lights," not by the general will or by what the government-protected monopoly of taxicabs wants. A liberalism—no slaves, the right to say no—is built into Smith's argument at the outset. *You* decide, not the government or the community, not the experts or the masters. You know best how to "economize" in using your own capital. It is a reasonable assumption, but one that all the statists firmly deny. And they deny that anyway an adult *should* in equal dignity be assumed to choose wisely—even if on occasion that adult does not. But the problem with statism is that only by an imposed assumption of political and administrative perfection will the general will choose better than the individual does. And always the statist general will takes away the dignity of individual choice. The general is a nasty master.

In a logic that economists finally got clear a century after Smith, economizing means "choosing the better way of doing it overall— Plan A rather than Plan B." What is "better," said the economists of the 1870s, is *not* "using the least labor" (Smith missed the point, and it led to a sadly mistaken picture of the economy as a supply chain, a picture believed always by the man in the street and by the statist enthusiasts for industrial policy). What is better is up to you to decide, considering how much *you value* what you get from Plan B compared with Plan A. The insight of the 1870s was that "value" is in this sense "subjective." Value is not an objective, physical, engineering fact, a matter of resources and supply chains. People with their own, personal knowledge of their own preferences—not expert central planners armed with engineering knowledge of the labor content of goods—decide what is valuable and therefore what to do. It is deeply liberal: no masters; instead, you.

Such an "economizer" argument leads naturally in Otteson's scheme to Smith's second, "local-knowledge" argument. Smith despised what he called in *TMS* "the man of system"—the bossy bureaucrat or the Communist Party official with the general will and engineering knowledge in hand. As he says, "What is the species of domestic industry which his capital can employ, and of which the produce is likely to be of the greatest value, every individual, it is evident can, *in his local situation*, judge much better than any states-man or lawgiver can do for him." The economist Friedrich Hayek would in 1945 call it "knowledge of the particular circumstances of time and place," wholly unavailable to an outside planner.[11] The free person possesses the relevant local knowledge, enjoys the benefits of wisely choosing Plan A, and bears the costs of not choosing Plan B. Free adults would want the credit or blame in choosing. They don't want to be treated like toddlers, who do *not* know what they want. They are free adults, willing in simple justice to pay the freight.

Smith puts his hostility toward outside busybodies (recall Hillel's formulation of the Golden Rule) this way: "The statesman, who should attempt to direct private people in what manner they ought to employ their capitals . . . would be nowhere so dangerous as in the hands of a man who had folly and presumption enough to fancy himself fit to exercise it." The expert economist who thinks he knows how to fine-tune the economy or the politician who is sure she can judge whether a high-speed rail should go from Boston to Worcester, Massachusetts, is, under Smith's reasoning, a dangerous fool.

The economizer argument and the local-knowledge argument then provide the basis for what Otteson calls Smith's "invisible-hand argument." According to Smith, "The annual revenue of every society is always precisely equal to the exchangeable value. . . . As every individual . . . endeavors as much as he can both to employ his capital [and labor and land] . . . [so] that its produce may be of the greatest value, every individual necessarily labors to render the annual revenue of the society as great as he can."[12] That is, people sell their goods and services in as efficient a way as they can, which makes the economy as a whole efficient in the exact sense of maximizing the annual revenue of the society. "The economy" is not something separate from the sum of transactions of the individuals in it. Then Smith articulates the apparent paradox, in one of only two places in his published writings using the theological phrase "invisible hand": "He intends only his own gain, and he is in this, as in many other cases, led by an invisible hand to promote an end which was no part of his intention."

Smith is not advocating gain achieved in any but ethical and peaceful means. Not "greed is good," or the Princeton boys' "in competition, individual ambition serves the common good." But "by pursuing his own interest he frequently [note the careful quali-fication of *frequently*] promotes that of the society more effectually than when he really intends to promote it." Smith is using the local-knowledge argument again. It was a feature of his own principled intellectual modesty called by two students of the matter "analytical egalitarianism."[13] He had written fiercely in TMS against the expert "man of system . . . [who] seems to imagine that he can arrange [by state compulsion guided by his conception of the general will, or more likely by his own selfish interest] the different members of a great society with as much ease as the hand arranges the different pieces upon a chess-board. He does not consider that . . . every single piece has a principle of motion of its own."[14] It's liberalism again: you have a right to a "principle of motion" of your own, as long as you do not physically damage other people.

Smith was reacting here against a view of society and economy dominant in 1776 and, alas, still vibrant—the view that government can pick winners by an "industrial policy," or that a black-letter law tells where taxes will ultimately fall, or that consumers need to be corrected in their consumption (recently revived in proposals to "nudge" people), or that natural liberty in running airlines or grocery stores or education in medicine needs to be closely regulated—lest we fall, as Bill Murray's cheeky Peter Venkman put it in the original

Ghostbusters, into apocalyptic "human sacrifice, dogs and cats living together—mass hysteria!" It ain't so.

§

Against the idea that grasping greed is the ethic for a commercial society, Smith wrote in the first line of *The Theory of Moral Sentiments* that "However selfish man may be supposed, there are evidently some principles in his nature, which interest him in the fortune of others, and render their happiness necessary to him, though they derive nothing from it except the pleasure of seeing it." He goes on to rebuke, we have noted, Thomas Hobbes and Bernard Mandeville, by name and at length (both practices unusual in Smith's writings), for depending on no ethic other than a selfish version of prudence, and reducing all motivation therefore to mere selfishness.

The Theory of Moral Sentiments was Smith's favorite of his two published books. He was what is known nowadays in departments of philosophy as a "virtue ethicist," in the tradition of Aristotle, Plutarch, Cicero, and Aquinas, with lively parallels in other cultures such as Hinduism and Confucianism. Smith was the last of the European tradition until the 1950s and 1960s, when a set of British female philosophers, including Elizabeth Anscombe and the novelist-philosopher Iris Murdoch, caused it to flower again. McCloskey in 2006 brought it over into economics, and in 2019, we have noted, Bart Wilson and another Smith, the Nobel laureate Vernon, carried on a Smithian economics under the rubric of humanomics.

Adam Smith, Vernon Smith, and the new tradition of humanomics treat economic actors as mixes of prudence with the other virtues which are more characteristically human than a prudence shared by grass and rats. From the seven principal virtues of courage, justice, temperance, prudence, faith, hope, and love, Smith chose four and a half (courage, justice, temperance, prudence, and a little bit of love, which his teacher Frances Hutcheson called "benevolence"). He was missing faith, hope, and the transcendent kind of love (Greek *agape*) because he, like Hume and Voltaire and others, had an aversion to conventional religion. They did not see that hope (having a project) and faith (having integrity) and transcendent love, the greatest of these (which is value in its widest sense), are human motivations in the office as much as in the church.

Of the seven virtues of classical and Christian theory, Smith paid particular attention to prudence in *Wealth of Nations*, temperance (chiefly, not solely) in *TMS*, and justice in a projected *Treatise on Jurisprudence*, a manuscript of which was burned at Smith's request when he died (but which lives on in elaborate notes by his students).

The approach McCloskey calls Prudence Only, however, reduces all virtues to vice, and in particular the sin of pride, which is the worship of the self. In "maximizing utility," as economists put it, you set yourself up as your only ethical end, a little god in the style of Trump. But a courageous man does not charge the enemy's guns for utility, or happiness, but for identity, for the very sake of being courageous. A loving wife does not love her husband because he is amusing or because he has yellow hair or because he can muscle open the tops of jars (although that is a very good thing, Carden's wife thinks). She loves him for himself alone. She is interested in his fortune beyond money. His happiness is necessary to hers, though she derives nothing from it but the pleasure of seeing it. It is an end worth pursuing for its own sake.

Smith's ethical theory is deeply social. People are accountable beings. As he put it in a letter to Gilbert Elliot some months after the publication of *TMS*, "Man is considered as a moral, because he is regarded as an accountable being. But an accountable being, as the word expresses, is a being that must give an account of its actions to some other, and that, consequently, must regulate them according to the good liking of this other." Though the accountable being "is, no doubt, principally accountable to God, in the order of time, he must necessarily conceive of himself as accountable to his fellow creatures."[15] We are accountable, one to another, and therefore to the judgment of the impartial spectator formed out of our lives with our fellow creatures. Unless we are Donald Trumps.

In 1600 or 1660, no one in England or Scotland would have thought to write a two-volume *Wealth of Nations*, treating a nation as a prudent project for the self-betterment of a bourgeois society and especially of its poorest members (though in 1662 Pieter de la Court wrote *Interest van Holland*, a best seller defending free trade and the republican government of the United Provinces; the Dutch were first). By Smith's time, though, the rhetorical ground in Europe had shifted, and an ethic of *acting* had started taking the place of an ethic of *being*.[16] Procedural correctness mattered. The new bourgeois society Smith theorized was pragmatic, prudent, non-utopian, and wary of both state power and monopolies.

Smith's formulation of the Bourgeois Deal embodied an ethic of self-ownership. He was especially indignant about restrictions on a worker's right to dispose of his labor as he saw fit. The English Settlement and Removal Acts, for example, would force the poor back to the parishes of their birth lest they overwhelm relief resources. The acts literally removed and resettled them, cleansing them from a locale by order of the general will. Smith observed, "To remove a man who has committed no misdemeanor from the parish where he chooses to reside is an evident violation of natural liberty and justice. . . . There is scarce a poor man in England of forty years of age, I will venture to say, who has not in some part of his life felt himself most cruelly oppressed by this ill-contrived law."[17] Compare immigration law and especially its administration in the Trump-era United States.

The invisible hand pushes people out of where they are wasting resources and into where they are creating wealth, in both cases as measured by people's willingness to pay with the fruits of their labors. But there is another invisible hand, a social one. We become polite members of our society by interacting on the social stage. Note: "inter-acting." Smith talked often in theatrical terms, and he did not believe that we could depend on natural niceness or natural greed-is-good nastiness for social peace on the world's stage. He emphasized that societies and selves shape people. As boys, he noted, the poet and the philosopher are little different, and this against the Blue-Blood pretense that the little lord got his nobility from his blood. Rather, they are playing on a social stage their whole lives, in never-ending improvisational comedy and conversation. As Smith put it, "everyone is practicing oratory on others through the whole of life."[18] Such commerce and conversation, whether social or financial, change us. You have to live in the world to become civilized, and you are a social—even a theatrical—product. As Shakespeare put it in *As You Like It*, "All the world's a stage, / And all the men and women merely players."

Above all, Smith articulated an ideology of the Bourgeois Deal. He showed his ethical standard for the denizens of the middle station in an unsigned memorial on a bourgeois friend, his very first publication, in 1758:

> To the Memory of Mr. William Crauford, Merchant of Glasgow

> Who to that exact frugality, that downright probity and plainness of manners so suitable to his profession, joined a love of learning, . . . an openness of hand and a generosity of heart, . . . and a magnanimity that could support . . . the most torturing pains of body with an unalterable cheerfulness of temper, and without once interrupting, even to his last hour, the most manly and the most vigorous activity in a vast variety of business . . . candid and penetrating, circumspect and sincere.[19]

It's not a tribute to Greed is Good or Prudence Only or Me First or even "in competition, individual ambition serves the common good." It praises the bourgeois virtues. The phrase is not an oxymoron.

§

Adam Smith's *Theory of Moral Sentiments*, like many modern novels, is about growing up, ethically speaking. In fact, liberalism is the political and economic and social theory of adulthood. The adult individual lives in a city with his family, and respects his community, but exercises Kant's "autonomy," Greek for self-rule.

The other two of the three great theories of society since 1776 are nationalism and socialism. If liberalism is the theory of being an adult, nationalism and socialism are nostalgic longings for the comforts of childhood. As Sigmund Freud noted, we long to return to the security of our father and mother. Nationalism reproduces our father, the king and country for which we are willing to die. Socialism reproduces our mother, who will protect and nourish us.

Modest versions of nationalism and socialism are not corrupting. It's harmless, even sweet, to celebrate the victories of the US women's soccer team. It is virtuous to provide for your children from your ability and according to their need. But many versions of the father-mother government have been disastrously bad for human welfare. Vladimir Putin's nationalism in the Russian Federation or Nicolás Maduro's socialism in Venezuela have not been harmless, sweet, or virtuous. Yet citizens of the United States are in a poor position to cast the first stone. Governments worldwide are too big, too bossy, too much the Hobbes-Rousseau "family" of masters over children.

We should wish to be free adults, perhaps with prompt protection by a modest government from invasion by Canada or COVID-19, or maybe taxed for an effective safety net to help the poor and handicapped—but mostly, liberated to venture. Which is, after all, the Bourgeois Deal.

Acknowledgments

Our intellectual debts are too numerous to list fully. McCloskey has been giving seminars and lectures on these topics around the world for more than two decades, and Carden has given numerous talks on the project at colleges and universities (many supported by generous grants from the Charles Koch Foundation)—including multiple visits to McKendree University just outside Saint Louis—and at student seminars sponsored by the American Enterprise Institute, the American Institute for Economic Research, the Fraser Institute, the Institute for Humane Studies, the Independent Institute, the Intercollegiate Studies Institute, the Nassau Institute, and Worth Publishers' EconEd conference. He presented the book in academic seminars at Troy University, Samford University, and Southern Methodist University as well as in sessions at the Southern Economic Association (with commentary from Steven G. Horwitz and Sarah Skwire) and the Public Choice Society (with commentary from Michael Munger, Randy Simmons, Roberta Herzberg, and Anne Bradley). Doug Stuart of the Libertarian Christian Institute read the manuscript and made valuable comments. The authors also benefited tremendously from conferences on the volumes of McCloskey's Bourgeois Era trilogy sponsored by the Competitive Enterprise Institute and the Mercatus Center. At various stages, students at Samford University and elsewhere have provided generous assistance. Hamilton Spivey helped with the project in its earliest stages in summer 2013 thanks to a generous grant from the Charles

Koch Foundation, and Oak Martin did a few explorations in the history of hymnody that ultimately didn't make it into the finished product but that are appreciated nonetheless. Harry David prepared the index. Howard Finch, dean of Samford University's Brock School of Business from 2011 to 2019, suggested that we make "Leave Me Alone and I'll Make You Rich" the title of the book rather than the subtitle or just a theme. Carden's family—wife Shannon and children Jacob, Taylor Grace, and David—deserve special mention for steady support and pleasant diversion as the project evolved. There is, no doubt, a great deal in this book which we get wrong or treat inadequately. Please let us know so that we can write an even better future edition.

Notes

We have kept notes to a minimum. When a fact or idea or even a quotation is easily found by looking it up online (e.g. *Federalist* 51), or when it is part of the common currency of economics or history, known to all serious students, and uncontroversial (e.g., Edward I took the throne of England in 1272; or modern economic growth per person is on the order of a factor of 30), we have resisted the academic temptation to add a note to exhibit our amazing erudition. But when a quotation would be hard to find, we want to help you follow up. When an idea or calculation is properly attributable to Professor N—and there are many of these that we have boldly appropriated: for example, Hans Rosling's brilliance—we wish to give due credit. If we have missed any of these, please forgive us, then tell us, and we'll fix it.

Epigraph

1. Amélie Oksenberg Rorty, "Experiments in Philosophical Genre: Descartes' *Meditations,*" *Critical Inquiry* 9, no. 3 (March 1983): 545–65, at 562.

Preface

1. U.S. Bureau of Labor Statistics, *Employed Full Time: Median Usual Weekly Real Earnings: Wage and Salary Workers: 16 Years and Over,* report source code LES1252881600Q, retrieved from FRED, Federal Reserve Bank of St. Louis, February 11, 2020, https://fred.stlouisfed.org/series/LES1252881600Q.

2. Examples are from Grace Pateras, "Yes, These Are Real: The Best Florida Man Headlines of 2019," *Tallahassee Democrat*, December 9, 2019, https://www .usatoday.com/story/news/nation/2019/12/09/florida-man-headlines-2019 -meme-florida-man-challenge-birthday/2629205001/.

3. He is in this thinking much influenced by David D. Friedman's *The Machinery of Freedom: Guide to a Radical Capitalism*, originally published in 1973 and published in a third edition in 2014 by Open Court, as well as Peter T. Leeson, *Anarchy Unbound* (Cambridge University Press, 2014); and Michael Huemer, *The Problem of Political Authority* (Palgrave, 2012).

4. Deirdre N. McCloskey, *The Bourgeois Virtues: Ethics for an Age of Commerce* (2006), *Bourgeois Dignity: Why Economics Can't Explain the Modern World* (2010), *Bourgeois Equality: How Ideas, Not Capital or Institutions, Enriched the World* (2016), all from the University of Chicago Press. See also Deirdre N. McCloskey, *Why Liberalism Works: How True Liberal Vales Produce a Freer, More Equal, Prosperous World for All* (Yale University Press, 2019).

Chapter 1

1. Branko Milanovic, *Global Inequality A New Approach for the Age of Globalization* (Harvard University Press, 2016; John V. C. Nye, "Economic Growth: Part I; Economic Growth and True Inequality," Library of Economics and Liberty, January 28, 2002, https://www.econlib.org/library/Columns/Nyegrowth .html; John V. C. Nye, "Economic Growth: Part II; Irreducible Inequality," Library of Economics and Liberty, April 1, 2002, https://www.econlib.org/ library/Columns/Nyepositional.html.

2. Donald J. Boudreaux, "Bonus Quotation of the Day," *Café Hayek* (blog), November 25, 2017, https://cafehayek.com/2017/11/bonus-quotation-day-86.html.

3. Doron Shultziner et al., "Causes and Scope of Political Egalitarianism during the Last Glacial: A Multi-Disciplinary Perspective," *Biology and Philosophy* 25, no. 3 (June 2010): 319–46.

4. Voltaire, *Philosophical Letters*, ed. and trans. E. Dilworth (1956; repr., New York: Modern Library, 1992), letter 10, pp. 154–55.

5. Adam Smith, *An Inquiry into the Nature and Causes of the Wealth of Nations*, 2 vols., ed. Ed. Edwin Cannan (London: Methuen, 1904), 2:184 (hereafter cited as *WN*).

6. Eric L. Jones, *Locating the Industrial Revolution: Inducement and Response* (World Scientific, 2010), 102–3.

7. Johnson and Strahan quoted in James Boswell, *The Life of Samuel Johnson* (1791; repr., Modern Library, 1967), 242. Boswell was recounting a conversation over breakfast with the two men on March 27, 1775.

8. Voltaire, *Philosophical Letters*, letter 10, p. 154.

9. César de Saussure, quoted in Tim Blanning, *The Pursuit of Glory: Europe 1648–1815* (Viking and Penguin, 2007), 110.

Chapter 2

1. Paul Collier, *The Bottom Billion: Why the Poorest Countries Are Failing and What Can Be Done about It* (Oxford University Press, 2007).

2. United Nations, Department of Economic and Social Affairs, Population Division, *World Urbanization Prospects: The 2018 Revision*, report no. ST/ESA/SER.A/420 (United Nations, 2019), https://population.un.org/wup/Publications/Files/WUP2018-Report.pdf; see also United Nations, Department of Economic and Social Affairs, Population Division, "Urbanization," accessed January 6, 2020, https://www.un.org/en/development/desa/population/theme/urbanization/index.asp.

3. William D. Nordhaus, "Do Real Output and Real Wage Measures Capture Reality? The History of Light Suggests Not," in *The Economics of New Goods*, ed. Robert J. Gordon and Timothy F. Bresnahan (University of Chicago Press for the National Bureau of Economic Research, 1997), 27–70, at 30.

4. John Mueller, "War Has Almost Ceased to Exist," *Political Science Quarterly* 124, no. 2 (Summer 2009): 297–321.

5. John Mueller, *Overblown: How Politicians and the Terrorism Industry Inflate National Security Threats, and Why We Believe Them* (Free Press, 2006).

6. Steven J. Pyne, *How the Canyon Became Grand: A Short History* (Penguin, 1999).

7. Barbara A. Hanawalt, *Crime and Conflict in English Communities, 1300–1348* (Harvard University Press, 1979).

8. Angus Deaton, *The Great Escape: Health, Wealth, and the Origins of Inequality* (Princeton University Press, 2013), xi.

9. See Hans Rosling, Anna Rosling Roennlund, and Ola Rosling, *Factfulness: Ten Reasons We're Wrong about the World—and Why Things Are Better Than You Think* (Flatiron Books, 2018).

Chapter 3

1. Edward Behr, *The Complete Book of "Les Misérables"* (1989; repr., Arcade, 2016), 39–42.

2. Jutta Bolt et al., "Rebasing 'Maddison': New Income Comparisons and the Shape of Long-Run Economic Development" (Maddison Project Working Paper no. 10, Groningen Growth and Development Center, University of Groningen, Netherlands, 2018). Monetary figures transformed into 2014 dollars using the Consumer Price Index on Measuringworth.com.

3. David Whitford, "The Most Famous Story We Never Told," *Fortune*, September 19, 2005.

4. For facts and statistics derived from them in this chapter, see H. Rosling, A. Rosling Roennlund, and O. Rosling, *Factfulness*, 52, 53, 55, 59–61, 67, 82, 84, 109, 92, 115.

5. The Roslings direct readers to gapm.io/womsuff, but as of February 11, 2020, the data were being updated and were not available. On New Zealand as the first nation to grant women full voting rights, see Melanie S. Gustafson, "Woman Suffrage," *World Book Encyclopedia* (Chicago: World Book, 2008); History.com, "New Zealand First in Women's Vote," last updated July 28, 2019, https://www .history.com/this-day-in-history/new-zealand-first-in-womens-vote.

6. Steven Pastis, "Pearls Before Swine," October 24 and 25, 2005, Go Comics, https://www.gocomics.com/pearlsbeforeswine/2005/10/24.

7. David Sipress, "Wasn't That Paul Krugman?" *New Yorker*, May 25, 2009, https://www.art.com/products/p15063504840-sa-i6847636/david-sipress -wasn-t-that-paul-krugman-new-yorker-cartoon.htm.

8. Steven Horwitz and Stewart Dompe, "From Rabbit Ears to Flat Screen: It's Getting Better All the Time," in *Homer Economicus: The Simpsons and Economics*, ed. Joshua C. Hall (Stanford University Press, 2014), 177–90.

Chapter 4

1. Tocqueville quoted in Leo Marx, *The Machine in the Garden: Technology and the Pastoral Ideal in America* (Oxford University Press, 1964), 190.

2. Jeffrey Tucker, *The Market Loves You: Why You Should Love It Back* (American Institute for Economic Research, 2019), 3–5.

3. Parts of what follows are from Deirdre N. McCloskey, "The Poverty of Communitarianism: A Review of *What Money Can't Buy: The Moral Limits of Markets*, by Michael J. Sandel," *Claremont Review of Books* 12, no. 4, (Fall 2012), https://claremontreviewofbooks.com/the-poverty-of-communitarianism/.

4. Michael Sandel, *What Money Can't Buy: The Moral Limits of Markets* (Farrar, Straus and Giroux, 2012), 64.

5. Sandel, *What Money Can't Buy*, 81.

6. Sandel, *What Money Can't Buy*, 110.

7. Sandel, *What Money Can't Buy*, 20.

8. Sandel, *What Money Can't Buy*, 46.

9. Stephen Landsburg, *The Armchair Economist: Economics and Everyday Life* (Free Press, 2012), 279.

10. Sandel, *What Money Can't Buy*, 78.

11. Jason Brennan and Peter M. Jaworski, *Markets without Limits: Moral Virtues and Commercial Interests* (Routledge, 2016), 10.

12. Brennan and Jaworski, *Markets without Limits*, 67.

13. Chris Kjorness, "Delta Dawn: How Sears, Roebuck & Co. Midwifed the Birth of the Blues," *Reason*, May 2012, https://reason.com/2012/04/19/delta-dawn/.

14. Tyler Cowen, *In Praise of Commercial Culture* (Harvard University Press, 2000).

15. Mario Vargas Llosa, "The Culture of Liberty," *Foreign Policy*, November 20, 2009, https://foreignpolicy.com/2009/11/20/the-culture-of-liberty/.

16. Alan Paton, *Cry, the Beloved Country* (1948; repr., Scribner, 1987), 32.

17. "We say 'according to the anecdote' because it is attested as far as we know only in Edmund Fuller, *2500 Anecdotes for All Occasions* (Crown, 1943), as cited in Clifton Fadiman and Andre Bernard, *Bartlett's Book of Anecdotes*, rev. ed. (Little, Brown, 2000). A good and statistically accurate story, though.

18. Ian Gazeley and Andrew Newell, "The End of Destitution: Evidence from British Working Households 1904–1937" (working paper no. 2, Economics Department, University of Sussex, 2010).

19. Tucker, *The Market Loves You*, 11.

Chapter 5

1. Statistics quoted in the first three paragraphs of this chapter are all from H. Rosling, A. Rosling Roennlund, and O. Rosling, *Factfulness*, 61–64.

2. Greg Lukianoff and Jonathan Haidt, *The Coddling of the American Mind: How Good Intentions and Bad Ideas Are Setting Up a Generation for Failure* (Penguin, 2018), 181–212.

3. H. Rosling, A. Rosling Roennlund, and O. Rosling, *Factfulness*, 66.

4. Hans Rosling quoted in H. Rosling, A. Rosling Roennlund, and O. Rosling, *Factfulness*, 51.

5. Nye, "Economic Growth: Part I"; Nye, "Economic Growth: Part II."

6. Graham Robb, *The Discovery of France: A Historical Geography* (W. W. Norton, 2007), 78.

7. Robb, *Discovery of France*, 78.

8. See Robert William Fogel, "Health, Nutrition, and Economic Growth," *Economic Development and Cultural Change* 52, no. 3 (April 2004): 643–58.

9. Robb, *Discovery of France*, 79.

10. Taine quoted in Robb, *Discovery of France*, 84.

11. Quoted from Moburg's memoir in Andrew Brown, *Fishing in Utopia: Sweden and the Future That Disappeared* (Granta, 2008), 9–10.

12. David Gilmour, *The Pursuit of Italy: A History of a Land, Its Regions, and Their Peoples* (Farrar, Straus, and Giroux, 2011), 20.

13. Fogel, "Health, Nutrition, and Economic Growth," 646.

14. Joseph A. Schumpeter, *Capitalism, Socialism and Democracy*, 3rd. ed., ed. Richard Swedberg (1950; repr., Harper Perennial, 2008), 67.

Chapter 6

1. Jonah Goldberg, *Suicide of the West: How the Rebirth of Tribalism, Populism, Nationalism, and Identity Politics Is Destroying American Democracy* (Crown Forum, 2018), 6.

2. Douglass C. North, *Understanding the Process of Economic Change* (Princeton University Press, 2005), 7.

3. T. B. Macaulay, "Southey's Colloquies on Society," in *Critical, Historical, and Miscellaneous Essays by Lord Macaulay*, vol. 1 (Boston, 1860), 184–87, at 185.

4. Edmund Phelps, *Mass Flourishing: How Grassroots Innovation Created Jobs, Challenge, and Change* (Princeton University Press, 2013), viii, x, 14, 15, 21.

5. Growth rates on India, China, and the world are from World Bank, "GDP Per Capita Growth (Annual %)—China, India," accessed February 25, 2020, https://data.worldbank.org/indicator/NY.GDP.PCAP.KD.ZG?locations=CN -IN; World Bank, "GDP Per Capita Growth (Annual %), accessed February 25, 2020, https://data.worldbank.org/indicator/NY.GDP.PCAP.KD.ZG.

6. Angus Maddison, *The World Economy* (Paris: Organization for Economic Cooperation and Development, 2006), 383. This 2006 edition comprises *The World Economy: A Millennial Perspective* (2001) and *The World Economy: Historical Statistic* (2003) bound as one volume. We are aware that China and India should be removed from the 1973–2003 rate to make the hypothetical exact. So the rate would be a trifle lower—say, 4 percent. But 4 percent world growth per person is still, as we say, unprecedented.

7. Dwight H. Perkins and Thomas G. Rawski, "Forecasting China's Economic Growth to 2025," in *China's Great Economic Transformation*, ed. Loren Brandt and Thomas G. Rawski (Cambridge University Press, 2008), 829–86.

8. Dwight H. Perkins, "The Transition from Central Planning: East Asia's Experience," in *Social Capability and Long-Term Economic Growth*, ed. Bon Ho Koo and Dwight H. Perkins (Macmillan, 1995), 221–41.

9. Schumpeter, *Capitalism, Socialism and Democracy*, 67–68.

Chapter 7

1. John Bates Clark, "The Society of the Future," *Independent* 53 (July 18, 1901): 1649–51, reprinted in Gail Kennedy, ed., *Democracy and the Gospel of Wealth* (Heath, 1949), 77–80.

2. Julian Simon, *The Ultimate Resource 2* (Princeton University Press, 1996).

3. Robert Wuetherick, personal communication with McCloskey, January 26, 2014.

4. Cahal Milmo, "GM Banana Designed to Slash African Infant Mortality Enters Human Trials," Independent, June 16, 2014, 9, https://www.independent.co.uk/news/science/gm-banana-designed-to-slash-african-infant-mortality-enters-human-trials-9541380.html.

5. Alan Barreca, Karen Clay, and Joel Tarr, "Coal, Smoke, and Death: Bituminous Coal and American Home Heating" (NBER Working Paper 19881, National Bureau of Economic Research, Cambridge, MA, 2014), 5, 37 (table 1).

6. Steve Chapman, "Capitalism and Climate Change," Chicago Tribune, September 25, 2014.

7. Niles Eldridge, Dominion (Henry Holt, 1995), 9.

8. Mikael Höök, Robert Hirsch, and Kjell Aleklett, "Giant Oil Field Decline Rates and Their Influence on World Oil Production," Energy Policy 37, no. 6 (June 2009): 2262–72.

9. "Historical Crude Oil Prices (Table): Oil Prices, 1946–Present," InflationData.com, accessed January 10, 2020, https://inflationdata.com/articles/inflation-adjusted-prices/historical-crude-oil-prices-table/.

10. Stephen Jarvis, Olivier Deschenes, and Akshaya Jha, "The Private and External Costs of Germany's Nuclear Phase-Out" (NBER Working Paper 26598, National Bureau of Economic Research, Cambridge, MA, 2019), https://www.nber.org/papers/w26598.pdf.

11. Robert Stone, "Pandora's Promise," transcript of CNN program aired November 7, 2013, http://transcripts.cnn.com/TRANSCRIPTS/1311/07/se.01.html, quoting studies following Chernobyl. One student of the matter concludes that "losses arising from Chernobyl were not of sufficient magnitude and the event was so long ago that the accident should not be definitive in decisions about investment in new reactors"; see Phil Simmons, "The 25th Anniversary of the Chernobyl Accident," International Journal of Climate Change: Impacts and Responses 3, no. 2 (2012): 1–14. At Australian Agricultural and Resource Economics Society, p. 12. Cleanup workers at Fukushima have had no discernible rise in disease; see Andrew C. Rivkin, "A Film Presses the Climate, Health and Security Case for Nuclear Energy," Dot Earth, New York Times, June 13, 2013.

Chapter 8

1. Macaulay quoted in G. K. Chesterton, Chesterton on Dickens (Ignatius Press, 1989), 361.

2. Quoted in Deirdre N. McCloskey, "Magnanimous Albion: Free Trade and British National Income, 1841–1881," Explorations in Economic History 17, no. 3 (July 1980): 303–20, at 304.

3. Smith, WN, 1:422.

Chapter 9

1. For all this, see McCloskey, *Why Liberalism Works*, 143–219.

2. Clark, "Society of the Future."

3. See Arthur M. Diamond, *Openness to Creative Destruction: Sustaining Innovative Dynamism* (Oxford University Press, 2019); Deirdre N. McCloskey, "The Myth of Technological Unemployment," *Reason*, August/September 2017, https://reason.com/2017/07/11/the-myth-of-technological-unem/.

4. Joel Mokyr, "Building Taller Ladders: Technology and Science Reinforce Each Other to Take the Global Economy Ever Higher," *Finance and Development* 55, no. 2 (June 2018), PDF version. By the way, his last name is pronounced *moh-KEER*.

5. Berkeley Breathed, "Bloom County," April 15, 1988, Go Comics, https://www.gocomics.com/bloomcounty/1988/04/15.

Chapter 10

1. Charles G. Sellers, *The Market Revolution: Jacksonian America, 1815–1846* (Oxford University Press, 1991), 6.

2. Michael Walzer, "Does the Free Market Corrode Moral Character? Of Course It Does," in Jagdish Bhagwati et al., *Does the Free Market Corrode Moral Character?* (John Templeton Foundation, 2008).

3. Thomas Mann, *Buddenbrooks*, trans. H. T. Lowe-Porter (Cardinal Giant, 1952), 42, 380, 209, 320, 144, 370, 34, 400.

4. Mann, *Buddenbrooks*, 124, 57, 215.

5. Mann, *Buddenbrooks*, 243.

6. Mann, *Buddenbrooks*, 215.

7. William Cowper, "The Task (Cowper)/Book 4—The Winter Evening," lines 553–55, Wikisource, last modified August 31, 2016, https://en.wikisource.org/wiki/The_Task_(Cowper)/Book_IV_%E2%94%80_The_Winter_Evening/.

8. Tyler Cowen, *Big Business: A Love Letter to an American Anti-Hero* (St. Martin's Press, 2019).

9. John Mueller, *Capitalism, Democracy, and Ralph's Pretty Good Grocery* (Princeton University Press, 1999).

10. Montesquieu, *The Spirit of the Laws*, trans. Thomas Nugent (Hafner Press, 1949), 316; emphasis added.

11. Donald Boudreaux, "And What about Those of Us Who Embrace Freedom?" *Cafe Hayek* (blog), August 23, 2018, https://cafehayek.com/2018/08/us-embrace-freedom.html.

Chapter 11

1. Quotation reprinted in Richard A. Easterlin, *The Reluctant Economist: Perspectives on Economics, Economic History, and Demography* (Cambridge University Press, 2004), 52.

2. Mary Douglas and Baron Isherwood, *The World of Goods* (Basic Books, 1979).

3. Mary Douglas, "Deciphering a Meal," *Daedalus* 101, no. 1 (Winter 1972): 61–81.

4. Richard Chalfen, *Snapshot: Versions of a Life* (Bowling Green University Press, 1987).

5. Marshall Sahlins, *Stone Age Economics* (Routledge Classics, 2017), xix.

6. Easterlin, *Reluctant Economist*, 53.

7. Daniel Horowitz, *The Morality of Spending: Attitudes toward the Consumer Society in America, 1875–1940.* (Johns Hopkins University Press, 1985), 168.

8. Richard A. Easterlin, "Living Standards," in *The Oxford Encyclopedia of Economic History*, 5 vols., ed. Joel Mokyr (Oxford University Press, 2003), 3:349.

9. Deirdre N. McCloskey, "Happyism: The Creepy New Economics of Pleasure," *New Republic*, June 28, 2012.

10. Christine Firer Hinze, "What Is Enough? Catholic Social Thought, Consumption, and Material Sufficiency," in *Having: Property and Possession in Religious and Social Life*, ed. William Schweiker and Charles Mathewes (Eerdmans, 2004), 162–88.

11. McCloskey, *Bourgeois Virtues*, 14.

12. The phrase is from the twentieth-century novelist (and in McCloskey's opinion more than slightly loony philosopher) Ayn Rand's novel *Atlas Shrugged*.

Chapter 12

1. Niall Ferguson, *Civilization: The West and the Rest* (Penguin, 2012).

2. Bart Wilson, *The Property Species: Mine, Yours, and the Human Mind* (Oxford University Press, 2020).

3. Lance E. Davis and Robert A. Huttenback, "Do Imperial Powers Get Rich Off Their Colonies?" in *Second Thoughts: Myths and Morals of US Economic History*, ed. Deirdre N. McCloskey (Oxford University Press, 1993), 26–33; Lance E. Davis and Robert A. Huttenback, *Mammon and the Pursuit of Empire: The Economics of British Imperialism* (Cambridge University Press, 1988).

4. McCloskey, *Bourgeois Dignity*, 232.

5. Emmanuel Le Roy Ladurie, *Montaillou: Cathars and Catholics in a French Village, 1294–1324*, trans. Barbara Bray (Penguin, 1980), 332.

6. Johnson quoted in James Boswell, *The Life of Samuel Johnson, LL.D.*, 2 vols., Everyman's Library (Dent, 1949), 2:447.

7. Franklin quoted in Gordon S. Wood, *The Americanization of Benjamin Franklin* (Penguin, 2004), 66.

8. Max Weber, "Chapter II: The Spirit of Capitalism," in *The Protestant Ethic and the Spirit of Capitalism*, trans. Talcott Parsons, Max Weber Archive, February 2005, https://www.marxists.org/reference/archive/weber/protestant -ethic/ch02.htm.

Chapter 13

1. Immanuel Wallerstein, *Historical Capitalism*, in *Historical Capitalism and Capitalist Civilization* (Verso, 1995), 13.

2. William Easterly, *The Elusive Quest for Growth: Economists' Adventures and Misadventures in the Tropics* (MIT Press, 2001).

3. Randal O'Toole, interview by Caleb O. Brown, *Cato Daily Podcast*, October 8, 2018, https://www.cato.org/multimedia/cato-daily-podcast/romance -rails.

4. Smith, *WN*, 2:184.

Chapter 14

1. Alexis de Tocqueville, *Journeys to England and Ireland*, ed. Jacob Peter Mayer, trans. G. Lawrence and K. P. Mayer (1958; repr., Transaction Books, 1988), 116.

2. The technical version of the argument is that the factor share is the elasticity of output with respect to percentage changes in the input. That is why 5 percent is properly thought of as low.

3. Robert William Fogel, *Railroads and American Economic Growth: Essays in Econometric History* (Johns Hopkins University Press, 1964).

4. See the splendid chart of prices around Europe over many centuries in Fernand Braudel and Frank Spooner, "Prices in Europe from 1450 to 1750," in *The Cambridge Economic History of Europe*, vol. 4, *The Economy of Expanding Europe in the Sixteenth and Seventeenth Centuries*, ed. E. E. Rich and C. H. Wilson (Cambridge University Press, 1967).

5. Alan Macfarlane, *The Origins of English Individualism: The Family, Property, and Social Transition* (Basil Blackwell, 1978).

6. Brennu-Njáls Saga, chap. 70. Njál is speaking to Mord at the Althing, the Icelandic gathering for trade and law reading and dispute settling. In the Project Gutenberg translation, it is for some reason in chapter 69, not 70.

7. Norman Yoffee, *Myths of the Archaic State: Evolution of the Earliest Cities, States, and Civilizations* (Cambridge University Press, 2005), 112.

8. On the positive and negative effects of Walmart, see Art Carden and

Charles Courtemanche, "The Evolution and Impact of the General Merchandise Sector," in *Handbook on the Economics of Retailing and Distribution*, ed. Emek Basker (Edward Elgar 2016), 413–32.

Chapter 15

1. Nicholas F. R. Crafts, S. J. Leybourne, and T. C. Mills, "Britain," in *Patterns of European Industrialization: The Nineteenth Century*, ed. Richard Sylla and Gianni Toniolo (Routledge and Fondazione Adriano Olivetti, 1991), 109–52, at 113; Charles H. Feinstein, "National Income Accounts: Investment and Savings," in Mokyr, *Oxford Encyclopedia of Economic History*, 4:41–48.

2. Ainslee Embree, ed., *Sources of Indian Tradition*, vol. 1, *From the Beginning to 1800*, 2nd ed. (Columbia University Press, 1988), 123.

3. Ludwig von Mises, *The Anti-Capitalistic Mentality* (1956; repr., Liberty Fund, 2006), 24.

4. Wallerstein, *Historical Capitalism*, 100. "Waste" such as decent housing for the formerly impoverished Chinese.

5. St. Thomas Aquinas, *Summa Theologica*, trans. Fathers of the English Dominican Province (Benzinger Brothers, 1918), Second Part of the Second Part, Q. 77, art. 4, p. 327, "I answer that."

6. John W. Danford, "'Riches Valuable at All Times and to All Men': Hume and the Eighteenth-Century Debate on Commerce and Liberty," *Liberty and American Experience in the Eighteenth Century*, ed. David Womersley (Liberty Fund, 2006), 319–47, at 328–29.

Chapter 16

1. See sense number 5b in the *Oxford English Dictionary on Historical Principles*.

2. David Mitch, "Human Capital," in Mokyr, *Oxford Encyclopedia of Economic History*, 3:1–7. Cf. David Mitch, *The Rise of Popular Literacy in Victorian England* (University of Pennsylvania Press, 1992).

3. Jason Long, "The Surprising Social Mobility of Victorian Britain," *European Review of Economic History* 27, no. 1 (February 2013):1–23, quotation at 1.

4. Johnson quoted in Peter Mathias, *The Transformation of England: Essays in the Economic and Social History of England in the Eighteenth Century* (Columbia University Press, 1979), 296.

5. Jonathan Daly, *The Rise of Western Power* (Bloomsbury, 2013), xii.

6. Joel Mokyr, *A Culture of Growth: Origins of the Modern Economy* (Princeton University Press, 2016).

7. Morgan Kelly, Cormac Ó Gráda, and Joel Mokyr, "Precocious Albion:

A New Interpretation of the British Industrial Revolution," *Annual Reviews of Economics* (School of Economics, University College Dublin), July 2013, 1.

8. Ralf Meisenzahl and Joel Mokyr, "The Rate and Direction of Invention in the British Industrial Revolution: Incentives and Institutions," in *The Rate and Direction of Inventive Activity Revisited*, ed. Josh Lerner and Scott Stern, NBER Books (University of Chicago Press, 2012), 443–79, at 447.

9. Witt Bowden, Michael Karpovich, and Abbott Payson Usher, *An Economic History of Europe since 1750* (American Book, 1937), 311. It was Usher who wrote the technological history in the book.

10. Karine van der Beek, "England's Eighteenth Century Demand for High-Quality Workmanship: Evidence from Apprenticeship, 1710–1770," in *Institutions, Innovation, and Industrialization: Essays in Economic History and Development*, ed. Avner Greif, Lynne Kiesling, and John V.C. Nye (Princeton University Press, 2015), 268–74.

11. Matt Ridley, "The Myth of Basic Science," *Wall Street Journal*, October 23, 2015, https://www.wsj.com/articles/the-myth-of-basic-science-1445613954.

Chapter 17

1. Quoted in Emmanuel Martin, "The Economics of Peace," in *Peace, War, and Liberty*, ed. Tom Palmer (Jameson Books, 2014), 38.

2. Luigi Einaudi, *From Our Italian Correspondent: Luigi Einaudi's Articles in "The Economist" 1908–1946*, ed. Roberto Marchionatti (Olschki Editore, 1923), 273.

3. Tojo quoted in R. A. C. Parker, *Struggle for Survival* (Oxford University Press, 1989), 84.

Chapter 18

1. Thomas Sowell, *Race and Culture: A World View* (Basic Books, 1994), 187, and Goldberg, *Suicide of the West* (Crown Forum, 2018), 33.

2. Sowell, *Race and Culture*, 187; Sowell, *Wealth, Poverty, and Politics: An International Perspective*, loc. 2592, Kindle, citing Robert C. Davis, *Christian Slaves, Muslim Masters: White Slavery in the Mediterranean, the Barbary Coast, and Italy, 1500–1800* (Palgrave Macmillan, 2003), 23, and Philip D. Curtin, *The Atlantic Slave Trade: A Census* (University of Wisconsin Press, 1969), 72, 75, 87.

3. David Richardson, "Slave Trade," in Mokyr, *Oxford Encyclopedia of Economic History*, 4:508–12.

4. Kenneth Pomeranz and Steven Topik, *The World That Trade Created: Society, Culture, and the World Economy 1400 to the Present* (M. E. Sharpe, 2006), 131–32.

5. Robert Paul Thomas and Richard Nelson Bean, "The Fishers of Men: The Profits of the Slave Trade," *Journal of Economic History* 34, no. 4 (1974): 885–914, esp. pp. 887, 910–11.

6. Alan L. Olmstead and Paul W. Rhode, "Cotton, Slavery, and the New History of Capitalism," *Explorations in Economic History* 67 (January 2018): 1–17. Other criticisms of the "New History of Capitalism" literature come from (among others) Eric Hilt, "Economic History, Historical Analysis, and the 'New History of Capitalism," *Journal of Economic History* 77, no. 2 (2017): 511–36; Stanley Engerman, review of *The Business of Slavery and the Rise of American Capitalism, 1815–1860*, by Calvin Schermerhorn, and *The Half Has Never Been Told: Slavery and the Making of American Capitalism*, by Edward E. Baptist, *Journal of Economic Literature* 55, no. 2 (2017): 637–43; and Robert Margo, "The Integration of Economic History into Economics," *Cliometrica* 12, no. 3 (2018): 377–406.

Chapter 19

1. Lewis calls this an upper-bound estimate. See H. Gregg Lewis, *Union Relative Wage Effects: A Survey* (University of Chicago Press, 1986), 9. He finds the wage-raising power of US unions to be mostly small, with exceptions such as electricians and doctors.

2. Price Fishback, *Soft Coal, Hard Choices: The Economic Welfare of Bituminous Coal Miners, 1890–1930* (Oxford University Press, 1992).

Chapter 20

1. Jack A. Goldstone, "Efflorescences and Economic Growth in World History: Rethinking the 'Rise of the West' and the Industrial Revolution," *Journal of World History* 13, no. 2 (Fall 2002): 323–89.

2. Behind an average cost paywall. See William D. Nordhaus, "Schumpeterian Profits in the American Economy: Theory and Measurement" (NBER Working Paper 10433, National Bureau of Economic Research, Cambridge, MA, 2004).

3. Alexander Gerschenkron, "Mercator Gloriosus," *Economic History Review* 24, no. 4 (November 1971): 653–66, at 655.

4. Ludwig von Mises, *Money, Method, and the Market Process: Essays by Ludwig von Mises* (Kluwer Academic Publishers and Ludwig von Mises Institute, 1990), 305.

5. Terence Kealey, "Back to the Future," *Buckingham at 25: Freeing Universities from State Control*, ed. James Tooley (Institute of Economic Affairs, 2001), 228–46.

6. David G. Green, *Reinventing Civil Society: The Rediscovery of Welfare without Politics* (Civitas, 1993), 26.

7. David T. Beito, *From Mutual Aid to the Welfare State: Fraternal Societies and Social Services, 1890–1967* (University of North Carolina Press, 2000); John E. Murray, *Origins of American Health Insurance: A History of Industrial Sickness Funds* (Yale University Press, 2007).

8. Sibylle Lehmann-Hasemeyer and Jochen Streb, "Does Social Security Crowd Out Private Savings? The Case of Bismarck's System of Social Insurance," *European Review of Economic History* 22, no. 3 (August 2018): 298–321.

9. Adam Thiere, *Permissionless Innovation: The Continuing Case for Comprehensive Technological Freedom* (Mercatus Center at George Mason University, 2014).

10. Thomas W. Hazlett, *The Political Spectrum: The Tumultuous Liberation of Wireless Technology, from Herbert Hoover to the Smartphone* (Yale University Press, 2017).

Chapter 21

1. Donald J. Boudreaux, "Deirdre McCloskey and Economists' Ideas about Ideas," *Liberty Matters*, Online Library of Liberty, July 2014, https://oll.libertyfund.org/pages/lm-McCloskey.

2. Phelps, *Mass Flourishing*, 27–28.

3. Joel Mokyr, *The Enlightened Economy: An Economic History of Britain 1700–1850* (Yale University Press, 2010); Stephen Davies, *The Wealth Explosion: The Nature and Origins of Modernity* (Edward Everett Root, 2019).

4. Quoted in Jacques Barzun, *From Dawn to Decadence: 500 Years of Western Cultural Life 1500 to the Present* (HarperCollins, 2000), 370.

5. Alexis de Tocqueville to Francisque de Corcelle, 17 September 1853, quoted in Richard Swedberg, *Tocqueville's Political Economy* (Princeton University Press, 2009), 280. Of course, if you define "institutions" broadly enough, as North sometimes does, and his followers such as Avner Greif regularly do, then "institutions" explain everything because laws have been merged with *moeurs*, or with anything else outside the naked and unsocialized will that leads people to do things.

6. Abraham Lincoln, "First Joint Debate at Ottawa: Mr. Lincoln's Reply," August 21, 1858, Bartelby.com, https://www.bartleby.com/251/12.html.

7. Daron Acemoglu and James A. Robinson, *Why Nations Fail: The Origins of Power, Prosperity, and Poverty* (Crown Business, 2012), 450.

8. Deirdre N. McCloskey, "Women's Work in the Market, 1900–2000," in *Women in Twentieth Century Britain: Economic, Social and Cultural Change*, ed. Ina Zweiniger-Bargielowska (Longman/Pearson Education, 2001), 165–79.

9. Fishback, *Soft Coal, Hard Choices*.

10. Deirdre N. McCloskey, *Knowledge and Persuasion in Economics* (Cambridge University Press, 1994), 347.

11. John R. Searle, *Making the Social World: The Structure of Human Civilization* (Oxford University Press, 2010).

12. Raymond Tallis, review of *Incomplete Nature*, by Terrence Deacon, and *Who's in Charge?* by Michael S. Gazzanga, *Wall Street Journal*, November 12, 2011.

Chapter 22

1. Keith Thomas, *The Ends of Life: Roads to Fulfillment in Early Modern England* (Oxford University Press, 2009), 114, 122.

2. David Crystal and Ben Crystal, *Shakespeare's Words: A Glossary and Language Companion* (Penguin, 2002).

3. Adam Smith, *The Theory of Moral Sentiments*, Glasgow ed., ed. D. D. Raphael and A. L. Macfie (Oxford University Press, 1976; reprinted by Liberty Fund, 1982), 138 (hereafter cited as *TMS*).

4. McCloskey's *Bourgeois Dignity* gives much more evidence on all this.

5. *Oxford English Dictionary*, s.v. "innovation," accessed February 25, 2020, https://www.oed.com/view/Entry/96311?redirectedFrom=innovation#eid.

6. *Oxford English Dictionary*, s.v. "novelty," accessed February 25, 2020, https://www.oed.com/view/Entry/128781?redirectedFrom=novelty#eid.

7. Margaret Jacob, *The First Knowledge Economy: Human Capital and the European Economy, 1750–1850* (Cambridge University Press, 2014), 78.

Chapter 23

1. Quoted in Lord Peter King, ed., *The Life of John Locke* (Henry Colburn, 1829), 88, https://books.google.com/books?id=AuFSCJWCcwEC&printsec=frontcover&dq=The+Life+of+John+Locke&hl=en&newbks=1&newbks_redir=0&sa=X&ved=2ahUKEwj1-sq8qprnAhUCPq0KHUiXAo8Q6AEwB3oECAcQAg#v=snippet&q=nature%20subservient%20&f=false.

2. Quoted in Pascal Bruckner, *Perpetual Euphoria: On the Duty to Be Happy*, trans. Steven Rendall (Princeton University Press, 2010), 1.

3. Alexander Pope, *An Essay on Man*, in *An Essay on Man and Other Poems by Alexander Pope*, vol. 2 (John Sharpe, 1829), 35, 45, 47.

4. William Butler Yeats, "Fragments," Poetry (website), accessed January 23, 2020, https://www.poetry.net/poem/39332/fragments.

5. Alexis de Tocqueville, *Democracy in America*, vol. 1, trans. James T. Schleifer (Indianapolis: Liberty Fund, 2012), 51. The original French phrase is "la liberté bourgeoise et démocratique."

6. Rosemary Moore, *The Light in Their Consciences: The Early Quakers in Britain, 1646–1666* (Pennsylvania State University Press, 2000), 3.

7. Quoted in Darrin M. McMahon, *Happiness: A History* (Atlantic Monthly Press, 2006), 176.

8. David Wootton, *Power, Pleasure, and Profit: Insatiable Appetites from Machiavelli to Madison* (Harvard University Press, 2018), 1.

9. David Wootton, "What's Wrong with Liberalism?" *History Today* 68, no. 12 (December 2018), https://www.historytoday.com/archive/feature/what%E2%80%99s-wrong-liberalism.

10. Wootton, *Power, Pleasure, and Profit*, 8.

11. Quoted in Wootton, *Power, Pleasure, and Profit*, 8.

12. John Stuart Mill, "The Mind and Character of Jeremy Bentham," *Westminster Review*, 1838, excerpted in Charles Dickens, *Hard Times* (Norton Critical Edition, 2016), 316–18.

Chapter 24

1. Laura Favero Carraro, "The Language of the Emerging Financial Market and Early Eighteenth-Century English Plays," *Essays in Economic and Business History* 37 (2019): 206–41.

2. Basil Willey, *The English Moralists* (Norton, 1964), 221.

3. Thomas Dekker, *The Shoemaker's Holiday*, in *English Renaissance Drama: A Norton Anthology*, ed. David Bevington, Lars Engle, Katherine Eiseman Maus, and Eric Rasmussen (Norton, 2002), act 1, scene 2, lines 3–6.

4. Laura Stevenson, "Anti-Entrepreneurial Attitudes in Elizabethan Sermons and Popular Literature," *Journal of British Studies* 15, no. 2 (Spring 1976): 1–20, at 4.

5. George Lillo, *The London Merchant*, in *Eighteenth-Century Plays*, ed. Ricardo Quintana (Modern Library, 1952). Subsequent quotations are from this edition.

6. Joyce Appleby, *The Relentless Revolution: A History of Capitalism* (Norton, 2010), 36.

7. W. A. Speck, "Eighteenth-Century Attitudes towards Business," in *The Representation of Business in English Literature*, ed. Arthur Pollard (Liberty Fund, 2009), 8–34, at 21.

8. Jane Austen, *Pride and Prejudice* (Penguin, 2003), 103.

9. Jane Austen to Fanny Knight, 18 November 1814, in R. W. Chapman, ed., *Jane Austen: Selected Letters*, 2nd ed. (Oxford University Press, 1985), 175.

10. Jane Austen to Martha Lloyd, 29–30 November 1812, in Deirdre Le Faye, *Jane Austen's Letters* (Oxford University Press, 2011), 205.

11. Marilyn Butler, introduction to R. Chapman, *Jane Austen: Selected Letters*, xxvi.

12. Nimish Adhia, "The Role of Ideological Change in India's Economic Liberalization," *Journal of Socio-Economics* 44 (June 2013): 103–11.

Chapter 25

1. This is how it is put, most persuasively, by Mokyr, *Culture of Growth*.

2. Rodney Stark, *The Victory of Reason: How Christianity Led to Freedom, Capitalism, and Western Success* (Random House, 2005), 48.

3. Appleby, *Relentless Revolution*, 35.

4. Calestous Juma, *Innovation and Its Enemies: Why People Resist New Technologies* (Oxford University Press, 2016), 44-67, describes efforts to ban coffee.

5. Andrew Pettegree, *The Invention of News* (Yale University Press, 2014), 11, 368.

6. Helmut T. Lehmann, introduction to *Three Treatises*, 2nd ed. (Fortress Press, 1970), 4.

7. David Daniell, *William Tyndale: A Biography* (Yale University Press, 1994), 383.

8. Daniell, *William Tyndale*, 79, quoting an account by Richard Webb.

9. Quoted in Martin Luther, *On Commerce and Usury (1524)*, ed. Philipp Robinson Rössner (Anthem Press, 2015), 90.

10. Robert Nisbet, "Idea of Progress: A Bibliographical Essay," Online Library of Liberty, last modified April 13, 2016, https://oll.libertyfund.org/pages/idea-of-progress-a-bibliographical-essay-by-robert-nisbet.

Chapter 26

1. See Vernon Smith and Bart J. Wilson, *Humanomics* (Cambridge University Press, 2019); McCloskey, *Bourgeois Dignity*; McCloskey, *Bourgeois Equality*; McCloskey, *Bourgeois Virtues*; Deirdre N. McCloskey, *Bettering Humanomics: Beyond Behaviorism and Neo-Institutionalism* (University of Chicago Press, forthcoming); Arjo Klamer, *Speaking of Economics: How to Get in the Conversation* (Routledge, 2007); Arjo Klamer, *Doing the Right Thing: A Value Based Approach* (Ubiquity Press, 2017). See also the works of predecessors such as Albert Hirschman, John Maynard Keynes, John Stuart Mill, and above all Adam Smith.

2. If your curiosity extends to wonder what we are talking about here (to our economist colleagues), see McCloskey, *Bettering Humanomics*; or McCloskey, *Knowledge and Persuasion in Economics*.

3. The economist and intellectual historian Keith Tribe argues that the Germans in the late nineteenth century who discussed the problem were in fact smarter about it than the English understanding of their writings. Keith Tribe, "*Das Adam Smith Problem* and the Origins of Modern Smith Scholarship," *History of European Ideas* 34, no. 4 (2008): 514–25.

4. Smith, *TMS*, 13.

5. John Stuart Mill, *On Liberty*, chap. 5, Library of Economics and Liberty, accessed January 26, 2020, https://www.econlib.org/library/Mill/mlLbty.html ?chapter_num=5#book-reader.

6. David Boaz, *The Libertarian Mind* (Simon and Schuster, 2015), 1.

7. Editorial, *Washington Post*, November 17, 2019.

8. Smith, *WN*, 1:250.

9. James R. Otteson, *Honorable Business: A Framework for Business in a Just and Humane Society* (Oxford University Press, 2019), esp. 38.

10. Smith, *WN*, 1:419. All subsequent quotations are from the same chapter, searchable via Project Gutenberg, https://www.gutenberg.org/files/3300/ 3300-h/3300-h.htm#chap27—and many other websites.

11. Friedrich A. Hayek, "The Use of Knowledge in Society," *American Economic Review* 35, no. 4 (September 1945): 519–30), at 521.

12. Smith, *WN*, 1:421. Smith in fact applies it only to "capital" in a strict sense, which leads him to a fallacious view that investment at home is better than investment overseas. But his treatment of the allocation of labor elsewhere in the book comes to similar conclusions, though his connection between labor and product markets leads him into another fallacy, the labor theory of value. Smith is our hero. But real human heroes are not without faults.

13. Sandra J. Peart and David M. Levy, eds., *The Street Porter and the Philosopher: Conversations on Analytical Egalitarianism* (University of Michigan Press, 2008).

14. Smith, *TMS*, 233–34.

15. Adam Smith to Gilbert Elliot, 10 October 1759, in Adam Smith, *Correspondence of Adam Smith*, Glasgow ed., ed. E. C. Mossner and I. S. Ross (Clarendon Press of Oxford University Press, 1977), 52.

16. Charles Taylor, *Sources of the Self: The Making of Modern Identity* (Harvard University Press, 1989), 503; cf. Anna Wierzbicka, *English: Meaning and Culture* (Oxford University Press, 2006), 80–82.

17. Smith, *WN*, 1:142.

18. Adam Smith, *Lectures on Jurisprudence*, Glasgow ed., ed. R. L. Meek, D. D. Raphael, and P. G. Stein (Clarendon Press of Oxford University Press, 1982), 352. Originally published 1762–1766.

19. Adam Smith, *Essays on Philosophical Subjects*, Glasgow ed., ed. W. P. D. Wightman and J. J. Bryce (Clarendon Press of Oxford University Press, 1980), 262.

Index